LITTLE BOSS

Burns: A Biography of Robert Burns
Vagabond of Verse: A Biography of Robert Service
William Wallace: Brave Heart
The Eye Who Never Slept: A Life of Allan Pinkerton
Michael Collins: A Life
Sounds Out of Silence: A Life of Alexander Graham Bell
The Man Who Invented Himself: A Life of Sir Thomas Lipton (forthcoming)

LITTLE BOSS

A Life of Andrew Carnegie

JAMES MACKAY

MAINSTREAM
PUBLISHING

EDINBURGH AND LONDON

To Margaret and Hamish Thomson

First published in 1997 by
MAINSTREAM PUBLISHING COMPANY (EDINBURGH) LTD
7 Albany Street
Edinburgh EH1 3UG

ISBN 1 85158 832 9

A catalogue record for this book is available from the British Library

Typeset in 12 on 14pt Van Dijck MT
Printed and bound in Great Britain by Butler & Tanner Ltd

Contents

Introduction

FORTY YEARS AGO, WHEN I WAS A STUDENT AT GLASGOW university, I worked during the summer vacations at what was then the railway hotel in Dornoch, the pretty little county town of Sutherland in the far north of Scotland. One year I had to resit the examination in constitutional history the following September, so much of my free time that summer was spent in the public library. Dornoch, with its medieval cathedral, might rank as a city in ecclesiastical terms, and it might be a royal burgh to boot, but in reality it was only a village. Yet it possessed a magnificent library, whose facilities and book stock were astounding and certainly out of all proportion to the size or importance of Dornoch itself.

The clue to this disproportionate library lay in its name, for it was a Carnegie library; and not just any Carnegie library but one with which its benefactor had close personal ties, because Dornoch was the town nearest to Skibo, the great castellated mansion of Andrew Carnegie who had risen from a dollar-a-week bobbin boy in a Pittsburgh mill to become the richest man in the world. His was the rags-to-riches story *par excellence*.

Carnegie himself had died in 1919, many years before my time, but he had left a relatively young widow who had been, if anything, more in love with Skibo even than Carnegie himself, and the people of Dornoch spoke of Louise Whitfield Carnegie with real affection. She, too, was now dead, but her daughter, the sole issue of the marriage, was still very much a living force in Dornoch and the surrounding district. Margaret was a child of Carnegie's old age, born when the great tycoon was sixty-two. After her mother's death in 1946

7

Margaret Carnegie Miller took on the role of châtelaine of Skibo, spending her summers there and fulfilling her part as *grande dame* of the district in magnificent style. She took an active part in the life of the community, at a certain rarefied level, to be sure, and her endowments and benefactions, though on a much more modest scale than her famous father's, were substantial and cost effective.

More importantly, perhaps, she gave Dornoch and Skibo of her time, unstintingly, presiding over local events or at least gracing them with her presence. The first time I saw her was at a distance, at the Highland Games held on the outskirts of Golspie: a small figure, dressed in black, with what I took to be a rather haughty, disdainful mien. Mrs Carnegie Miller was pointed out with rather hushed breath, not because of her wealth and position, but because she was recently *divorced*. Back in those days, this was a post-marital status only briefly encountered in the newspapers but never observed at first-hand, far less touching one's own life, and it made the little old lady an even greater object of curiosity, an even more distant figure.

The following summer, however, I was back at Dornoch Hotel having cheerfully sought, and obtained, demotion from assistant control clerk to lounge waiter, because I could earn in tips in a single evening as much as a clerk earned in a week. This brought me into close contact with the hotel guests, as they drank their coffee and sipped their liqueurs in the lounge after dinner. In one of the alcoves Sir David and Lady Robertson held court most evenings. He was the member of Parliament for Caithness and Sutherland and, lacking a permanent home in his constituency, took up long-term residence in the hotel. He was then a Conservative MP but would later have the unenviable distinction of being disowned by his party and serving the rest of his term as an Independent.

The staff of the hotel fell into three groups: the professionals drafted in for the season from other British Transport hotels, the Embos (inhabitants of a nearby village of that name who, disconcertingly, all seemed to rejoice in the surname of Mackay) and the students, a few of whom came from Ross Hall catering college but were, for the most part, talented amateurs like myself. With rare percipience Sir David quickly divined that I was definitely not one of the professionals, and that, despite my surname, I did not hail from

Embo. He soon discovered that I was a history student and that I was wrestling with Taswell-Langmead, the bible of constitutional history, which I had obtained from the magnificent local library.

One evening the Robertsons had a guest, and Sir David made a point of introducing me to her with the words that I was making very good use of her father's library. At this the lady's face lit up and she beamed a smile which I have never forgotten. She asked me what I hoped to do when I had graduated. Did I intend to teach? I shook my head vigorously and, God help me, blurted out that my ambition was to be a writer.

'My father was a writer,' she said simply. This was news to me. I cudgelled my brains furiously trying to remember what I knew of the great Andrew Carnegie, but could only recollect that he had made his money from steel and founded libraries with his fortune. Mrs Carnegie Miller was speaking again. 'What will you write?'

At that time I had written essays but published nothing; yet I found myself confiding that I was writing a historical novel, vaguely woven around an ancestor who had been a Covenantor. She regarded me intently before commenting in her low, even, only faintly American voice, 'Write about *real* people, young man. They are much more interesting than fictional characters.'

'Perhaps he'll write a book about your father some day,' quipped Sir David, and at this all three of them, the MP, his lady and Mrs Carnegie Miller laughed heartily. I think I mumbled something like, 'Oh, I could never do *that*.' Flushed with intense embarrassment, I scooped up the drinks tray and made as dignified an exit as I could, studiously avoiding that alcove for the rest of the evening, or at least until the Robertsons and their guest had departed.

I never met Margaret Carnegie Miller again but this, my first encounter with anyone remotely connected to a celebrity, let alone someone who was a legend in his own lifetime, left an indelible mark. I soon made up for the deficiency in my knowledge and read Carnegie's *Autobiography*, followed by some of his earlier books. And I struggled manfully through Hendrick's two-volume biography as well as the much shorter and pithier hatchet-job by John Winkler. Then, in 1970, there appeared Joseph Frazier Wall's monumental work. Reading this immensely detailed book of almost 1200 pages I felt a pang of regret; Professor Wall had clearly had the wholehearted co-operation of Mrs Carnegie Miller. Then, on reflection, I felt that while this had decided advantages it also had its drawbacks, for no matter how much a biographer may be given a free hand by the family of his subject, there is always the need to show restraint and perhaps to retouch the portrait or interpret events in a certain favourable way.

Many years later, my interest in Andrew Carnegie was rekindled by the news that Skibo was up for sale. Then, two years later, the 150th anniversary of Carnegie's birth was celebrated in a low-key, one might almost say apologetic, manner. I was involved, in a modest way, with the issue of a commemorative aerogramme by the Scottish Postal Board; Carnegie's sesquicentenary ought to have merited an issue of stamps, if not in the land of his birth then certainly in his adopted country, but it was ignored by both. Celebrations, such as they were, appear to have been confined to Dunfermline, staged in October, a month ahead of the actual anniversary and actually presenting a colourful pageant of Dunfermline's 900 years of history which put Andrew Carnegie in his true, historical perspective. Two of the eleven scenes, entitled 'The Green Gate' and 'The Infeftment Ceremony', respectively described an episode in the early life of Carnegie and that momentous day for the town, in November 1903, when he fulfilled a boyhood dream by handing over Pittencrieff Glen to the people of Dunfermline.

The Dunfermline of the present day is very far removed from the weaving town of Carnegie's boyhood. Like every other industrial town it has enjoyed prosperity and suffered decline. Post-industrial Dunfermline has been largely transformed. The eastern link road of the 1980s cut a broad swathe through disused, derelict and decayed factories and mills but mercifully skirted the inner city which has been refurbished and renovated. The Abbey, Refectory, Abbot House and Royal Palace are tangible reminders of the time when Dunfermline was the Scottish capital, but the city also has its Carnegie Library, Carnegie Centre, Carnegie Clinic and even a Carnegie Hall – not perhaps on the same scale as its world-famous New York counterpart, but the home of live entertainment in Dunfermline to this day. There is also the Lauder Technical College, named after Carnegie's favourite uncle and, with more than 5000 students, virtually a university. Pass through the Louise Carnegie Gates and you enter Pittencrieff Park which Carnegie gave to the people of Dunfermline and today boasts a fine statue of him, vying with the tower of Malcolm Canmore as one of the town's principal landmarks.

And there is the humble cottage in Moodie Street, with the impressive Birthplace Museum alongside. Actually, the Carnegie home is only half of the cottage, and one cannot but marvel at the fact that William and Margaret Carnegie raised three children in such cramped quarters, *and* provided the space for William's workshop as a damask weaver. The tiny, spartan abode of the Carnegies contrasts with the solid opulence of the museum, with its glass cases containing the medals and decorations, the honorary degrees, the ornamental keys that ceremonially unlocked the doors to so many Carnegie libraries, and the extravagantly bejewelled burgess caskets. In the museum shop you can purchase packets of shortbread with Carnegie's portrait on the label. The brand name 'Sweetness and Light' seems odd, but is in fact derived from Carnegie's own favourite words to describe the benefits he delighted in conferring on his native town. Dunfermline has done well from Carnegie and continues to do well by him.

In the year of the 150th anniversary Simon Goodenough produced his excellent book entitled *The Greatest Good Fortune: Andrew Carnegie's Gift for Today*. This is a magnificent tribute to the enduring legacy of Andrew Carnegie, outlining the history of each of the trusts and benefactions which he endowed, their activities over the years and even their assets to the last penny. More than anything else, that volume highlights the magnitude of Carnegie's philanthropy, but inevitably only a broad outline of the man himself was given.

My own interest in Carnegie as the possible subject of a biography was kindled in the 1980s as a result of my work with the Burns Federation and latterly in connection with research into the great Burns Temple Hoax of 1904. The previous August Carnegie had visited Kilmarnock, received the freedom of the burgh and laid the foundation stone of the Loanhead School. All went well until the chairman of the school board, over dinner, hinted that perhaps Mr Carnegie might like to part with a modicum of the £60,000,000 he was then giving away. 'You have spoiled my day,' was the unexpected reply of the multi-millionaire, and the subsequent proceedings interested him no more. This brusque response affected some of the town wags to such an extent that they resolved to have their revenge. The following February Provost Hood was very agreeably surprised to receive a letter allegedly from Hew Morrison, Carnegie's Scottish agent, intimating that the great man proposed to spend half a million pounds on the erections of a great temple dedicated to Robert Burns, his favourite bard. Kilmarnock, as the mecca of Burns lore, would be the location for this huge building. Sadly, it later transpired that the proposal was a hoax, but not before it hit the headlines around the world.

I was intrigued by Carnegie's angry response at the time, and this led me to examine some of his benefactions at the beginning of the century when he embarked on the prodigious task of giving away the better part of $500,000,000. Gradually a picture emerged of conditional philanthropy and what I can only describe as leveraged benefaction. This, in turn, led me to a much more thorough exploration of the background of this remarkable man and a detailed examination of the convoluted strands of his character. Carnegie's regard for Robert Burns assumed the magnitude of a religion; his conversation and his writings were frequently peppered with quotations from Burns. For this reason I make no apology for having drawn all of the quotations in the chapter headings of this book from the same source. One quotation I have forborne to apply in the book itself I shall now take the liberty of giving here. It comes from Burns's celebrated 'Ode to a Louse':

> O wad some Power the giftie gie us,
> To see oursels as ithers see us!
> It wad frae monie a blunder free us,
> An foolish notion;
> What airs in dress an gait wad lea'e us,
> An ev'n devotion.

In writing this book I have made use of the facilities of libraries that owe their existence to the generosity of other men: of James Dick the gutta-percha millionaire who endowed the Dick Institute in Kilmarnock, and of Stephen Mitchell the tobacco magnate who endowed the Mitchell Library in Glasgow; but for sixteen years my studies owed much to the library in Dumfries, named in honour of

William Ewart MP, architect of the Free Libraries Act, but actually one of the earliest libraries to have been funded through the munificence of Andrew Carnegie. My thanks are due to the staff of these libraries, as well as the many men and women of the Glasgow University Library, the National Library of Scotland and the British Library in the United Kingdom, and the Library of Congress, the New York Public Library and the Public Library of Pittsburgh on the other side of the Atlantic for much of the information that has been distilled into this volume.

I must also record my indebtedness to a number of individuals such as Robert Steward, Archivist of Highland Region, Jane Paterson and Moira Scott of the Carnegie United Kingdom Trust, Sara Engelhardt of the Carnegie Corporation of New York, John Lane of the Carnegie Institute, Bill Runciman of the Carnegie Dunfermline Trust and the Carnegie Hero Trust, the late Ian Barr of the Scottish Post Office Board and John Holman of Royal Mail, Derrick Barclay, Curator of the Andrew Carnegie Birthplace Museum, and last but by no means least, George Robertson, whose knowledge of Dunfermline's most famous son is prodigious.

A special word of thanks is also due to my editor, Judy Diamond. This has not been the easiest of projects, but she has coped with the many problems arising from it with her customary cheerfulness and efficiency.

James Mackay
Glasgow, April 1997

ONE

Dunfermline

1835–48

A bonie, westlin weaver lad
Sat working at his loom;
He took my heart, as wi a net,
In every knot and thrum.
> Robert Burns, 'To the Weaver's Gin You Go'

CARNEGIE IS AN ANCIENT NAME IN THE SCOTTISH COUNTY OF Angus, a corruption of the Gaelic *Caither an eige*, the fort of the gap; but where this fort was cannot be ascertained, for it disappeared a thousand years ago. The name Carnegie first appears in a charter of David II in 1350 from which the Earls of Southesk and Northesk traced their origins.

About 1755 a young man named James Carnegie drifted into the picturesque hamlet of Patiemuir, a cluster of thatched or red-tiled cottages nestling in a fold of the moorland hills about a mile above the Firth of Forth. Patiemuir was a sleepy little place, off the beaten track and just the spot for a man with a past to settle. James became a hand-loom weaver and about 1758 married a village lass, Charlotte Walker. Later, the story would go that James was the grandson of Sir James Carnegie, fifth Earl of Southesk who had been out in the Jacobite rebellion of 1715 and had died in exile in France in 1729. It was theorised that Sir James's son had also been a Jacobite and had fought for Bonnie Prince Charlie in 1745–46; that he had gone into hiding after Culloden and raised his children to respect the secret of their past.

In support of this romantic mystery an incident of 1770 was cited. In that year James Carnegie took an active part in the Meal Riots, for

15

which he was imprisoned on a charge of sedition. While in prison he was visited by a mysterious lady who conversed earnestly with him and, on taking her leave, gave him a jewelled snuffbox with the initials J.C. and the date 1712 engraved on the lid. 'James never explained either the visit or the gift, and the family had only the small snuffbox upon which to build their legends,' noted one biographer.[1]

Suggestions of an aristocratic origin came relatively late in the life of Andrew Carnegie, and seem to have arisen in an attempt to explain the phenomenon of the weaver's son who became the world's richest man by his own efforts. Significantly, Andrew Carnegie himself made no mention of this family legend in his *Autobiography*, stating merely that he was 'of poor but honest parents, of good kith and kin'.[2] And Burton Hendrick, writing soon after Carnegie's death, tells how a professional genealogist once told Carnegie that he was descended from Scottish kings, hinting that, for a suitable sum, he could be furnished with an illustrious pedigree. 'I am sorry to hear that,' replied Carnegie, 'because my wife married me under the impression that I was the son of a weaver.'[3]

The present whereabouts of the jewelled snuffbox are not known; amid the artefacts, papers and memorabilia of a man whose life was extremely well documented, its absence is conspicuous. Furthermore, Carnegie is a very common surname in Angus and Fife. That James Carnegie was an outspoken radical is well attested. Even among the weavers, a class of men noted for their radical politics, he stood out. Apart from his qualities of leadership, however, there was nothing in either his character or outlook of the aristocratic background suggested by some writers at the beginning of the twentieth century. Andrew Carnegie and the seventh Earl of Southesk would become close friends and often greet each other as 'cousin' but this was nothing more than jovial banter, and not meant to be taken seriously.

Between 1759 and 1782, James and Charlotte produced six daughters and three sons. After the fifth daughter, James's eldest son Andrew was born on 13 April 1769.[4] In turn he followed his father into the weaver's trade. It was the usual practice for weavers to travel in groups when they went to neighbouring towns to sell their finished webs. Young Andra Carnegie, however, preferred his own company and invariably travelled alone, singing lustily as he tramped the rutted country roads to Dunfermline or, farther afield, to Stirling or Perth.

Probably on one of these forays, about 1792, he met Elizabeth Thom, the daughter of Elizabeth Wilkie and George Thom, a prosperous shipmaster in the port of Limekilns. Andra, who had a good conceit of himself, courted the lively girl, much to her father's disgust. Captain Thom threatened to cut his daughter off without a penny if she married her weaver lad, but Elizabeth stood up to her father and told him, 'Better to marry for love and work for siller than to marry for siller and work for love.' In defiance of her father she went off to Patiemuir as Andra's bride.[5] Captain Thom was as good as his word, and Elizabeth was cut out of his will. Each of her three sisters, Agnes, Margaret and Henrietta, eventually received one of the Thom ships as her patrimony, but misfortune overtook them all, whereas Elizabeth and Andra, though they seldom had much money, had plenty of loving, and ten children.[6]

According to family legend, Elizabeth did eventually try to effect a reconciliation with her father. George Thom was inclined to put aside his rancour provided that Elizabeth name her next child, her eighth, after one of his family. Elizabeth promised that if the child was a boy he would be named after her father, and if a girl, named after one of her sisters. The baby was a girl, and on the day of the christening Captain Thom and his daughters gathered in the seceders' chapel in Limekilns for the formal act of reconciliation. But this capitulation was too much for Andra Carnegie, who could be just as thrawn as his father-in-law. When the Revd William Hadden asked for the girl's name Andra spoke out, 'She's to be called Ann, for my aunt of the same name.' The Thoms flounced out of the little church in high dudgeon and no further communication between the Thoms and the Carnegies was attempted.[7]

This dour, obstinate streak in Andra contrasted sharply with the qualities by which he was fondly remembered. He had an outgoing personality, and was lively, engaging and curious about the world beyond the confines of Patiemuir. Like many other weavers of the time he was a voracious reader, feeding his hungry intellect with an astonishing range of literature. He became the natural leader of the parish intelligentsia, noted for his wit and debating skills. He acquired the nickname 'Professor' and held court in a long, narrow single-roomed cottage in the village which some wag dubbed 'the College'. The building was later preserved by the Carnegie Trust of Dunfermline as a sort of shrine to the family intellect, and for many years served the village as a community centre. This contradicted an old but persistent myth that the Professor had held his seminars over a beer barrel in the Bull Head Tavern. In truth, the convivial gatherings under Andra's jovial chairmanship were little more than an outlet for the menfolk after a hard day's toil at their looms, but they pooled their slender resources to purchase the latest books as well as the twice-weekly *Scotsman* from Edinburgh. These were read aloud, and passages then discussed at great length. Fortified by a few drams, the Professor and his cronies would debate the issues of the day, theological, political, philosophical, social or economic, invariably reflecting the robust radicalism which gave them their solidarity. Radical – almost republican – in politics, the Patiemuir weavers were seceders to a man, having deserted the Church of Scotland in favour of the Secession movement led by Ebenezer Erskine.

It has to be said that Andra was never as diligent a damask weaver as his father James, being only too easily deflected from the loom if there was a political meeting or a country dance. He was no idle spectator, and had always to be in the thick of the argument. One old man in Patiemuir would tell Andra's famous grandson many years later: 'Eh, mon. I hae seen the day when your grandfaither and I could hae hallooed ony reasonable man oot o' his jidgment.'[8] Andra had a reputation for practical jokes; well into his seventies he was still dressing up at Hogmanay and frolicking with the youngsters as they went about the village 'first-footing'. Andrew Carnegie recalled the old man with pride:

> I think my optimistic nature, my ability to shed trouble and to laugh through life, making 'all my ducks swans', as friends say I do, must have been inherited from this delightful old masquerading grandfather whose name I am proud to bear. A sunny disposition is worth more than fortune.[9]

The sixth child and second son of the Professor was William Carnegie, born at Patiemuir on 19 June 1804 and baptised two days later. William was a sickly, diffident, quiet and introspective child, the very antithesis of his extrovert father. He inherited none of Andra's rougher qualities, but he was just as devoted to radical politics. While Andra was noted as a lusty singer of folk ballads, William would be chiefly remembered for his gentle tenor voice, beautifully pitched, in which he rendered the love songs of Robert Burns. He took immense pride in his skills as a weaver, producing webs of the finest damask.

In the 1820s, however, all the skill and artistry of the handloom weaver could not compete with the new technology which would soon wipe out this cottage industry. In place of the independent weavers working their looms at home there would emerge vast mills, employing hundreds and thousands of hands who tended the great steam-powered machines. The demand for hand-made webs declined and William was forced to go farther and farther afield in search of purchasers. Realising how remote and cut-off Patiemuir was, he and his elder brother James decided to leave the hamlet and settle in the neighbouring town of Dunfermline. For a time the brothers prospered, obtaining work from the mills which gave out the webs and took back the finished cloth. Their father and other members of the family followed them two or three years later, settling in a small, single-storey house at the corner of Priory Lane and Moodie Street.

Dunfermline in the third decade of the nineteenth century was developing rapidly. Situated on high ground overlooking the Firth of Forth, some fourteen miles north-west of Edinburgh, the Auld Grey Toun had been in medieval times the capital of Scotland, developing around the magnificent abbey built by St Margaret, wife of King Malcolm Canmore. It had lain in ruins ever since it was sacked by the English in 1304, but it was a place of national veneration, as the burial place of several Scottish kings as well as its saintly founder. A few years before the Carnegie family moved to the town, there had been considerable excitement when, in 1818, workmen digging the foundations for the new abbey church discovered the tomb of Robert Bruce and briefly disinterred the warrior-king's bones, still wrapped in a shroud of gold thread. The remains were placed in a lead coffin sealed with pitch and buried with appropriate ceremony. To mark the occasion the great central tower of the new abbey church was topped by masonry letters reading on the four sides KING ROBERT THE

BRUCE.[10] This curious structure, a major landmark to this day, reflects the exuberance of the town in the early nineteenth century and the intense civic pride in its ancient glories.

In the Maygate, not far from William Carnegie's modest loom-shop, was the much more commodious dwelling and shop of Thomas Morrison, one of the town's leading shoemakers. His father John, born about 1740, had settled in Edinburgh as a prosperous leather merchant. Both Thomas and his brother Robert had received a good education, and in due course Thomas had taken over the family business. He married Ann Hodge, the daughter of a well-to-do Edinburgh merchant. The eldest children of this marriage were Seaton and Thomas Junior and both would later recall an idyllic childhood when they lived in a fine house in the New Town and had their own ponies to ride.[11] According to family legend, it was not long after the birth of his fourth child, a daughter named Margaret, that Thomas Senior speculated unwisely and lost his fortune, leaving his family with a lifelong aversion to stockmarket ventures. The Morrisons are said to have left Edinburgh as a result, and settled in Dunfermline. An examination of the birth registers of Dunfermline, however, shows that the move to the Auld Grey Toun took place at least a decade earlier, for Thomas Junior was born in Dunfermline, and baptised there on 11 November 1803, as were his brother William in February 1808 and his three younger sisters.[12]

Starting at the bottom again, and plying the cobbler's trade he had learned as a young man, Thomas Morrison gradually won back respectability. Alluding to this drastic change in circumstance, Morrison wrote to his friend William Cobbett: 'Blessed be God, I learned in my youth to make and mend shoes; the awls were my resource and they have not failed me.' Cobbett published this letter in the form of an article, under the title 'Heddekashun and Handication' in his *Political Register* of 21 December 1833, with the comment: 'I am tempted to call it the very best communication I ever received in my life for the *Register*.' Morrison's letter was a savage indictment of the educational system of the period and made a strong plea for vocational training. Characteristically, he condemned the system of primary education because it inculcated servility in the working classes. The Shorter Catechism, so rigorously drummed into children from the earliest age, also came in for severe criticism:

'Is it at all surprising that, under this damnable *heddekashun*, children of sensitive feeling and lively imagination should go mad, or become imbecile through life?' Tom Morrison's philosophy was succinctly put:

> How sweet, in my experience, is the bread which one earns with his own hand! . . . To form one of a congregation composed of the high and holy order of 'workies'; all sober, clean, well-dressed, polite, acute, rational and intelligent; to hear and join their occasional arguments, criticism, encomiums, or laughter — these are to me sources of the purest and highest enjoyments . . . I am no knowledge-society man, condescending to teach the 'workies'; no working man's companion, designing to mislead them; no demagogue, wishing to make them a ladder by which I may leave my order and ascend to the grade of the *heddekated* and 'rispictible'; but the working man's self, having no expectation, scarcely ever a transient wish, but to make and mend shoes, as long as I have strength to bore with the awl or sight to put through the bristles.

Encouraged by Cobbett, who had come to Dunfermline to address a political rally, Tom Morrison founded his own periodical which he aptly named *The Precursor*. This twopenny monthly was so radical and inflammatory that no printer in Dunfermline would touch it, and he was compelled to take the manuscript all the way to Edinburgh to get it set in type. Only three erratic numbers ever appeared. No copies of the inaugural number, dated January 1833, have survived, although it was apparently a four-page paper. The second number, dated 1 February 1833, came out on time. Congratulating himself on the feat of actually getting the paper out at all, Morrison adopted a defensive tone, obviously in response to attacks made upon him over the primitive form of communism he had advocated in his essay 'The Rights of Land' in the inaugural issue. In answer to accusations of 'levelling principles', he now set the record straight:

> We say, — honour to wisdom and worth, comfort and independence to industry and frugality; the accidents of birth we regard not, titles and orders we despise; and *mere wealth* we will not worship. If this is 'levelling', we plead guilty to the charge; but if we are

represented as enemies to all distinction in society and as desirous
. . . of making an equal division of property without regard to the
respective merits of the producers and just rights of the holders, we
despise the charge, and the ignorant or wicked beings who prefer it,
too much to descend to a refutation.

This retreat from his initial extremism was not enough to silence
his critics or, more importantly, to win him a larger circulation. After
one more issue *The Precursor* sank into oblivion. Tom Morrison was
not comfortable with compromise anyway. Although he never again
attempted to provide a voice for the radicalism of south-east
Scotland, he remained a vociferous critic of the Establishment in
matters political and religious. In the latter arena he was what would
now be called a fundamentalist. One writer later described him as
living in a Puritan environment[13] and that was an understatement.
Morrison, stiff and unbending, even seceded from the Seceders when
they proved too liberal for his taste. In time he became the head of a
small Baptist sect and earned a reputation as a preacher that
extended as far as Edinburgh itself, where his pulpit oratory was
much in demand.

In the year that the Great Reform Act passed Parliament by a
majority of one and set the ball rolling that would slowly and
painfully transform Britain into a true democracy, Tom Morrison was
a busy man. When he was not nurturing his infant magazine and
thundering from the pulpit of the Baptist chapel, he was trying to
organise the weavers of Dunfermline into a political union. With its
stirring motto 'Knowledge, Union, Fraternization', it aimed at 'the
diffusion of political knowledge, the improvement of the national
institutions, and, specifically, to effect a reform of the Commons
House of Parliament'. As disillusionment over the Reform Act set in,
Morrison's Weavers' Political Union, and other bodies like it, gained
support. In a list of council members of this union dated 1834
appears the name of William Carnegie of Priory Lane.

William, now past thirty years of age, was as yet unmarried. He
was initially attracted to Tom Morrison because his politics were
very similar to Professor Andra's, if rather more articulate and
refined in expression. But William soon came under a spell of another
kind. Tom, a widower since 1814, had raised a son and four daughters

single-handed. The second daughter was Margaret, born on 19 June 1810, and thus six years William's junior to the very day; but she had an old head on her shoulders and from the outset seems to have been the dominant partner in the relationship that developed between them. In December 1834 they were wed,[14] and William installed his young bride in the tiny cottage that served as both home and workshop. Andra Carnegie and Old Tom Morrison both lived long enough to see their first grandson, who was born on 25 November 1835. In accordance with Scots tradition, the boy was named after his paternal grandfather. Eight years later, when the marriage was blessed with a second son, he was named after his maternal grandfather. A daughter Ann, named after Margaret's late mother, was born on 5 January 1838 but this sickly infant died a year later.[15]

Andrew Carnegie's birthplace was typical of the weavers' cottages in Dunfermline. Built in the late eighteenth century, it was a solid grey sandstone structure with a red-tiled roof and two dormer windows. Two doors at ground level led into two separate dwellings. The Carnegies occupied one half of the ground floor area, and another weaver and his family had the other half. The family's living quarters, in fact, consisted of a single attic room with its sloping ceiling and tiny window. Today it is preserved as a museum to the town's most famous son, and visitors can marvel at the cramped bunk-beds hemmed in by the partition and the eaves, and the little room which served a man, his wife and three children as their kitchen, dining-room, living-room and bedroom. The ground floor was the workshop, entirely taken up with William's loom and the impedimenta of his trade. When he was at work, the deafening clack of the loom penetrated the thin ceiling and floorboards separating it from the family quarters upstairs.

The modest rental for this accommodation was a pound a quarter, but William was so hard pressed to make ends meet that when Margaret's time drew near he could not afford the services of a professional midwife. Instead, he called on Ella Ferguson (Mrs John Henderson), Margaret's best friend, to deliver the baby. A few months later the roles were reversed and Margaret delivered Ella's first child.

As time dimmed reality, this humble cottage came to have a very special place in Andrew Carnegie's affections. Andrew, who could recite many of the poems of Burns before he could read and write, would often think of his birthplace as akin to the cottage described by his poet-hero in 'The Cottar's Saturday Night'. In his *Autobiography* Carnegie hardly mentions his father at all. There is a passing reference, alluding to some time in 1839 or early 1840:

> As my father succeeded in the weaving business we removed from Moodie Street to a much more commodious house in Reid's Park. My father's four or five looms occupied the lower storey; we resided in the upper, which was reached, after a fashion common in the older Scottish houses, by outside stairs from the pavement. It is here that my earliest recollections begin, and strangely enough, the first trace of memory takes me back to a day when I saw a small map of America. It was upon rollers and about two feet square. Upon this my father, mother, Uncle William, and Aunt Aitken were looking for Pittsburgh and pointing out Lake Erie and Niagara. Soon after, my uncle and Aunt Aitken sailed for the land of promise.[16]

The move to the house in Edgar Street, opposite Reid's Park, took place late in 1836. That had been a very good year for the handloom weavers; despite a lowering in the price paid for webs, business had been brisk and those weavers prepared to put in longer hours and redouble their efforts earned good money. William Carnegie profited by the increased demand for heavy damasks and took a gamble by moving to larger premises, where he could install more looms and hire several apprentices. The house was much larger than the half-cottage on Moodie Street but had the same configuration of a working area on the ground floor and living quarters in the garret above. Aunt Aitken was Margaret's younger sister Annie who had married Andrew Aitken. Her twin sister Kitty had married Tom Hogan. Together, the Aitkens and the Hogans emigrated to Pennsylvania in 1840.

About his mother, Andrew wrote candidly: 'I cannot trust myself to speak at length . . . Perhaps some day I may be able to tell the world something of this heroine, but I doubt it. I feel her to be sacred to myself and not for others to know. None could ever really know her – I alone did that.'[17] He claimed that she had inherited from her mother the dignity, refinement and air of the cultivated lady. 'After my father's early death she was all my own,' he added revealingly. When he published his first book, *An American Four-in-Hand in Great Britain* (1883), he fulsomely dedicated it 'To my favorite Heroine My Mother'.

Margaret Morrison Carnegie would later be recalled by her contemporaries in Dunfermline as a young woman of positive likes and prejudices, warm-hearted but of controlled emotions. No beauty, her strong features betrayed the rugged individualism of her character. Early photographs show a rather dumpy woman, her black hair parted in the centre and swept back severely to reveal a plain, rather masculine face with a square jaw and determined chin. The only redeeming feature was the eyes, large, lustrous, dark and penetrating. She had the same intellectual and spiritual restlessness as her father, and her favourite reading matter consisted of the theological writings of William Ellery Channing, one of the founders of American Unitarianism. William Carnegie, who never had a great deal to say for himself, was captivated by this creature as she flitted demurely about her father's house, deferring to Old Tom and her brilliant brother, also called Tom, as they debated political issues endlessly. Someone more acute than William might have noted that Margaret's demure behaviour concealed a steely mind and a strength of character. After their marriage he discovered that this strange woman could be alarming at times; although always resourceful, she could be ruthless in her determination to have her own way. He never understood this but had the good sense to give way. Margaret was a model housewife, frugal, neat, clean and hard-working. Like her father and brother, she had learned the cobbler's trade and eked out William's meagre earnings by taking in boot and shoe repairs. As the demand for fine damask linen receded, Margaret came to be more and more the breadwinner of the family, a fact that was not lost on their sharp elder son.

Little Andy, as he was affectionately known, was the apple of his mother's eye. In him were invested all her hopes and longings; she indulged him and – so far as her straitened circumstances allowed – spoiled him. Andy developed into a dumpling of a boy. From his father he inherited the flaxen colour of his hair but little else. In every other respect he was a Morrison, from his bright, piercing eyes to his short, sturdy legs. An elderly great-aunt who helped nurse him recalled his gargantuan appetite and astonishing precocity. There is a vivid pen-portrait of the lusty infant seated at the table, beating a loud tattoo with a spoon in each hand 'wherewith to shovel double portions of porridge into his mouth', punctuated with cries of 'Mair! Mair!' as his fond parents marvelled at their little prodigy. Despite this nurturing, however, he never grew tall. As a fully grown man Andrew stood little more than five foot two inches tall. When he shed his puppy fat he was actually quite slight of figure. This and his tow head gave him a very boyish appearance that belied his age and his maturity, often leading business colleagues and rivals to under-estimate him.

Little Andy's prodigious appetite was matched by his precocity. Many of his contemporaries later testified to his astonishing feats of memory. As well as the works of Burns, he could repeat verbatim lengthy passages of books read to him; and from an early age he liked to pepper his conversation with proverbs, old saws and apt quotations, a habit that remained with him all his life, and was also reflected in his voluminous writings. At an early age he also displayed a rare talent for persuading and manipulating people. This skill, which he would eventually hone with frightening precision, was evident when he was scarcely out of infancy.

One Sunday, when Andy was about six, he and his father were returning from the seashore, the boy perched on his father's back. The three-mile climb uphill from the coast had wearied the elder Carnegie and when they came to the steep rise leading into Dunfermline, William suggested mildly that Andy might enjoy walk-ing the rest of the way.

'Ah, faither,' soothed the boy, drawing his arms tighter about the man's neck, 'never mind. Patience and perseverance makes the man, ye ken.'

Shaking with laughter, William trudged on. Andy had learned the practical benefit of getting on the good side of people.[18]

Several other anecdotes have survived from Andy's early child-hood. At the head of Moodie Street was a communal well from which the womenfolk drew buckets of water. The supply was scanty and irregular and sometimes a dozen or more women had to wait in line. In some cases the well could only fill sufficiently if left overnight, and in that case the wifies would leave their buckets in a line, so that they could reclaim their positions at dawn. There was an unwritten law about everyone taking their turn in the proper order, but little Andy would sail into the midst of them, elbowing and butting his way through to fill his pail first. The poor old dames clucked and tutted and put him down as an awful laddie, but he would flash his dazzling smile and get away with his aggressive behaviour. 'In this way I probably developed the strain of argumentativeness, or perhaps combativeness, which has always remained with me,' commented Carnegie disingenuously.

In his *Autobiography* he tells how:

> One of the chief enjoyments of my childhood was the keeping of pigeons and rabbits. I am grateful every time I think of the trouble my father took to build a suitable house for these pets. Our home became headquarters for my young companions . . . there was nothing [my mother] and my father would not do to please us and the neighbors' children who centered about us.
>
> My first business venture was securing my companions' services for a season as an employer, the compensation being that the young rabbits, when such came, should be named after them. The Saturday holiday was generally spent by my flock in gathering food for the rabbits. My conscience reproves me today, looking back, when I think of the hard bargain I drove with my young playmates, many of whom were content to gather dandelions and clover for a whole season with me, conditioned upon this unique reward – the poorest return ever made to labor. Alas! what else had I to offer them! Not a penny.[19]

One imagines that Carnegie had his tongue in his cheek as he penned these lines.

Before the birth of Tom Carnegie in 1843, Andy was virtually an only child. Of course, there had been a little sister Ann, but her life was so brief that her presence seems hardly to have been registered. Carnegie himself never mentioned her in any of his autobiographical writings. With a father absorbed in his workshop and a mother busy with shoe repairs as well as housework, the solitary child was often left to his own devices. When he was just past his fourth birthday Andy found that his devoted mama suddenly had far less time for

him, as she tried to cope with her sickly baby. Feeling a sense of
rejection, little Andy soon discovered how to unlatch the door that
led to the outside stairs, and thus escape from the house into the park
across the street. Soon he was roaming farther afield, exploring the
town. From the top of the High Street, on a clear day, he could gaze
out over the Forth and see the spires and smoke-stacks of Auld
Reekie. There was also the ruined abbey to explore and thrill to the
exploits of Wallace and Bruce.

And then there was the great Glen of Pittencrieff which contained
Malcolm's Tower and the remains of the monastery and palace which
Malcolm Canmore had built for his English queen. The estate of
Pittencrieff had been purchased by the Hunt family who erected a
high stone wall around it, secured by stout iron gates. Once a year
the townspeople were permitted to enter and view the historic ruins
and admire the newly landscaped grounds. This concession was
granted to all the town's inhabitants, with a few notable exceptions.
As a result of a bitter quarrel between James Hunt and Old Tom
Morrison, the entire Morrison clan (including the Carnegies) were
banned. James Hunt vowed that no Morrison would ever set foot on
his estate, and Tom Morrison was too proud to put the matter to the
test. For Andy, who had to wait outside the gates until his playmates
returned and regaled him with stories of the peacocks and the other
wonders of Pittencrieff, his chagrin must have been unspeakable. In
his *Autobiography*, he mentioned Pittencrieff Glen in passing, only
commenting that 'The child privileged to develop amid such
surroundings absorbs poetry and romance with the air he breathes,
assimilates history and tradition as he gazes around.'[20] There was no
mention of his family being excluded, nor of the bitter resentment he
nurtured at the rank injustice of this. But the memory remained with
him all his life, and one may imagine the tremendous sense of
satisfaction he got when the day came that Pittencrieff Glen was *his*
– to give to the citizens of Dunfermline for their public and
perpetual use.

Having discovered how to escape from the house in Edgar Street,
and before the time when he was enrolled in the nearby school,
Andy's favourite haunt was the shop of his uncle, George Lauder,
who had married Aunt Seaton (Margaret Morrison's eldest sister).
Seaton died young, leaving a son, George Junior, who was a great

comfort to his grieving father. George Lauder had a grocery business which gave him ample time for his own son and his inquisitive nephew. He would chat for hours on end to the two small boys, and Carnegie would later remember him with great affection:

> My uncle possessed an extraordinary gift of dealing with children and taught us many things. Among others I remember how he taught us British history by imagining each of the monarchs in a certain place upon the walls of the room performing the act for which he was well known. Thus for me King John sits to this day above the mantelpiece signing the Magna Charta, and Queen Victoria is on the back of the door with her children on her knee . . .
>
> In the list of the monarchs which I learned at my uncle's knee the grand republican monarch [Oliver Cromwell] appeared writing his message to the Pope of Rome, informing His Holiness that 'if he did not cease persecuting the Protestants the thunder of Great Britain's cannon would be heard in the Vatican'. It is needless to say that the estimate we formed of Cromwell was that he was worth them 'a' thegither'.
>
> It was from my uncle I learned all that I know of the early history of Scotland – of Wallace and Bruce and Burns, of Blind Harry's history, of Scott, Ramsey [sic], Tannahill, Hogg, and Fergusson. I can truly say in the words of Burns that there was then and there created in me a vein of Scottish prejudice (or patriotism) which will cease to exist only with life. Wallace, of course, was our hero. Everything heroic entered in him.[21]

Little Andy could not say 'George' so he called his uncle and cousin 'Dod' instead. The Lauders, father and son, called Andy 'Naig', from the middle syllable of his surname which, in Scotland, is invariably pronounced 'Car*naig*ie' with the stress on the middle syllable – not '*Car*negie', stressed on the first syllable the way Americans pronounce it.

Uncle Lauder (whom Carnegie normally referred to by his surname) encouraged Dod and Naig to recite Scottish poetry and even to enact playlets at Hogmanay. *Rob Roy* and other works by Sir Walter Scott provided an abundance of suitably patriotic sketches for this purpose.

When 'a wicked big boy at school' told Andy that England was larger than Scotland, he brought this doleful news to his uncle. Lauder refuted this, saying that 'If Scotland were rolled out flat as England, Scotland would be the larger, but would you have the Highlands rolled down?' Oh never! That was balm of Gilead for the wounded young patriot. Later on, the greater population of England was forced on Andy. Again Uncle Lauder had the ready answer: 'Yes, Naig, seven to one, but there were more than that odds against us at Bannockburn.'

Returning home from Uncle Lauder's house at night Andy had the choice of two routes, the longer but well-lit route along Maygate, or the shorter way through the eerie, unlit abbey churchyard. It was a point of honour for the boy to take the latter route, whistling to keep his spirits up and imagining what his great hero Wallace might have done in similar circumstances, had he encountered any foe natural or supernatural.

The ruins of the medieval abbey had a powerful effect on the boy's imagination; but the great mass of the new abbey church seems to have held little or no interest for him. This was the bastion of the Established Church which, when Andy was eight, was suddenly and dramatically rent in two by the great schism which led to the creation of the Free Church. These dramatic events did not touch the Morrisons or the Carnegies. By that time Andy's parents were disenchanted with the Baptists, Margaret seeking the answers in the writings of William Channing while her husband flirted with the Swedenborgians who had rented an austere little building as their chapel. Margaret refused to accompany William to this chapel, but did not prevent him taking Andy. Sitting on a hard wooden bench one Sunday morning, listening to the pastor droning on, Andy looked up at the window and saw that it had a narrow border of blue and red glass. The sun glinting through the window produced a chequered pattern on the bare wooden floor. Andy was suddenly moved by this sight and his eyes welled with tears.[22]

When Andy was five he should have been enrolled at the local primary school, but remarkably he raised an objection to this and his ever-indulgent parents gave way, saying that he need not attend school until he himself asked to do so. There must have been many times over the ensuing three years when they wished they had not made such a rash promise, but they never reneged on the deal. Andy roamed the streets while his contemporaries were confined to the classroom, though more often than not he was seated in a corner of Uncle Lauder's shop absorbing a vast amount of general knowledge. Eventually Margaret asked Robert Martin, master of the Lancastrian School in Rolland Street, if he would take Andy out for a stroll some Saturday afternoon with some of his playmates and gently explain to the boy the untold advantages of going to school. Martin must have been very persuasive, for that night Andy announced that he would attend school, from Monday morning onwards. All his life, he would take decisions on personal grounds.

Soon Robert Martin became one of Andy's heroes, and he applied himself to his schoolwork with characteristic single-mindedness. The schoolroom in Rolland Street was drab and bleak, but in Andy's eyes it was transformed into an Aladdin's cave of educational treasures. In one large, cold, draughty room, 'Snuffy' Martin presided over a single class numbering about 180 pupils of all ages from five to twelve. The Lancastrian method of teaching relied heavily on the endless repetition of facts, or arithmetical tables, recited by the younger children and supervised by the older children. The latter got their instruction direct from the schoolmaster and they, in turn, imparted it to the infants. By this means a single teacher could control a large number of pupils and thus keep the cost of tuition down to a few pence a week. But as a method of educating children it was virtually useless and one suspects that Andy learned infinitely more at Uncle Lauder's knee. Martin maintained a rigid discipline with frequent use of the Lochgelly tawse, a stout leather strap. With several groups chanting and reciting different lessons simultaneously the school-room must at times have resembled bedlam.

A system that relied so much on learning by rote appealed to a boy with a photographic memory. Early on, Andy realised that he had a knack for memorising passages, and in his *Autobiography* he held this up as a good example: 'I cannot name a more important means of benefiting young people than encouraging them to commit favorite pieces to memory and recite them often.'[23] Every morning each pupil was expected to memorise two verses of the psalms and recite them before the class. Andy never gave this chore a thought until the moment when he set out to walk the short distance to Rolland Street.

In the space of four or five minutes he would have mastered the requisite portion and as the recitation was the first lesson of the day he passed this ordeal successfully. 'Had I been asked to repeat the psalm thirty minutes afterwards the attempt would, I fear, have ended in disastrous failure.' He retained only what was of interest to him, while other matters, such as the psalms, which did not impress him, soon faded from his memory.

Andy also recalled with pride the first penny he ever earned, or received from anyone beyond the family circle. It was given to him by Mr Martin for reciting before the whole school Burns's doleful poem 'Man was made to Mourn'. Andy smirked as Martin patted his tow head, but on the way home from school that afternoon, as he rubbed the penny in his trouser pocket, he was confronted by some of his schoolmates who jeered at him and taunted him with cries of 'Teacher's pet!'. Most boys, in similar circumstances, would instinctively have turned on their tormentors and given fight; but Andy, with that self-control instilled in him by his mother, held up his head and studiously ignored the rabble, sensing that behind the taunts lay envy, and that envy, in the circumstance, was a compliment. Though naturally combative and pugnacious, he always had the good sense to know when it was more prudent to ignore the challenge. Thus, at a very early age, Andy learned to get his own way by subtler methods.

'It is impossible to exaggerate the influence of the national poet on this particular worshipper,' wrote one biographer.[24] Andy's father and favourite uncle were themselves avid devotees of Burns, but they stopped well short of the uncritical adulation accorded by the boy. Burns remained Carnegie's favourite – and not just as a poet but as a philosopher, guide and mentor – all his life. As some men turned to their bible for guidance, so Carnegie turned to his well-thumbed Burns. The ploughman-poet was the single most important influence in his religious and political outlook. As an adult, Carnegie was a voracious and wide-ranging reader, but his studies as a man discovered few truths that his favourite bard had not enunciated or forecast. Most of all, he admired Burns's unswerving championship of the working classes. Never half-hearted in any of his enthusiasms, Carnegie's intense feeling for Burns was one of idolatry. (This eventually took the very real form of stipulating that a bust of Burns should be prominently displayed in every library endowed by Carnegie, leading to the curious situation that, at one time, there were more statues of Burns in the United States than of Columbus and Washington put together.)[25] In later life, when all other authors failed him, Carnegie could still turn to Burns for consolation, even in his deepest moods. 'I gloated over the gems of Burns like a Prince of Ind over his jewels,' he wrote. Above all, the radical songs of Burns, penned in the white heat of revolutionary fervour in the 1790s, had the greatest appeal for Andy, and this remained with him all his life, blind to the contradictions between his principles and his practice.

John Morley, the Liberal politician and a great friend of Carnegie in later life, once said that a few lines of Burns had done more than the millions of editorials ever written to improve the social and political conditions of the people; this dictum had Carnegie's warmest endorsement. On one occasion Carnegie asked his friend which particular lines he had in mind, and Morley replied, 'No need to name them to you,' perhaps thinking of an occasion when Carnegie's familiarity with Burns showed to good advantage.[26]

The years in which Andrew Carnegie spent his boyhood were a time of great political tumult, economic vicissitude and social upheaval. The Reform Act of 1832, far from quelling the spirit of revolution that arose in the aftermath of Waterloo, merely fuelled the fires of unrest. By enfranchising those who paid a rental of at least ten pounds a year, it strengthened the middle classes, but left the working classes largely unrepresented and even more discontented than before. The Industrial Revolution that destroyed handloom weaving and other cottage industries soon created many new jobs in coal and steel, in heavy engineering and shipbuilding, and in countless other industries undreamt of a generation earlier, but the transformation of Britain into the world's manufacturing base was not accomplished without considerable hardship and distress. At the same time, traditional methods of farming and landholding were giving way to new crops and techniques and, above all, to the enclosure of common land. Thousands of cotters and labourers were driven from the land and drifted into the new towns and cities that mushroomed almost overnight. The east of Scotland was not quite so deeply affected by these changes as the west, and for that reason the political development of the working classes was less extreme, less militant, than it was in the area around Glasgow and Paisley.

In 1838 the People's Charter, formulated in London, was published at a mammoth demonstration in Glasgow, and its tenets spread like wildfire across the country. Soon, however, the Chartists divided into two main groups, the advocates of physical and moral force respectively. The former were mainly to be found in the Glasgow area, whereas the latter were stronger in Edinburgh, Dundee and other manufacturing towns of the east. In Dunfermline, the names of Morrison, Lauder and Carnegie were soon prominent in the Chartist movement. Old Tom had died in 1837 – he was actually taking part in a political rally in England at the time – so he did not live to see the promised land; but the gauntlet was ably taken up by his son Tom and his sons-in-law, George Lauder and William Carnegie. These three men were staunch supporters of John Fraser, leader of the Constitutionalist or moderate wing of the Chartists, who founded the *Edinburgh Monthly Democrat* in July 1838. In the very first issue of this journal, Fraser published a comment boldly headed 'Splendid triumph of democracy in the western district of Fife'. After warmly congratulating the men of Dunfermline, he praised the writer of a letter which he extolled fulsomely with the rhetorical question: 'Who that has the soul of a man within him cannot read it without feelings of exultation and brightening hopes for the redemption of his country! . . . Men of Edinburgh and Mid-Lothian, see what those patriots have done. Go ye and do likewise!' The letter itself appeared below:

> To the Editor of the Democrat.
>
> Sir, – the Working Men's Association of Dunfermline, at a meeting of their Committee, held last night (July the 1st), for the purpose of despatching our petition, found it contained 6,106 signatures, which trebles the number appended to this petition above any ever sent from Dunfermline.
>
> The work goes on gloriously here. Some of our friends have gone to the surrounding towns and villages, and I am happy to state they were most enthusiastically received, and their labours crowned with

the most cheering success. The Association is very strong in number, still increasing, and every man is nobly doing his duty. Indeed, we flatter ourselves, were all the country as the 'Western district of Fife', the advocates of misrule and corruption would soon have to give place to a better order of things; but

'It's comin' yet for a' that'

&c. Will Carnegie

Early euphoria, however, soon gave way to disillusionment as that brotherhood of man that Burns had forecast seemed just as far off as ever. Gradually the physical force element won the ascendancy, but revolution, when it came in 1839, was confined to an abortive rising in south Wales, easily put down by the authorities and swiftly followed by savage repression. For a time, the government seemed to have the situation firmly under control, but the outward calm concealed a dangerous groundswell of discontent that erupted again, in the summer of 1842, in a wave of strikes and riots. At first the moral force men tried to stand aloof, but when the coalminers of Clackmannanshire came out on strike in late August, Tom Morrison and his friend William Fleming promptly organised the Cessation-from-Labour Committee. Naïvely, they hoped that the best way to solve the growing problem of industrial unrest was to call a peaceful general strike. At Tom's instigation, leaflets to this effect were printed and sent to every town in Scotland and England where Chartist and Working Men's Associations were known to exist. Morrison sincerely believed that, under his leadership, a spontaneous movement of the working classes would strengthen the position of the moral force men within Chartism, and prevent the riots and violence from getting out of hand.

In Dunfermline itself, Tom's call to down tools was readily accepted. Across the town the looms were silent, the shops were shuttered and even the collieries of the outlying district were deserted. The response of the mill-owners and mine bosses was swift. Ready to hand was an army of unemployed, half-starved and desperate for any work at any cost. The strikers soon found themselves permanently out of work as their places were taken by scabs and blacklegs. After seven days, the general strike was confined to Dunfermline itself, and pockets of Clackmannanshire and Lanarkshire, round Tillicoultry and Airdrie.

Early on, there had been a potentially ugly incident when Morrison chaired an open-air meeting on the boundary between Fife and Perthshire, broken up by the sudden appearance of the county sheriff and his deputies. Tom had persuaded his followers to withdraw in good order across the river dividing the counties and continued the meeting in full view of the enraged sheriff who was powerless to pursue them beyond his own jurisdiction. A few days later, however, the government sent in the Inniskilling Dragoons, backing a large posse of special constables, to forestall a rally planned for the following Saturday at Torryburn, and arrest the ringleaders. Morrison was seized in his bed, while Fleming and Andrew Henderson, president of the local Chartist Association, were apprehended on their way home from a political rally in Kirkcaldy.

One of Andy's earliest memories was of being awakened by a rap on his window near the outside staircase. He heard his father get up and go to the door, and listen as someone broke the news that Tom Morrison had been taken. The following morning the boy heard the whole story from his parents. Later in the day the town was placarded with leaflets urging the raising of a defence fund, and talk of a gaol-break was rife. (Many years later, Andrew Carnegie obtained one of the hand-bills appealing for £300 for the defence; he had it framed and displayed prominently on the wall of Skibo Castle. When King Edward VII visited Skibo and tentatively suggested a baronetcy, Carnegie politely turned down the honour, and proudly pointed to the poster, saying that *that* was his title to nobility.)

Uncle Tom's reputation as a rabble-rouser was more imaginary than real. To be sure, he was well known in Dunfermline as a determined heckler at political meetings. His personal appearance was not particularly striking, as he was below average height; but his beady eyes and florid face, framed by bushy beard, side-whiskers and an unruly mane, gave him a wild mien. A contemporary report in the *Dunfermline Journal*, admittedly a Conservative paper, gives the flavour of Tom Morrison's behaviour:

> The manner in which he heckles the speaker is most disgusting and
> the low contemptible sneer with which it is frequently accompanied,
> and with which he can laugh at the most sacred emotions of the

human heart, too often characterises his public conduct, and renders
it an abomination to every well-regulated mind.[27]

Morrison's actions belied his appearance, however, and he showed
commendable restraint when his friends marched on the gaol with
the intention of breaking him and his fellow prisoners out. A
frightened provost appealed to Morrison to calm his angry followers.
Through the bars of his cell he called out to them, saying that if they
followed his moral force principles they must put away their weapons
and depart in peace.

'All my friends fold their arms,' he said solemnly. Almost everyone
obeyed the injunction.

'Now walk peaceably to your homes and obey the law.'

The crowd assented and melted away. Within minutes the streets
were deserted. The following morning three of the town's leading
citizens put up the bail money and the trio were released. The
authorities thought it more prudent to let the matter drop, and the
defendants were never brought to trial. The effect of this incident
was to enhance Tom Morrison's standing in the community, and at
the forthcoming municipal elections he was voted on to the town
council. In the fullness of time he became a magistrate and ever
afterwards was known as Bailie Morrison, one of Dunfermline's most
highly respected citizens.

Matters dragged on indecisively. Somehow William Carnegie
continued to find work, even though weavers were reduced to a single
web a week, for which they were paid the paltry sum of four shillings.
In 1843, shortly after the birth of his second son, Tom, William was
forced to sell one of his looms for a few shillings, a fraction of its
original cost, and let go the most recent apprentice. Soon a second
and then a third loom had to be sold for whatever he could raise.
Reduced to a single loom once more, and barely finding enough work
for himself, William was obliged to give up his premises in Edgar
Street and move back to a humble half-cottage on Moodie Street,
quite close to the house where he had started married life with
Margaret almost ten years earlier. When there was scarcely any work
for the last remaining loom, Margaret converted the front of the
workshop into a tiny grocery where she sold farm produce to her
neighbours. The meagre return from the little shop was augmented

by taking in shoe repairs, at which Margaret laboured long and hard, far into the night. By her side sat her son, valiantly threading needles for her when her eyes were too tired. This experience left an indelible impression on eight-year-old Andy:

> Shortly after this I began to learn what poverty meant. Dreadful days came when my father took the last of his webs to the great manufacturer, and I saw my mother anxiously awaiting his return to know whether a new web was to be obtained or that a period of idleness was upon us. It was burnt into my heart then that my father, though neither 'abject, mean nor vile' as Burns has it, had nevertheless to
>
> > Beg a brother of the earth
> > To give him leave to toil.
>
> And then and there came the resolve that I would cure that when I got to be a man.[28]

Clearly this situation could not go on indefinitely. William had to face the fact that the day of the independent handloom weaver had gone for good. The only solution was to emigrate. Margaret's sisters Kitty and Annie, with their husbands Tom Hogan and Andrew Aitken, were now sending back glowing reports from Allegheny City, Pennsylvania. Margaret's brother William was also doing well on a farm in Ohio, while Andrew Hogan, Tom's brother, was already making his mark in real estate. Quite a number of families had left Dunfermline and settled in Pennsylvania. It would be almost a home from home, except that the prospects were endless for those prepared to work hard – and hard work was something that neither Margaret nor William had ever shirked.

The decision to leave Scotland was not lightly taken, however. Surviving family correspondence shows that Margaret had given the matter serious thought as far back as 1840, but she was then put off by reports from her sisters of the economic depression in the United States at that time, not yet recovered from the panic of 1837. 'My dear Margaret, things being in such an unsettled condition in this country at present, it would be the height of folly to advise you to venture out in this season at any rate,' wrote Annie. Andrew Aitken added a note to his brother-in-law George Lauder: 'I wish I had taken your advice & not come to America this soon – the banking system has made sad havoc here – business is at a stand here.'[29] In 1842 things were no better, Annie writing to Margaret, 'I would not advise any person to come out at present who can get a lively hood [*sic*] at home, as trade is very dull here.' Two years later, however, the situation had improved considerably. On 30 May 1844 Annie wrote to her sister:

> Business here is much better now, as most individuals can find employment, although some are out of a job yet, & the wages are considerably reduced . . . This country's far better for the working man than the old one, & there is room enough & to spare, notwithstanding the thousands that flock into her borders. As for myself, I like it much better than at home, for in fact you seem to breathe a freer atmosphere here; but as Andw. Hoggan says no wonder them women like it, for they are so much thought of in this country. Indeed you would be surprised to see how kind men are to their wifes; they seem so anxious to let them have an easy life although they toil very late themselves.

America, the Land of the Free, was always being held up by the Chartists as a model democracy. Yet, despite the attraction of this Utopia and the blandishments of his relatives who had made the move, William Carnegie remained indecisive and timid, alarmed at the prospect of giving up everything for something unknown. What concentrated his mind in the end was the harsh winter of 1847 which followed the failure of the potato harvest for the second year in succession. The working classes of Scotland, as in Ireland, were re-duced to starvation and utter destitution, and now emigration became imperative if the Carnegies were to survive at all. With the coming of spring in 1848, the Micawberish William hoped that the situation would somehow improve and they would not have to uproot themselves after all; but then all Europe was convulsed by revolution. There was a sudden dramatic resurgence of Chartism (which had been in the doldrums for several years). A huge demonstration was planned in Fitzroy Square, London, to be addressed by the great demagogue Feargus O'Connor. It was expected that over 150,000 people would flock to the rally, but in the event fewer than 23,000 turned up, and they were heavily outnumbered by the police and military drafted in for the occasion. O'Connor meekly agreed to the police request that he must present his petition to Parliament without a procession of his followers. The giant petition, said to contain 5,700,000 names, was duly delivered, but afterwards found to contain fewer than 2,000,000 names, many of doubtful authenticity. The People's Charter was thus laughed out of court, and the movement collapsed.

This cruel farce finally persuaded William and Margaret that there was no point in remaining in Scotland. But although their minds were made up, they had the painful problem of raising sufficient money for the passage to America. The disposal of their few remaining possessions left them pitifully short of the necessary amount. At a crucial moment, Margaret's friend Ella Henderson came to the rescue with the loan of twenty pounds. George Lauder deplored their decision to leave, but when he realised that his sister-in-law was set on the move he organised the very cheapest fares he could get for them.

On 16 May 1848 the Carnegies set off on their great adventure. The previous evening William's sister, Charlotte Drysdale, had called round at the cottage, now completely denuded of all but a borrowed chair, and there found her brother, his head in his hands, in deepest despair. When she held out her hand and proffered two pounds ten shillings, Will burst into tears. 'If ever I've anything,' he sobbed, 'I'll mind ye.'[30] By contrast, Margaret told her brother Tom, 'I'll make a spoon or I'll spoil the horn', an old Scottish saying that meant that the move to America would make or break them; she would succeed or die in the attempt.

Early the following morning the Carnegie family boarded the horse-drawn omnibus that ran from Dunfermline to Charlestown, one of the little ports on the Firth of Forth. Margaret, William and their sons were accompanied by Dod, Uncle Lauder, Uncle Tom and a few family friends including Provost Walls. Andy was heartbroken at the decision to leave his beloved Dunfermline, and on the bumpy ride down to the coast stood at the rear of the omnibus, staring through his tears at the receding view. The last thing he could see was the square tower of the new abbey church. 'Bruce's monument,' he wrote to cousin Dod fourteen years later, 'I remember that was the last thing I saw of Dunfermline, and I cried bitterly when it could be seen no more.'[31]

At Charlestown the convoy boarded the little ferryboat, rowed across the choppy firth to the steamer bound from Edinburgh to Glasgow on the Forth and Clyde Canal. As the Carnegies were transferring from the launch to the steamer, Andy clung frenziedly to his beloved Uncle Lauder, crying, 'I cannot leave you! I cannot leave you!' and it took a burly seaman to prise the sobbing child from George Lauder and place him in the well of the boat beside his disconsolate parents. Once the canal boat got under way, however, Andy recovered his composure and was soon staring around him with wide-eyed interest, as new scenery and landmarks passed before his excited gaze. By the time the canal boat reached Port Dundas in Glasgow, the boy was experiencing a sense of exhilaration he had never felt before. Dirty, grimy, bustling Glasgow had already overtaken douce Edinburgh to become Scotland's largest city. As the Carnegies tramped down through the city to the docks along the Broomielaw, Andy must have been overawed by the tall tenements and other unfamiliar sights, though strangely this experience passed without comment in any of his autobiographical writings. The family, along with other steerage passengers, were herded aboard their ship and assigned to their bunks. Fatigued by the longest day of their lives, the Carnegies promptly fell asleep.

At dawn on 17 May 1848, the 800-ton sailing vessel *Wiscasset*, a whaling schooner built in Maine which had been square-rigged for the merchant service, weighed anchor and beat down the Firth of Clyde on the ebbing tide. Margaret and William, with twelve-year-old Andy and five-year-old Tom, would become part of the statistics; in 1848 no fewer than 188,233 people migrated from Britain to the United States, a record figure. For the next seven weeks this ageing schooner with its cramped quarters and abominable victuals would be home to the family, and many others like it, driven from Scotland by poverty and sustained only by hope.

TWO

Allegheny City

1848–53

– nurst in the peasant's lowly shed,
To hardy independence bravely bred,
By early poverty to hardship steel'd
And train'd to arms in stern Misfortune's field –
Robert Burns, 'The Brigs of Ayr'

ALMOST AS SOON AS ANDY SAW THE GREAT SQUARE-RIGGED SAILS
fill with wind overhead, any sense of being overawed disappeared.
He stood on deck, facing westwards in the fresh spring breeze, and
suddenly the world was his oyster. In the days and weeks ahead, while
most of the passengers lay in their bunks, wallowing in utter
wretchedness and their own vomit, Andy was up on deck, bright-
eyed and eager to learn everything about the little ship. Seasickness
was never to trouble him, and his lively, cheery spirit soon endeared
him to passengers and crew alike. Certainly, within twenty-four
hours, there could have been no one aboard who did not know the
little tousle-haired boy. He quickly became the ship's mascot, always
ready and willing to run errands for everyone, always keen to learn
the arcane mysteries of seamanship and navigation. Soon he was
being employed by the crew to pass on messages or orders to the passengers and Andy relished every moment of his exalted position.

I was able to direct the passengers to answer the call of the
boatswain for, the ship being undermanned, the aid of the
passengers was urgently required. In consequence I was invited by

42

the sailors to participate on Sundays, in the one delicacy of the
sailors' mess, plum duff. I left the ship with sincere regret.[1]

On the fiftieth day out from Glasgow the *Wiscasset* dropped anchor off Castle Garden, Manhattan. No previous experience had prepared Andy for the bewildering sight that was New York, 'the first great hive of human industry among the inhabitants of which I had mingled, and the bustle and excitement of it overwhelmed me'. Yet what impressed the boy most of all about the brief sojourn in New York, was an incident as the family passed through Bowling Green. There they ran into Robert Barryman, one of the *Wiscasset*'s crew, now splendidly attired in his shore uniform of blue jacket and white trousers. 'I thought him the most beautiful man I had ever seen.' Barryman took his erstwhile shipmate to a refreshment stand and stood him a glass of sarsaparilla which Andy drank 'with as much relish as if it were the nectar of the gods'.

The Carnegies' only contact in New York City was James Sloane, a fellow weaver whose wife, Euphemia Douglas, had been one of Margaret's closest friends. Their sons William and John would one day own a famous Fifth Avenue firm of carpetmakers; in 1900 Willie Sloane bought land adjacent to the Carnegie residence in New York for his two married daughters 'so that our children of the third generation became playmates as our mothers were in Scotland'. The Carnegies did not tarry in New York but called at the Immigration Society for advice on the best (or cheapest) way to get to Pittsburgh. The direct route was expensive and complicated, involving a journey by stagecoaches, canals and finally an inclined-plane railcar from Philadelphia. Instead, the immigration agents recommended a rather circuitous trip at a third of the cost per mile, and thus the family came to travel to Pittsburgh on the overnight steamer up the Hudson to Albany and thence by canal boat to Buffalo, a journey of 364 miles that would take ten days alone. If the Atlantic crossing had been decidedly uncomfortable, the trip along the Erie Canal was hell on earth. For ten days they journeyed without being able to change their clothing, sleeping at night on a narrow bench in an unventilated cabin in the heat and humidity of a New York summer. Margaret and little Tom slept in the women's cabin, while William and Andy shared the privations of the men's quarters. By the standards of the

Forth and Clyde Canal, this journey was primitive in the extreme. The canal boat was drawn by a single horse and moved at a leisurely pace. In fine weather, however, the passengers could lie on the roof of their quarters. Those who had a little money could even step ashore when the boat paused at towns and villages along the way, and purchase food and drink to vary the monotony of the shipboard diet. While, for Margaret and William, this journey was something only to be endured as stoically as possible, their elder son enjoyed every moment, enchanted by the ever-changing scene as they passed through little settlements with outlandish names like Palmyra, Utica and Syracuse.

At Buffalo they transferred to a steamer for the journey across Lake Erie to Cleveland; the sight of this great inland sea took Andy's breath away. At Cleveland there was no time to marvel at the city as they joined the bustling throng of immigrants, bewildered by the shouts of rival canal agents touting for business. Next the Carnegies boarded another barge for the ride along the Ohio and Erie Canal to the village of Akron, where they would transfer to another boat that would take them eastwards again, to Beaver in Pennsylvania. Akron, which would one day become the rubber metropolis of the world, was then a frontier town filled with dingy drinking-dens and cheap boarding-houses that served the passing canal trade. The Carnegies took one look at this tawdry sight and promptly boarded the first canal boat going east to the headwaters of the Ohio. The journey from New York to Pittsburgh took all of three weeks; a few years later Andy would do it in less than ten hours by rail. 'Nothing comes amiss to youth, and I look back upon my three weeks as a passenger upon the canal boat with unalloyed pleasure,' he later wrote.

> All that was disagreeable in my experience has long since faded from recollection, excepting the night we were compelled to remain upon the wharf-boat at Beaver waiting for the steamboat to take us up the Ohio to Pittsburgh. This was our first introduction to the mosquito in all its ferocity. My mother suffered so severely that in the morning she could hardly see. We were all frightful sights, but I do not remember that even the stinging misery of that night kept me from sleeping soundly. I could always sleep soundly, never knowing 'horrid night, the child of hell'.[2]

44

By now the family had been constantly on the move for more than ten weeks, and must have been bewildered not only by the vastness of the United States but by the fact that, having gone so far west, they were now heading back east. It was as if they were going round in circles. But after their horrendous night on the wharf at Beaver at the mercy of the mosquitoes, the welcome sight of the paddle-steamer from Cincinnati buoyed them up. Soon they were on the last lap of their epic journey. At Beaver, the Ohio River might still be described as picturesque, but the farther they progressed upstream the muddier the river became, until it was a turgid broth of effluent and scum from the heavy industries around Pittsburgh. This presaged the nature of their destination, but even that could not have prepared the Carnegies for the appalling sight that met their gaze as the steamer rounded the last bend and the city of Pittsburgh came into view. In the 1840s, when Chicago was still a country town and cows grazed north of Wall Street in New York, Pittsburgh was already regarded as the dirtiest and ugliest city in America. The smoke and grime of Glasgow were as nothing to the filth and the awful stench of the vast, sprawling industrial complex at the junction of the Allegheny and Monongahela Rivers.

The inner district of the city had been wiped out by fire only three years previously, but already the buildings hastily thrown up in the aftermath of the conflagration were so heavily patinated with soot that it was impossible to distinguish them from the older surviving structures. The narrow, congested thoroughfares were crammed with horse-drawn vehicles of every kind and the noise of this traffic was deafening. Margaret and William had never seen such a frenzy of activity, and they were frightened by it; but to their twelve-year-old elder son, the streets had a vibrancy that he relished. Deposited unceremoniously at the downtown wharf, the Carnegies eventually got a ferry across the river and set off to trudge the two miles through the suburb of Allegheny to the district where Margaret's two sisters and their husbands lived.

Andrew Aitken had recently died, and his widow Annie had moved in with her sister Kitty and Tom Hogan who lived in a frame house on Rebecca Street which they rented from Tom's brother Andrew. Annie still owned the tiny shack at the back of the Hogan lot and, in turn, had let it out to Andrew Hogan as a weaving workshop. The two small upper rooms of this building were empty, and this is where the Carnegies took up residence. The small wooden house was dingy in the extreme and looked out on to a seedy back alley that was a dust-bowl in summer and a quagmire at all other seasons. The Carnegies quickly realised that poverty and squalor, like everything else in this strange new country, were on a larger scale than anything they could have imagined at home. In Dunfermline they might have been poor, but at least they had always lived in solidly built stone houses with good tiled roofs. Here they were reduced to living in what was little more than a shanty town, where the flimsy wooden shacks gave scant protection against the elements. Officially, their address was 336½ Rebecca Street, Allegheny City; unofficially, the place where they lived was derisively known as Slabtown.

Andrew Hogan had now given up weaving, finding a much more profitable line in erecting shacks for new migrants and speculating in land deals. He was only too happy to let William have the use of his loom. Soon the elder Carnegie was happily at work, turning out his best quality damask linens once more. Weaving fine tablecloths was one thing, but selling them proved to be another matter entirely. In the evenings William hawked his wares from door to door but soon found that there was depressingly little demand for his superior product. 'The returns were meagre in the extreme' is how Andrew Carnegie tersely described it later.[3] Once more Margaret came to the rescue. Next door but one on Rebecca Street lived Henry Phipps, an English cobbler. Margaret told him that she had been trained in boot and shoe repairs and begged him for some out-work for binding shoes. Thus, in addition to her household chores, Margaret now worked far into the night, just as she had done in Dunfermline, stitching shoe-leather – only now the task of threading the needles and waxing the thread fell to five-year-old Tom. This work, which occupied her at odd moments during the day and often till midnight or beyond, brought in the princely sum of four dollars a week, sufficient to clothe and feed the family. Describing this in his *Autobiography*, Carnegie took the opportunity to insert a moralising passage:

> This is where the children of honest poverty have the most precious of all advantages over those of wealth. The mother, nurse, cook,

governess, teacher, saint, all in one; the father, exemplar, guide, counselor, and friend! Thus were my brother and I brought up. What has the child of millionaire or nobleman that counts compared to such a heritage?'[4]

And he waxed lyrical on the same theme when, in 1896, he had addressed himself to the youth of the nation, at a time when America was in the grip of a deep depression:

> It is because I know how sweet and happy and pure the home of honest poverty is . . . that I sympathize with the rich man's boy . . . It seems, nowadays, a matter of universal desire that poverty should be abolished. We should be quite willing to abolish luxury, but to abolish honest, industrious, self-denying poverty would be to destroy the soil upon which mankind produces the virtues which enable our race to reach a still higher civilization than it now possesses.[5]

Only someone who had never known the meaning of real poverty could have penned such smug, self-righteous lines. Poverty was relative, and elsewhere in his *Autobiography* Carnegie admitted that 'We were not reduced to anything like poverty compared with our neighbors. I do not know to what lengths of privation my mother would not have gone that she might see her two boys wearing large white collars, and trimly dressed.'[6] 'Honest poverty', a phrase borrowed from Burns of course, would become a cliché which Carnegie used on countless occasions throughout his life. It would always be 'sweet and happy and pure', because that was how it had seemed to him in his childhood, or how it increasingly came to be idealised as he became more and more successful in adulthood. So also democracy would mean only the absence of titled nobility, because that was what Uncle Tom Morrison had inculcated. Carnegie's basic attitudes, formed as a small boy, never altered as he grew older, and he would continue to regard all later events in terms of personal experience and, paradoxically, personal detachment.

Central to the young Carnegie's philosophy was the view that 'the Lord helps them that help themselves'. No one was going to give him a helping hand, so he must seize his opportunities whenever they presented themselves. The 'awful laddie' that barged his way to the head of the water line, who ingratiated himself with 'Snuffy' Martin at Rolland Street and made himself indispensable to the crew of the *Wiscasset*, became streetwise in Slabtown in a remarkably short time. It was not much, but even here, amid the dismal streets and dingy alleys, there were opportunities for getting on in life. His own experience coloured his later outlook, and he never quite grasped that there might be other roads to advancement. 'I congratulate poor young men upon being born to that ancient and honorable degree which renders it necessary that they should devote themselves to hard work,' he told the graduates of Curry Commercial College in 1885.

> The partner's son will not trouble you much, but look out that some boys poorer than yourselves, whose parents cannot afford to give them the advantages of a course in this institute, advantages which should give you a decided lead in the race – look out that such boys do not challenge you at the post and pass you at the grandstand. Look out for the boy who has to plunge into work direct from the common school and who begins by sweeping the office floor. He is probably the dark horse that you had better watch.[7]

The youthful audience would have been in no doubt as to the 'dark horse' Carnegie was referring to.

Margaret Carnegie worked eighteen and sometimes twenty hours a day. In addition to shoemaking out-work, she took in laundry and made herself useful in many other ways to her neighbours. A few cents here, a dime there, Margaret began putting by the occasional hard-won silver dollar; more than a hundred of them would be required to repay Ella Henderson's generous loan, but Margaret placed this at the top of her priorities. There was no suggestion of Andy returning to school. He was now approaching his thirteenth birthday, and the four years spent at Rolland Street were quite adequate to have given him a basic education. He had a neat pen, could count quickly and accurately, had a good command of English and even the rudiments of Latin. What more did an eager youth need to get started in life? The question was, what was there for him to do?

Andrew Hogan came up with the idea that a bright lad like Andy would do well as a pedlar, hawking all manner of knick-knacks along the city wharves. This suggestion was put to Margaret as she sat, Tom on her lap, sewing shoe-leather. Later Andy would describe the scene as 'the most tragic I have ever witnessed':

I never knew what an enraged woman meant till then. My mother was sitting sewing at the moment, but she sprang to her feet with outstretched hands and shook them in his face.

'What! my son a peddler and go among rough men upon the wharves! I would rather throw him into the Allegheny River. Leave me!' she cried, pointing to the door, and Mr Hogan went.

She stood a tragic queen. The next moment she had broken down, but only for a few moments did tears fall and sobs come. Then she took her two boys in her arms and told us not to mind her foolishness. There were many things in the world for us to do and we could be useful men, honored and respected, if we always did what was right . . . It was not because the occupation suggested was peaceful labor, for we were taught that idleness was disgraceful; but because the suggested occupation was somewhat vagrant in character and not entirely respectable in her eyes. Better death. Yes, mother would have taken her two boys, one under each arm, and perished with them rather than that they should mingle with low company in their extreme youth.[8]

Poor Hogan was only trying to be helpful, but he had not reckoned with the blazing fury he unleashed. Andy had never seen his mother in such a temper, and the memory was seared into his soul. 'Anything low, mean, deceitful, shifty, coarse, underhand or gossipy was foreign to that heroic soul,' he wrote in his *Autobiography*. 'Tom and I could not help growing up respectable characters, having such a mother,' and, as an afterthought he added, 'and such a father, for the father, too, was one of nature's noblemen, beloved by all, a saint.'[9]

Not long after this incident William Carnegie gave up handloom weaving and obtained a position in a cotton mill run by a Mr Blackstock, 'an old Scotsman in Allegheny City'. William, in turn, secured employment for his elder son as a bobbin boy at $1.20 a week. This time Margaret did not demur. William and Andy would rise at six o'clock and breakfast in the dark, then trudge to the factory before sun-up. Apart from a very short meal-break at midday, they would work till after dark. 'The hours hung heavily upon me,' wrote Carnegie, 'and in the work itself I took no pleasure; but the cloud had a silver lining, as it gave me the feeling that I was doing something for my world – our family.' Not all his millions ever gave him half as much pleasure as his first meagre wage: 'I was now a helper of the family, a breadwinner, and no longer a total charge upon my parents.'[10]

When John Hay, who had known the Morrisons back in Dunfermline, offered Andy two dollars a week to come and work in his bobbin factory, the boy accepted with alacrity. William appears to have left Blackstock's employment about the same time, and gone back to the uncertainties of his own loom. He wove chequered tablecloths that no sensible person would purchase since machine-made cloths were much cheaper, but William was oblivious to this and was quite happy to sit at his treadle, singing 'auld Scots sangs' and working away in his own little world while his wife and son got on with the real business of making ends meet. The separation from his father, and having to go off to the factory every morning on his own, only emphasised the boy's own unhappiness at this period. To his disgust, Andy soon found that work in the bobbin factory was even more irksome than it had been in Blackstock's mill. His main task was to run a small steam engine and to stoke the fire for the boiler in the basement. It was a terrifying experience for a young lad who had been brought up with a loathing of machinery of any kind:

> I found myself night after night, sitting up in bed trying the steam gauges, fearing at one time that the steam was too low and that the workers above would complain that they had not power enough, and at another time that the steam was too high and the boiler might burst.[11]

At least the job was relatively clean, as the boiler used woodchips instead of coal. Andy kept his fears to himself, for his parents had enough troubles of their own to contend with. Margaret was no doubt thankful that this job kept her young son apart from the uncouth, common workforce. In fact, it cut him off completely from any contact with the other workers. Every day this lonely, frightened boy toiled in the fetid cellar, fervently praying that something better would turn up. Then, one day, the chance presented itself. Hay had to make out some bills, and having no clerk, was compelled to deal with this chore himself. Being a poor penman he asked Andy what kind of hand he could write, and gave him some clerical work to do. John Hay was evidently satisfied with Andy's bold, open hand-writing, for thereafter he gave him the weekly statement of accounts to write out. Instinctively Andy knew how to cut an appealing figure and play upon the protective feelings of others: 'besides, dear old man, I believe he was moved by good feeling toward the white-haired boy, for he had a kind heart and was Scotch and wished to relieve me from the engine . . .'

There was not sufficient clerical work in the factory to keep a boy fully employed, so Andy had to combine the tasks of making out the bills and keeping the accounts with a modicum of manual labour. The new duties did not involve machinery, but were almost as objectionable as the boiler-room: he had to bathe the newly made spools in vats of oil. While Andy relished the fact that he still had a room all to himself, so that he did not have to mix with the other workers, he could barely tolerate the overpowering stench of the oil:

> I never succeeded in overcoming the nausea produced by the smell of the oil. Even Wallace and Bruce proved impotent here. But if I had to lose breakfast, or dinner, I had all the better appetite for supper, and the allotted work was done. A real disciple of Wallace or Bruce could not give up; he would die first.[12]

Till the end of his days Carnegie could not abide the smell of oil; even as an old man, an unexpected encounter with the merest whiff of machine oil would reawaken ghastly memories and make him physically sick.

Rebecca Street was the headquarters of a little gang known as the Bottom Hooshiers. Andy and little Tom were not immediately admitted to this select band because their speech and manners marked them out as different. Andy's broad Scots accent was an immediate source of amusement to the ragamuffins as much as his diminutive stature, pale pink skin and flaxen hair. More than half a century later one of these street kids, Thomas N. Miller, reminded Carnegie of those times when the Bottom Hooshiers hollered 'Scotchie! Scotchie! Scotchie!' after him and Andy riposted, 'Aye, I'm a Scotchie, and I'm prood o' the name!'[13] In no time at all, though, Scotch Andy won acceptance and became one of the gang. The Bottom Hooshiers turned out to be a cradle of millionaires and public leaders. In truth, most of them were of Scots blood, if not actually Scottish immigrants like Andy, and they probably owed something of their later success to the half-pint who rapidly became their leader. One was Robert Pitcairn who became vice-president of the Pennsylvania Railroad and one of the richest men in the state. Another was David McCargo who developed the Allegheny Valley Railroad, while Henry W. Oliver made a vast fortune from the iron ore deposits of north-western Pennsylvania. On the other hand, two of Andy's closest chums died young in very tragic circumstances. John Phipps, son of the neighbourhood cobbler, was killed by a runaway horse while still in his teens, and William Cowley succumbed to disease during the American Civil War. Andy was deeply affected by the death of John, who was his closest confidant; afterwards he transferred his affections to John's younger brother Henry. Many years later Henry Phipps Junior would recall with pleasure not so much his erstwhile playmate but that boy's mother:

> Her home has been to me a second home, and she has been to me like a mother and her sons like brothers. When a young child, Mrs Carnegie taught me to tell the time of day; in later years she endeavored to teach me the value of time. I have listened to Mrs Carnegie's telling, in a manner pleasant and suited to the childish ear, the first stories I ever heard of Scottish history. How deeply they sank into the young minds of those who listened! With what pleasure the neighbors' children would listen with bright eyes to Mrs Carnegie reciting from memory portions of the 'Lady of the Lake', 'Marmion' and other poems.[14]

The clerical side of Andy's duties made him aware of the fact that the only way he would ever escape from dirty or unpleasant manual labour would be to develop the skills of the white-collar worker. Hay kept his accounts in the old-fashioned single-entry system, but 'hearing that all great firms kept their books in double entry', Andy resolved to learn the rudiments of modern book-keeping. He discussed it with John Phipps, Thomas Miller and William Cowley, and persuaded them to join him in a course of tuition from an accountant named Williams. During the winter months the four boys tramped over to Pittsburgh two or three evenings each week for lessons. Andy, who had a natural bent for mathematics, took to accountancy like a duck to water, savouring the precision of the double-entry system.

One of his biographers says that Andy 'never had the opportunity to revolutionize Hay's accounts' because he moved on 'early in the spring of 1849';[15] but Carnegie's *Autobiography* implies that he remained in Hay's employment until early in 1850, and there is no reason to doubt this. Another biographer takes a middle view, saying that 'The vat and boiler-room held Andrew captive for something less than a year'.[16] At any rate, Carnegie himself explained graphically how a dramatic change in circumstances arose through the slightest of events.

One evening, over a game of draughts, David Brooks, manager of the O'Reilly Telegraph Company in Pittsburgh, casually remarked to Andrew Hogan that he was looking for a bright messenger boy. 'Upon such trifles do the most momentous consequences hang,' wrote Carnegie, offering another piece of homespun philosophy. 'A word, a look, an accent, may affect the destiny not only of individuals, but of nations. He is a bold man who calls anything a trifle . . . The young should remember that upon trifles the best gifts of the gods often hang.'[17]

The pay would be $2.50 a week. Hogan immediately suggested his brother's nephew, knowing that this sum was a vast improvement over his present wage. Brooks agreed to interview the lad the following morning, so Hogan rushed off to give the good news. Andy was 'wild with delight' at the prospect of giving up his troglodyte existence, and Margaret was relieved, especially as her husband was now unemployed once more. Characteristically, the one objector to the change was William, timid and conservative as ever. He reasoned that for such a large wage Brooks must be looking for a much bigger, more robust boy. Andy was too wee, too childish in appearance, to be entrusted with such a responsible task. He might be sent out on

dark nights; he might be compelled to go long distances; it was plain
that the situation involved all kinds of physical and moral dangers:
'Ye better let weel alane.' Andy, he reasoned, stood no chance of
getting the job; it would be a waste of time and the loss of a day's
pay to go after such a hopeless quest. But in answer to his wife's
arguments and his son's entreaties, William finally agreed to consult
John Hay on the matter. Although he was likely to lose a promising
employee, Hay told William that the boy ought to be given the
chance to try for the position, and reassured the timid Carnegie by
saying that if Andy did not get the job he could always come back to
the bobbin factory.

The following morning, clad in his one decent suit, Andy set out
with his father to cross the river and call on Mr Brooks. William had
insisted on accompanying the boy but when they arrived at the
telegraph office, on the corner of Third and Wood Streets,[18] Andy
asked his father to wait outside. 'I insisted upon going alone upstairs
to the second or operating floor to see the great man and learn my
fate. I was led to this, perhaps, because I had by that time begun to
consider myself something of an American.'[19] Probably it was rather
a fear that William's awkward and diffident manner might prejudice
Brooks that induced Andy to abandon his father on the doorstep.

The interview was short and sweet. Brooks quickly sized up the
boy. To be sure, he was very small for his age, but he had a quality of
alertness and confidence that impressed the manager. Andy was
careful to explain that he did not know Pittsburgh, and that he might
not be strong enough, but he wanted a trial. Brooks swept this aside
and merely asked how soon he could start. Quick as a flash Andy
responded that he was ready to start immediately. Another
messenger boy, George Maclean, was called in and told to show young
Carnegie the ropes. Some time later, Andy remembered that he had a
father loitering outside, and went down to tell him that he could go
home and tell Margaret that he had got the job.

Andy was exhilarated at the change in his circumstances:

> From the dark cellar running a steam engine at two dollars a week,
> begrimed with coal dirt, without a trace of the elevating influences
> of life, I was lifted into paradise, yes, heaven, as it seemed to me,
> with newspapers, pens, pencils, and sunshine about me. There was

scarcely a minute in which I could not learn something or find out
how much there was to learn and how little I knew. I felt that my
foot was upon the ladder and that I was bound to climb.[20]

At first Andy was worried that some other, bigger, brighter boy
might turn up and wrest the precious job away from him. Now he lay
awake at night, not worrying about steam pressures, but trying to
memorise the names and addresses of all the businesses in the
downtown section of the city, and then trying to recall the names
and faces of the individuals to whom he had already delivered
telegrams. This proved to be a valuable exercise, not only in
improving his already remarkable memory, but in 'winning friends
and influencing people' as Dale Carnegie (no relation) would later
express it. This facility to recognise people in the street gave Andy
the edge over the other messengers. If he succeeded in delivering a
telegram on the street he not only saved himself a long climb up
flights of stairs to the relevant office, but brought himself to the
attention of businessmen who would ever afterwards remember the
alert youth who had expedited their messages. One of these was the
lawyer Edwin M. Stanton, afterwards Secretary of War in Lincoln's
Cabinet, whom Carnegie singled out as someone who 'was good
enough to take notice of me as a boy'.

The company which Brooks managed was the O'Reilly Telegraph
Company which handled all the traffic from the eastern states over
the Eastern Telegraph Line. Its rival, handling the western traffic,
was located next door in the basement of the St Charles Hotel. As
business expanded, it became necessary to take on additional staff.
The original messenger boy, George Maclean, was promoted to
telegraph operator and Andy now became the senior messenger,
given the task of finding another junior. It was then that Andy
secured a position for his friend David McCargo and instructed him
in his duties. When a third messenger was required, Andy had no
hesitation in proposing his pal Robert Pitcairn. These three Scots
musketeers, Andy, Davy and Bob, relished the work, feeling that
they had the whole communications between Pittsburgh and the
East Coast in their hands. In due course two other Scottish lads were
recruited to the expanding messenger service. These were Henry
Oliver and Will Morland, subsequently the head of the great manu-

facturing business of Oliver Brothers and a prominent Pittsburgh lawyer respectively. When James D. Reid, the Dunfermline-born general superintendent of the company, visited the Pittsburgh office, the five messenger boys were lined up for his inspection. Although smartly turned out, each boy was clad differently. Reid decided there and then that they should have a corporate livery, and sent them to a nearby tailor to be kitted out in a smart uniform of dark green jacket and matching knickerbockers. Thereafter the Green Mercuries as they were nicknamed became a familiar sight in the city streets.

This was an intensely competitive business, as the boys often received tips or payment in kind, perhaps some fruit or cookies. Squabbles over who should deliver the messages which, being beyond the downtown area, were guaranteed to produce a dime tip, frequently led to fisticuffs, until Andy came up with the solution. Henceforward cash tips should be pooled, and then shared out equally among the messengers at the end of the month. 'This pooling of extra earnings,' he was at pains to explain, 'not being intended to create artificial prices was really co-operation. It was my first essay in financial organization.'[21]

As well as being dean of the messenger corps and treasurer of the pool, Andy took it upon himself to protect the morals of his colleagues. Henry Oliver and Will Morland, in particular, found him overbearing and bumptious. Not being aware of young Carnegie's family background, they assumed that he was some sort of religious fanatic. If one of the boys cracked a dirty joke, Andy would get up from his desk and flounce out of the room with an exaggerated air of disapproval. Even when he tried to unbend a little and indulge in what he considered to be a harmless frolic, his associates found him stiff and awkward in this unaccustomed role. Half a century later David McCargo gently reminded Carnegie of this:

> The whole trend of your mind seemed to be towards big things. Indeed, I recall that your efforts to do the pranks of the average boy struck me at times as being almost grotesque. You would not follow the fashions in dress, because, I supposed, you believed it to be the evidence of a little mind.[22]

Andy had a strongly puritanical streak in him and never disguised his contempt for those weak enough to indulge in tobacco or alcohol. He even found it necessary to reprimand Bob Pitcairn for his excessive consumption of sweets. As treasurer of the pool he felt it his duty to inform the confectioner next door to the telegraph office, where some of the boys ran up accounts, 'that he would not be responsible for any debts contracted by the too hungry and greedy boys'.[23] When he scolded Pitcairn, Bob replied that he had live things in his stomach that gnawed his insides until fed upon sweets.

Although acutely aware of the fact that the other boys heartily resented his overbearing manner, his frugal habits and his officious meddling in their affairs, Andy never made any attempt to court their popularity; he was far too busy ingratiating himself with his superiors. John P. Glass, who managed the front office on the ground floor, came to depend more and more on the tow-headed youngster to handle some of the more routine administrative details of the office and 'mind the shop' during his absence. As Glass, a highly popular man with political aspirations, was increasingly absent from the office, Andy deputised for him more and more, taking messages from the public. Soon he was also receiving the incoming messages from the operating room and assigning them to the other boys for delivery. One Saturday evening, when the boys lined up for their monthly pay, Glass waved Andy aside and paid all the other boys. For one horrible moment young Carnegie thought that he had unwittingly committed some terrible sin and was about to be dismissed in disgrace; but when the other messengers had left the room Glass took the boy behind the counter and counted out not the usual $11.25 but $13.50. He told Andy that his services were worth that much more to the company and that henceforward this would be his monthly pay. Andy dashed home and turned over to his mother the usual sum, but kept the additional $2.25 in his pocket. He wished to savour a little longer in private the pleasure of this bonus.

Only once he was in bed that night with his brother did Andy confide his secret to Tom, solemnly telling him that this was only the beginning. Some day they would go into business together. They would have a large firm. Andy was vague as to its nature but he was sure that it would carry an impressive sign inscribed 'Carnegie Brothers'. They would all be rich and father and mother would yet ride in their own carriage through the streets of Pittsburgh (this would be a recurring fantasy). The following morning, over Sunday breakfast, Andy produced the extra money with a flourish and proudly handed over his bonus to his mother. 'Then father's glance of loving pride and mother's blazing eye soon wet with tears, told their feeling. It was their boy's first triumph and proof positive that he was worthy of promotion.'[24] In one of his calculating moods Andy figured out that three hundred dollars a year would keep the family in comfort. Now his raise, together with his mother's income of four or five dollars a week, attained that goal. William, who still managed to dispose of the occasional tablecloth, seems not to have been taken into the reckoning.

As Andy became familiar with the shops and offices that habitually sent and received telegrams, he also picked up interesting titbits of business gossip, many of which were stored away in that retentive memory of his. Some day they might come in useful . . . Although now unofficially promoted to senior messenger, Andy still had to sweep out the operating room, a chore which the boys took in turn. This brought him at close quarters to the telegraph instruments and, overcoming his in-built aversion to machinery, he began studying them with curiosity. From this it was but a short step to practising with the Morse key early in the morning before the operators came on duty. Soon he was tapping out messages to boys at the other telegraph stations 'who had like purposes to my own'.

Early one morning, while sweeping out the room, Andy heard the Pittsburgh call-sign being rapped out with vigour, indicating that someone had an urgent message to transmit. Andy only hesitated a moment before tapping out the signal that he was ready to start receiving. Philadelphia came on the line saying that there was an urgent death message; could he take it? Andy responded that he would, if it were transmitted slowly. He succeeded in getting the message and ran out with it to await the arrival of David Brooks. Handing him the slip, he confessed what he had done. Luckily, Brooks complimented his over-eager messenger on his initiative, but warned him to be careful not to make mistakes. This bold gamble paid off and it was not long before Andy was being called upon to watch the instrument while the operator absented himself; in this casual manner he learned the art of telegraphy.

It was a relatively easy matter to make the leap from messenger boy to telegraph operator. 'We were blessed at this time with a rather indolent operator, who was only too glad to have me do his work,'[25] Carnegie noted smugly. In face of such overweening ambition, indolence stood no chance. Such rapid promotion, from junior messenger boy to fully fledged operator in the space of eighteen months, would have satisfied most teenagers, but not Andy. At that period incoming messages were punched on to a running slip of paper from which the operator read to a copyist. Andy, however, had heard rumours that a telegraphist out west had learned to read by sound, and could really take a message by ear. This set the boy to thinking, and when George Maclean, who was also by now an operator, found that this was feasible, Andy decided to try as well, and was surprised at the ease with which he learned the new language. Soon he was taking all his messages by ear, and became something of a celebrity, not only among his fellow operators but among the local businessmen who popped into the operating room to witness this feat.

Sixteen-year-old Andy's big chance came when Joseph Taylor, the operator at Greensburg thirty miles away, requested two weeks' leave. A temporary replacement had to be found and Brooks asked Carnegie if he felt up to the work. Andy nodded vigorously. The following day found him on the stagecoach bound for Greensburg, noting approvingly that his fellow passengers were the well-known lawyer David Bruce and his sister, and a Mr MacLaren – all fellow Scots of course. This was Andy's first excursion away from home and the Greensburg hotel was the first public house in which he had ever taken a meal. 'I thought the food wonderfully fine,' he added.

When not engaged on telegraph work, Andy explored the little town and surrounding countryside. Most mornings he took a walk through the great cuttings and along the embankments being made for the Pennsylvania Railroad, little dreaming that one day he himself would enter the service of that great corporation. Andy's eagerness for work, however, was almost his undoing. One night he sat in the office during a storm, not wishing to cut off the connection, when a flash of lightning struck the building, sending thousands of volts through the wire to the transmitter key and knocking the slight youth off his stool. 'After that I was noted in the office for caution during lightning storms.' Fortunately he survived the experience and in due course returned to Pittsburgh, having completed his stint to everyone's satisfaction. As a result, James D. Reid, the general superintendent of the telegraph company ('another fine specimen of the Scotsman'), promoted him to full-time operator and authorised a rise in Andy's wages to twenty-five dollars a month. Many years later Carnegie was able to repay the kindness of his fellow Fifer when he secured for Reid the position of American Consul in their native Dunfermline.

In the spring of 1851 a flood on the Ohio River destroyed telegraphic communication between Steubenville and Wheeling. Andy was despatched to Steubenville to take the eastern traffic coming by wire from Pittsburgh and transmit the messages by riverboat to Wheeling, where they could be relayed westwards. For over a week, pending repairs to the lines, Andy had sole responsibility for keeping telegraphic communications open to and from the entire Ohio valley. One evening when he took despatches to the river steamer bound for Wheeling, Andy ran into his father on board ship, with a bale of tablecloths which he hoped to sell in Cincinnati. It was a cold spring night and he was shocked to discover that William did not have the money for a cabin but was planning to spend the night on deck. Suddenly the contrast in their status struck Andy: the youth already an up-and-coming business executive entrusted with a major assignment of vital importance to the nation's commerce and revelling in the challenge, and the father, defeated yet unable to come to terms with the harsh reality of his circumstances, persisting with a trade that was already dead. Andy's words of comfort to William were: 'Well, Father, it will not be long before Mother and you shall ride in your carriage.' The older man responded characteristically:

> My father was usually shy, reserved and keenly sensitive, very saving of praise (a Scotch trait) lest his sons might be too greatly uplifted; but when touched he lost his self-control. He was so upon this occasion, and grasped my hand with a look which I often see and can never forget. He murmured slowly: 'Andra, I am proud of you.'
>
> The voice trembled and he seemed ashamed of himself for saying so much. The tear had to be wiped from his eye, I fondly noticed, as he bade me goodnight and told me to run back to my office. Those

words rang in my ear and warmed my heart for years and years. We understood each other. How reserved the Scot is! Where he feels most he expresses least. Quite right. There are holy depths which it is sacrilege to disturb. Silence is more eloquent than words.[26]

This passage is much more revealing than Carnegie intended, betraying a curious insensitivity to the feelings of those who had failed. Oblivious to the pain and embarrassment felt by William at this encounter, Carnegie could only record fatherly pride at his own eager promise of a carriage.

These exploits at Greensburg and Steubenville indicate that Andy, despite his youth, was regarded highly not only as a dependable operator but as something of a troubleshooter. More importantly for the immediate future, Carnegie was now a name on the lips of major businessmen who insisted that when they had particularly important messages to send, he should be the operator to handle them. By cutting out the copyist, Andy considerably accelerated the reception of telegrams, and this soon brought him even greater responsibilities. At this period all foreign news for the Pittsburgh press was received by wire from Cape Race. One operator was entrusted with this extremely exacting and important task and soon it was tacitly assigned to him.

> The lines in those days worked poorly, and during a storm much had to be guessed at. My guessing powers were said to be phenomenal, and it was my favorite diversion to fill up gaps instead of interrupting the sender and spending minutes over a lost word or two. This was not a dangerous practice in regard to foreign news, for if any undue liberties were taken by the bold operator, they were not of a character likely to bring him into serious trouble.[27]

Not dangerous, perhaps, to the 'bold operator' who was ready to cut corners – and Andy would later prove singularly adept at this – but the effect of such a dubious practice on the trustworthiness of the news submitted to the press was quite a different matter. One can speculate how much of what appeared in the Pittsburgh newspapers in 1852–53 was an accurate rendering of foreign despatches, and how much was the product of the 'phenomenal guessing powers' of a sixteen-year-old boy. Andy, it seems, was giving quite a new meaning to the expression 'free press'. At any rate, he got away with it, and was soon adding fresh lustre to his laurels, and lucre to his pockets. The five newspaper offices in the city pooled their resources by hiring one man at seven dollars a week to take down the foreign despatches and make copies for each of them. This individual, in turn, asked Andy if he would make five copies of all press despatches for him, for which he undertook to pay the boy a dollar a week. This was modest remuneration, but it brought Andy's monthly pay up to thirty dollars. One biographer avers that 'that extra dollar a week was not turned into the family fund. He considered it his own, his first capital. Little acorns, mighty oaks . . .'[28] Carnegie's version, however, was merely 'The family was gradually gaining ground; already future millionairedom seemed dawning'.

Around this time the Hogans left Allegheny to keep house for Tom's brother William at East Liverpool, Ohio, where he had prospered. This left the Hogan house available for the Carnegies, who promptly moved from their little shack at the rear. By now the hundred dollars required to repay Ella Henderson had been garnered and translated into a bank draft for twenty pounds. At one stroke the family was out of debt and settled in much more commodious surroundings. Hogan was keen to sell the house and set a price of $700 on it, but a bad flood on the Allegheny River caused some water damage to the ground floor and when he could not get the original asking price, Hogan dropped it to $550. In March 1853 the Carnegies took the plunge and made Hogan an offer, the sum to be paid off in instalments over a period of two years. At that time a four-roomed house such as this commanded a monthly rent of six or eight dollars, so Andy calculated that the risk was worth while.

All work and no play makes Jack a dull boy; in Andy's case even his leisure time would be utilised to the full. On a number of occasions he escorted a young lady named Lou Atherton to evening parties and brought her safely home, but this was purely a business arrangement, for which he was paid twenty-five cents by the girl's parents.[29] Andy had no interest in girls as such, and his autobiographical writings and the many anecdotes about his youth are entirely silent on the subject.

The Bottom Hooshiers were transformed, under Andy's guidance, into a little debating society which used to gather in the Phipps workshop in the evenings after the journeymen cobblers had gone home. Many years later, in 1903, Tom Miller reminded Andy of a time when he had once spoken for an hour and a half without pause on the subject 'Should the judiciary be elected by the people?'. Later Andy persuaded his five trusty companions and fellow messengers to join Webster's Literary Society. 'I know of no better mode of benefiting a youth than joining such a club as this,' he wrote. 'Much of my reading became such as had a bearing on forthcoming debates, and that gave clearness and fixity to my ideas.'[30] The self-possession he later had before an audience he attributed to the experience gained in this debating society.

One of the perks of being a telegraph operator in Pittsburgh was receiving complimentary tickets to concerts and theatrical performances, and Andy made the fullest use of this facility. Not content merely to watch a Shakespeare play, he would afterwards read the text and study it carefully, committing the great soliloquies to memory, just as he had previously learned the poems of Burns. He hungered for knowledge, any knowledge, and read every book he could lay his hands on, making full use of his circle of friends and acquaintances for this purpose. When he had exhausted this source, he happened to read in the local newspaper that Colonel James Anderson of Allegheny would open his personal library of four hundred volumes each Saturday afternoon to any young working boy who wished to borrow a book for the following week. A selection of the books which Andy subsequently borrowed from Anderson are now preserved in the Carnegie Birthplace Memorial Building in Dunfermline and reveal the scope of his reading: books on history and geography, especially about his adopted country, and weighty tomes on science and sociology. Ever since leaving Dunfermline, Andy had conducted a frequent and often lengthy correspondence with the Lauders and these letters are extremely illuminating about the boy's intellectual development. His Scottish patriotism was as fervent as ever, but subtly at first and later more stridently, comparisons between America and the old country took over. While social and political conditions were gradually improving in Britain, the United States was invariably held up as infinitely superior in every respect. When Andy confessed that he could no longer pronounce *sow crae* (pig-sty) in the approved Dunfermline manner, his Americanisation seemed complete. These letters to cousin Dod and Uncle Lauder make frequent reference to the books he was reading, as a result of Anderson's generosity; in his *Autobiography* Carnegie devoted a chapter to his intellectual benefactor,[31] and undoubtedly this greatly influenced his own desire to provide free libraries. Appropriately, when the Carnegie Library was opened in Allegheny, Carnegie unveiled a monument to Colonel Anderson in Diamond Square whose plinth concluded with the words:

> This monument is erected in grateful remembrance by Andrew Carnegie, one of the 'working boys' to whom were thus opened the precious treasure of knowledge and imagination through which youth may ascend.

When Anderson's original experiment proved successful, the colonel doubled his collection and moved it to a separate building. The Mechanics' and Apprentices' Library became Allegheny's first public library, with an annual subscription of two dollars, but free of charge to all apprentices. When Andy paid his first visit to the new library he was confronted not by the generous Anderson but a salaried librarian who informed him haughtily that, as he was not an apprentice, he would have to pay his two dollars. Although this was not unreasonable, Andy was scandalised, claiming that Anderson's intention had obviously been to continue the free library privileges to all those who had enjoyed them previously. The librarian being unmoved by this argument, Andy fired off a letter to the *Pittsburgh Dispatch* on 9 May 1853:

> Mr Editor:
>
> Believing that you take a deep interest in whatever tends to elevate, instruct and improve the youth of this country, I am induced to call your attention to the following. You will remember that some time ago Mr Anderson (a gentleman of this city) bequested a large sum of money to establish and support a Library for working boys and apprentices residing here. It has been in successful operation for over a year, scattering precious seeds among us, and although fallen 'by the wayside and in stony places' not a few have found good ground. Every working boy has been freely

admitted only by requiring his parents or guardian to become surety. But its means of doing good have recently been greatly circumscribed by new directors who refuse to allow any boy who is not learning a trade and bound for a stated time to become a member. I rather think that the new directors have misunderstood the generous donor's intentions. It can hardly be thought that he meant to exclude boys employed in stores merely because they are not bound.

A Working Boy though not bound.

A week later the librarian responded, explaining that the terms of the gift had specifically designated apprentices. 'Working Boy' returned to the attack on 17 May, reiterating his view that Colonel Anderson had never meant to exclude any working boys from the free use of the library. Three days later, a brief notice on the editorial page asked 'Working Boy' to call at the newspaper office. The following day Andy called at the *Dispatch* and was told that Colonel Anderson's attention had been brought to the recent correspondence, and that as a result he had graciously reworded the terms of his gift so that all working boys, whether apprentices or not, below a certain age, would be granted free access.

It was Andy's first triumph, and his first literary success. Seeing his words 'in guid black prent' as his favourite bard had put it, fed his vanity, and for a time he seriously contemplated a career in journalism. Although he never embarked on that course professionally, Carnegie would devote a not inconsiderable amount of his energies to journalism of one sort or another until the end of his days.

Towards the end of his life, Carnegie discovered that his own father had been one of the five weavers responsible for starting the first circulating library in Dunfermline. To be sure, this must have been a very modest affair, for it was recorded that when the little library moved to a new location, the founders carried the precious books in their aprons and two coal-scuttles; but it was the principle that mattered, and enabled Andy to boast that he had never heard of a lineage for which he would exchange that of a library-founding weaver. 'I followed my father in library founding unknowingly – I am tempted to say providentially – and it has been a source of intense satisfaction to me.'[32]

For a brief period Andy himself was involved in librarianship. In Allegheny William Carnegie had resumed his affiliation to the Swedenborgian Society which had a small congregation. William was a regular attender at Sunday services and for a time Andy himself, mainly under the influence of his Aunt Aitken (who hoped that he might become a preacher), took part in the Sunday School, sang in the choir, acted as teller at business meetings and ran the little library of theological and devotional works for several years. The Sabbath school ran a newsletter entitled *Dewdrop* and Andy was an occasional contributor. The only piece still extant, however, was obviously written in 1854 because it was a denunciation of war, with particular reference to the Battle of the Alma which took place in that year. Andy argued that weapons and the instruments of war should be confined to museums, and not paraded. 'Let war be shown to the young men in its true light, and all will be well.'[33]

An abhorrence of war and militarism was a recurring theme of Andy's letters to the folks back in Scotland, and would become a dominant factor in the last years of his life. Another issue on which he had trenchant views was slavery which he heartily detested, though he was at pains to explain the circumstances behind the great debate then raging in America between the free and slave states and the vexed question of whether slavery should be extended to Kansas and Nebraska. Already, in the 1850s, the seeds of dissension that would lead to the Civil War were being sown, but for the moment Andy was proud of the fact that the People's Charter, of which the workers back home could still only dream, was an accomplished fact in his adopted land. In a letter to Dod, dated 8 February 1854, he claimed, 'We believe that we have a great mission to fulfill with our independence a new light dawned upon the world.' But, already, by the time that letter was written, Carnegie was on the move, ever onward and upward, with new goals in his sights.

THREE

My Boy Andy

1853–59

There's a youth in this city, it were a great pity
That he from our lasses should wander awa;
For he's bonie and braw, weel-favor'd witha',
An his hair has a natural buckle an a'.
                    Robert Burns, 'There's a Youth in this City'

A MAJOR LANDMARK IN PITTSBURGH'S DEVELOPMENT WAS THE
opening, on 10 December 1852, of the single-track railway line
connecting the city to the Atlantic coast. For some time, of course,
the Pennsylvania Railroad had to utilise the old state-operated
inclined-plane tracks that traversed the mountains. Nevertheless, the
new system gave Pittsburgh a direct connection with the East and
eliminated the long, roundabout route through rivers, lakes and
canals, reducing the travelling time beyond all recognition.
Overnight Pittsburgh became truly the Gateway to the West. As the
railroad neared completion, an increasing amount of business came
the way of the O'Reilly Telegraph Company. In particular, the
recently appointed superintendent of the Pennsylvania Railroad's
Western Division, Thomas A. Scott, was an increasingly frequent
caller at the telegraph office at night and on several occasions Andy
was the duty operator. Scott was impressed by the boy's energy and
efficiency and in no time at all he was insisting that his messages to
Herman Lombaert, the general superintendent at Altoona, should be
transmitted by no one else but young Carnegie. Andy responded to
this recognition and did everything he could to accommodate Mr
Scott. He was flattered that the personable young superintendent

should have singled him out. From the outset, Andy was greatly taken by Scott, 'an extraordinary man, one to whom the term genius in his department may safely be applied'.[1]

Thomas Scott was, indeed, an extraordinary man. Born in Franklin County in eastern Pennsylvania of Scottish parents in 1823, he had lost his father ten years later and at a very early age forced to work to support his widowed mother and ten siblings. His first break came at the age of seventeen when he became clerk to his brother-in-law James Patton, collector of tolls for the state-owned road and canal system. Six years later he became the Pennsylvania Railroad's stationmaster at Duncansville, at that time the western terminus of the line. When the line was extended to Pittsburgh in 1852, he was promoted to third assistant superintendent, in charge of the division from Altoona to Pittsburgh. Following his appointment he established his office in Pittsburgh. He was twenty-nine at the time and still a bachelor. Though almost entirely self-educated, with little more than two years' formal schooling, he was widely read and a man of considerable refinement and taste. He was, in every sense of the word, a gentleman: charming, handsome, gentle, affable and warmhearted. He would need all these charismatic qualities and more to cope with the problems of his new position, not the least being the overt animosity of many of the leading figures in the Pittsburgh business community, resentful of the Pennsylvania Railroad's monopoly which had effectively kept out the Baltimore and Ohio Railroad for several years. This, in turn, had served to keep Pittsburgh isolated and powerless to realise its full potential as an industrial and commercial hub. It speaks volumes for the diplomacy and charm of Tom Scott that he overcame this hostility and eventually gained the wholehearted backing of the city for his railroad.

To be sure, businessmen relented when the railroad reduced its freight rates to two and a half cents a mile, putting its tariffs on a level with the canal companies, but from the outset the railroad cut the travelling time so drastically that henceforward it transported the great bulk of the interstate freight traffic. Until the through line was completed in 1854, though, there were numerous operational difficulties to be overcome, especially concerning the transfer of freight and passengers to the antiquated inclined-plane system, but Scott handled them in a no-nonsense manner that endeared him to the shippers, accustomed as they were to breakdowns and delays in the waterborne traffic. To streamline this operation, Scott realised that the railroad would need to have its own telegraph system in constant communication with Altoona and points east. He put this extraordinary proposal to the railroad president, J. Edgar Thomson, and when he readily assented, Scott went to work on the concept with customary flair and energy. The necessary equipment was obtained and installed. All that remained was to hire an operator of the right calibre for such an exacting job.

One day Andy was surprised when one of Scott's assistants came into the operating room and casually remarked that his boss had wondered whether young Carnegie could be obtained as his clerk and telegraph operator. The young man had told Scott that this was unlikely as Carnegie was now a fully fledged telegraph operator.

Andy cut him short: 'Not so fast!' he cried. 'He can have me. I want to get out of a mere office life. Please go and tell him so.'

That, at least, is the version in Carnegie's *Autobiography*; his colleagues at the telegraph office told a somewhat different story. Tom David, writing to Carnegie about his move to the Pennsylvania Railroad half a century after the event, reminded him that:

> It took some persuasion on the part of John P. Glass to convince you that it offered better opportunities. I saw Mr Glass having an earnest talk, and to my question, 'What is the matter with Andy,' he intimated that you did not like to make a change.[2]

The truth of the matter is that Andy was holding out in the hope that the telegraph company might offer him a raise that would be sufficient to induce him to remain where he was. In fact James Reid, the superintendent, offered him a substantial increase, which would have brought him thirty-three dollars a month, not counting the five dollars from the press service; Tom Scott's offer of thirty-five dollars, without the perquisite from the press service, actually represented a net loss of three dollars a month. It is highly probable that Andy would have made the move anyway, regardless of the cash equation, as he could perceive the infinitely greater potential of working for the railroad, particularly under Thomas Scott. That much was evident in a long letter to Uncle George Lauder shortly afterwards:

I have some news to tell you. I left my old place in the telegraph office and am now in the employ of the Pennsylvania Railroad Co., one of (if not the first of) the three leading roads from our Atlantic cities to the Great West. It forms a continuous line from Philadelphia to Pittsburgh & here connects with Western roads & the Ohio River. Mr Scott he's the supt. of it with whom I became acquainted while in the office by often talking for him on business by telegraph, offered me 35 dollars per month to take charge of their Telegraph office which the Co. has in this City for its own exclusive use – & also to assist him in writing and auditing accounts which I accepted. The Teleg. co. would have increased my salary to $400 per year if I had remained there but we all thought that the new situation held out better prospects for the future – I resigned my station on the first of February & have been employed at my new place since that time. I am liking it far better than the old one – instead of having to stay every other night till 10 or 11 o'clock, I am done every night at 6, which is a great advantage, and am not so much confined. Although I thought my old berth a very good one for the present, still for the future, I felt it did not hold out great inducements – I must always have been an employee – & the highest station I could reasonably expect to attain to was Manager of an office with 7 or 8 hundred a year and I had begun to think that if another situation would turn up which would be better for the future, I would accept it even though the salary was less than at present when Mr Scott (without my application) offered me my present berth – he is having an office fixed up for his own use and I am to be along with him in it & help him – I have met with very few men that I like so well in this Country – & I am sure we will agree very well. There is not much telegraphing to do, but it is necessary for them to have an office – The line runs along side of the Road & as there is only one track laid yet – the time the different trains pass stations must be known.[3]

With shorter hours, higher wages and better opportunities, this new situation seemed idyllic, but there were certain drawbacks. 'From the operating-room of the telegraph office I had now stepped into the open world, and the change at first was far from agreeable.'[4] In his *Autobiography* Carnegie claimed that he had just reached his eighteenth birthday but, at the time, he was in fact not long past his seventeenth, a strange error to make, but justified by the ensuing comment: 'I do not see how it could have been possible for any boy to arrive at that age much freer from a knowledge of anything but what was pure and good.' He would have his readers believe that he had never uttered a bad word in his life up to that time 'and seldom heard one', though the testimony of some of his former colleagues from the messenger days might suggest otherwise. 'I knew nothing of the base and vile,' he continued. 'Fortunately I had always been brought into contact with good people.'

Now he began to realise what his mother had meant about 'rough men of the wharves' when she had blazed at Andrew Hogan. There was something sanctimonious about the ensuing passage:

> I was now plunged at once into the company of coarse men, for the office was temporarily only a portion of the shops and the headquarters for the freight conductors, brakemen, and firemen. All of them had access to the same room as Superintendent Scott and myself, and they availed themselves of it . . . The experience with coarse men was probably beneficial because it gave me a 'scunner' (disgust), to use a Scotism, at chewing or smoking tobacco, also at swearing or the use of improper language, which fortunately remained with me through life.[5]

Written many years after the trauma of suddenly being exposed to all manner of obscenity for the first time, Carnegie might claim that this was 'beneficial', but at the time the shock to such an innocent young man of being confronted with the facts of life must have been pretty horrific. It would explain why Carnegie took such a 'scunner' to sexual matters as well as tobacco. This drove him into the protective carapace of his loving and ever-protective family and the 'sweet and pure surroundings of home'. Precocious in so many ways, he was emotionally immature, and the death of his father not long afterwards made him cling to his mother more than ever.

In the ensuing weeks he frequently returned to his old office and, glossing over the harsher side of his new surroundings, regaled his former colleagues with his exciting, challenging new role. He soon recruited Davy McCargo and Bob Pitcairn for the railroad (the latter being appointed personal secretary to General Superintendent Lombaert), and after Tom Scott's private office was fitted out and Andy joined him in this inner sanctum, working conditions improved dramatically. Then he could regard the rougher elements in a detached and more charitable light:

> I do not wish to suggest that the men of whom I have spoken were really degraded or bad characters. Railroading was new, and many rough characters were attracted to it from the river service. But many of the men were fine young fellows who have lived to be highly respectable citizens and to occupy responsible positions. And I must say that one and all of them were most kind to me.[6]

The last sentence is very significant, revealing a quality that Carnegie was to utilise and exploit throughout life. At seventeen he was barely five foot tall, and, fully grown, he would never be much taller. He was a skinny kid, too, a tow-headed stripling with the fresh face of a choirboy. One can imagine the kind of coarse remarks directed at Tom Scott's protégé by the railroad roughnecks – not helped by Scott's constant reference to the lad as 'my boy Andy'. Scott's relationship with Andy seems to have been more that of a big brother than an employer; despite the twelve-year gap in their ages the lad habitually addressed his boss as Tom, in an era when the formalities between employer and employee were usually very strictly observed.

One of Andy's duties was to go across the Allegheny Mountains to Altoona to collect the monthly payrolls and cheques from Herman Lombaert. Tom Scott warned his young assistant that the General Superintendent was 'stern and unbending', a strict disciplinarian and a stickler for proper business etiquette. This was later confirmed by Bob Pitcairn, so it was with some trepidation that Andy was introduced to the great man. Imagine his surprise when Lombaert smiled and said affably, 'You must come down and take tea with us tonight.' He was even more surprised that evening when Lombaert introduced him to his wife with the words, 'This is Mr Scott's Andy.' Carnegie commented: 'I was very proud indeed of being recognized as belonging to Mr Scott.'[7] More importantly, it indicated that his name was already familiar to those at the highest level in the railroad organisation.

The following morning, with the brown-paper packet containing the payroll and bundle of cheques tucked into his waistcoat, Andy boarded the footplate of the locomotive running as far as Hollidays-burg where he had to transfer to the inclined-plane. Riding the foot-plate and chatting to the driver and fireman were new experiences, and Andy relished the ride, although it was exceedingly bumpy. After one particularly nasty jolt he felt uneasily for the package and was horrified to discover that it had become dislodged and fallen out on to the track. All too well aware that the loss of such an important packet would mean the end of his promising career, the boy implored the engine-driver to stop and reverse back down the line till he found it. Remarkably, the driver – 'kind soul' – agreed and the locomotive inched its way back while Andy, in a paroxysm of fear, scanned the trackside. Eventually he espied the package. As luck would have it, it had rolled down the steep bank of a river and lay within a foot of the water's edge. Andy scrambled down and retrieved it. For the remainder of that eventful journey he clutched it tightly in his little pink hands until he was safely back in Pittsburgh.

> It was long after the event that I ventured to tell the story. Suppose that package had fallen just a few feet farther away and been swept down by the stream, how many years of faithful service would it have required upon my part to wipe out the effect of that one piece of carelessness! I could no longer have enjoyed the confidence of those whose confidence was essential to success had fortune not favored me. I have never since believed in being too hard on a young man, even if he does commit a dreadful mistake or two; and I have always tried in judging such to remember the difference it would have made in my own career but for an accident which restored me to that lost package at the edge of a stream a few miles from Hollidaysburg. I could go straight to the very spot today, and often as I passed over that line afterwards I never failed to see that light-brown package lying upon the bank. It seemed to be calling: 'All right, my boy! the good gods were with you, but don't do it again!'[8]

While Carnegie was absolutely right about the good gods being with him, it is regrettable that he seldom if ever adopted the forgiv-ing stance he professed in this passage. In fact, an opportunity to put this to the test had occurred soon afterwards (and was described in the *Autobiography*). Carnegie seems to have been unconscious of the glaring discrepancy between what he preached and what he practised. Tom Scott was absent from Pittsburgh for a week or two and left his youthful aide in charge of the office. During that period there was an accident for which the ballast crew were blamed. Up to that point everything had gone well in Scott's absence, 'but that this accident should occur was gall and wormwood to me'. Without waiting for the superintendent's return, Carnegie summoned what he was pleased to call 'a court-martial', peremptorily dismissed the chief offender and suspended two others for their share in the catastrophe.

> Mr Scott after his return of course was advised of the accident, and proposed to investigate and deal with the matter. I felt I had gone too far, but having taken the step, I informed him that all had been settled. I had investigated the matter and punished the guilty. Some of these appealed to Mr Scott for a reopening of the case, but this I never could have agreed to, had it been pressed. More by look I think than by word Mr Scott understood my feelings upon this delicate point, and acquiesced.
>
> It is probable he was afraid I had been too severe and very likely he was correct . . . I had felt qualms of conscience about my action in this, my first court. A new judge is apt to stand so straight as really to lean a little backward.[9]

This trait of dictatorial ruthlessness in his young protégé must have been disagreeable to Scott, though he can hardly have been surprised at it, for already he had become aware that his boy Andy was more than an efficient clerk. Someone less easy-going than Tom Scott might have been disturbed at the way in which this arrogant and cocksure pint-sized teenager was usurping his own authority.

One morning, when Scott was absent from the office, Andy got a message from Altoona that a serious accident on the Eastern Division had delayed the westward express, and that the eastbound passenger train was proceeding with a flagman in front at every curve. The freight trains in both directions were held up in sidings. Andy thought for a moment and then decided to use his own initiative. The words of Lord Nelson, 'Death or Westminster Abbey', flashed before his mind, knowing that he risked dismissal, disgrace or even criminal prosecution if he made a mistake. But if he could pull it off, and get the freight trains moving again, it would be a considerable coup. Swiftly he began wiring orders in Scott's name, started every train, carried them from station to station, and had everything running smoothly when Scott finally put in an appearance. He had heard of the delays and anxiously wondered what was happening. Deferentially Andy told him what he had done, then showed Scott the messages and reports pinpointing every train on the line – freights, ballast trains, everything.

> All was right. He looked in my face for a second. I scarcely dared look in his. I did not know what was going to happen. He did not say one word, but again looked carefully over all that had taken place. Still he said nothing. After a little, he moved away from my desk to his own, and that was the end of it. He was afraid to approve what I had done, yet he had not censured me. If it came out all right, it was all right; if it came out all wrong, the responsibility was mine. So it stood, but I noticed that he came in very regularly and in good time for some mornings after that.[10]

It was a repetition of that early-morning telegram from Philadelphia which Andy, a mere messenger boy, had taken in the absence of the regular operator, but the consequences this time, had matters gone awry and trains collided on the single track, would have been infinitely more serious. Another boss would probably have dismissed Carnegie for his temerity and presumptuousness, but Andy knew how to play on the generosity of his employer. His hunch was confirmed the same evening when L.B. Franciscus, the freight supervisor, relayed to him the fact that Scott had been boasting of the latest exploit of 'that little white-haired Scotch devil of mine'. For a moment Carnegie had been full of remorse at his rash action, but after getting this reassurance from Franciscus his attitude changed. 'This satisfied me,' he bragged. 'Of course I had my cue for the next occasion, and went boldly in. From that date it was very seldom that Mr Scott gave a train order.'

If General Superintendent Lombaert had been held up as a stern, unbending individual, the very name of John Edgar Thomson was breathed with awe. The president of the railroad 'was the most reserved and silent of men, next to General Grant, that I ever knew

. . . He walked about as if he saw nobody when he made his periodical visits to Pittsburgh.' But even the great man greeted Carnegie warmly as 'Scott's Andy' after the train-running incident. Any youth that had the eye of the railroad president was bound to go far.

Thereafter, Andy raised his profile a notch or two. When criticism of the railroad recurred in the *Pittsburgh Journal*, it was robustly rebutted by a letter from an anonymous correspondent who demolished all the arguments put up by the business community. It was a remarkable performance by any standard and Niles A. Stokes, the company's chief lawyer, was intrigued as to the identity of the railroad's champion. From his residence at Greensburg he sent a wire to Scott asking him to try and find out the author. Andy himself handed the telegram to his boss, smirking that even Robert Riddle (the Scots-born editor of the *Journal*) did not know the answer. Then, with a wink and a knowing look, he made a clean breast of it. Scott seemed incredulous. He said he had read the letter that morning and wondered who had written it. 'His incredulous look did not pass me unnoticed. The pen was getting to be a weapon with me,' added Carnegie smugly.[11] As a result, Andy was invited to spend the following Sunday with Stokes and his wife.

> . . . the visit is one of the bright spots in my life. Henceforth we were great friends.
>
> The grandeur of Mr Stokes's home impressed me, but the one feature of it that eclipsed all else was a marble mantel in his library. In the center of the arch, carved in the marble, was an open book with this inscription:
>
> > He that cannot reason is a fool,
> > He that will not a bigot,
> > He that dare not a slave.
>
> These noble words thrilled me. I said to myself, 'Some day, some day, I'll have a library . . . and these words shall grace the mantel as here.' And so they do in New York and Skibo today.[12]

This was the first time that Andy had ever spent a night in a strange house, and such a splendid mansion immediately gave the youth a tantalising glimpse of the finer things in life, which his overweening ambition might some day bring him.

All in all, this record of Carnegie's activities during his first few months in the service of the Pennsylvania Railroad was impressive by any standards, and one can forgive the self-satisfaction with which he observed:

> The battle of life is already half won by the young man who is brought personally in contact with high officials; and the great aim of every boy should be to do something beyond the sphere of his duties – something which attracts the attention of those over him.[13]

Carnegie's detractors, most notably the biographer John Winkler, hint that the clerk and confidential man to the most influential railroad official in the region must have used his position to feather his own nest. 'Evidence is plentiful that our shrewd youth became a past master at the art of pleasing the Pennsylvania's customers, at a price,' says Winkler,[14] but without adducing a single shred of evidence in support of this contention. His colourful allegation that 'All his fingers seemed to have been dipped in glue' is not borne out by the facts. Of course, had Carnegie been taking bribes and sweeteners from the railroad's clients he would hardly have admitted this in his *Autobiography*, but a careful examination of Carnegie's accounts and memo notebooks of the period betrays no hint of any money other than what came to him by way of his monthly pay-cheque. Significantly, when the first opportunity arose to invest in stock, Andy had to borrow the necessary sum. Moreover, common sense should indicate that, in view of the fact that freight traffic was the life's blood of the railroad, priority would always be given to satisfying the needs of the larger customers, and that a bribe to the superintendent's confidential clerk would hardly be likely to ensure preferential treatment for any individual shipper. Carnegie put it succinctly in his *Autobiography* when he placed such a high value on his personal connections with influential executives of the company.

Apart from dressing well – and the dapper Carnegie was always fastidious in this matter – Andy had no extravagances. He walked to and from work each day and dutifully handed over the bulk of his pay to his mother who continued as household treasurer. One of Andy's duties was to write out the monthly payroll and when he came to Tom Scott's name for $125 he often wondered what he did with all that money. After a short time, however, Andy's salary was raised to $40 a month. He would take his pay-cheque to the bank and cash it, getting two bright and shiny gold double-eagles in exchange: 'They seemed to me the prettiest works of art in the world.'[15] The coins were handed over to Margaret and she presumably gave her elder son back a small amount of pocket-money. By such heroic self-denial, rather than the pocketing of bribes, Carnegie paid off the family debts. By the time he was twenty he had paid Andrew Hogan the remainder of the sum owing on the purchase of the lot at Rebecca Street, together with the two houses on it. Aunt Aitken, who had been responsible for getting the smaller dwelling for the Carnegies in the first place, was installed in that house. After Tom Hogan's death, his widow Kitty returned to Allegheny and took over the larger house, when the Carnegies left the district. Shortly before the last of the half-yearly payments were made to Andrew Hogan, however, William Carnegie died, on 2 October 1855. The precise cause of death is unknown, but it appears that Andy's father, having woven his last piece of unsaleable cloth, had just taken to his bed and given up the will to live. He was only fifty-one. 'Fortunately for the three remaining members life's duties were pressing. Sorrow and duty contended as we had to work. The expenses connected with his illness had to be saved and paid and we had not at this time much store in reserve.' Thus the death of his father was reduced to a temporary setback in Carnegie's finances. 'Mother kept on the binding of shoes; Tom went steadily to the public school; and I continued with Mr Scott in the service of the railroad company.'[16]

Tom was now twelve and about to enter high school. William's death could not have drawn Andy and his mother any closer together; they were already as close as humanly possible, and latterly William had been marginalised or excluded from their plans and deliberations. Andy would continue to look instinctively to Margaret for advice and support in every venture. She would not only give this unstintingly, but would insist on her right to give it. Winkler articulates a widely held notion when he speaks of:

the peremptory pledge to remain single during her lifetime which the irresistible Margaret Carnegie had exacted from her first born. There are indications that the canny youth welcomed the seemingly harsh inhibition. He and his oaken mother were in thorough agreement that no entangling romantic alliance must be permitted to thwart the career which both felt was to be notable.[17]

The idea of any such pledge seems highly fanciful. Besides, it was unnecessary. Andy was sufficiently hard-headed and single-minded to realise that marriage had no place in his foreseeable future. He enjoyed the company of his contemporaries of both sexes and as he came to manhood he enjoyed an active social life through church connections (not only the Swedenborgians but also the local Presbyterians) as well as the Webster Literary Society and other bodies. He had inherited the extrovert qualities of his grandfather and namesake and had a reputation for ready wit, joviality, good humour and a talent as a raconteur. He might not have been the most tuneful member of the Swedenborg choir, earning the occasional rap over the knuckles from choirmaster Ludwig Koethen, but he was a popular and lively member of the little church. In everything he did, he excelled; and everywhere he went, people took note of the diminutive flaxen-haired fellow. Andrew Carnegie was the sort of person who stood out in any crowd. Yet there was something of the loner in him too. Never afraid to speak his mind, even when it ran against the tide of popular opinion, he was a maverick in his politics. Something of the old Chartist radicalism persisted in his outlook which was generally more extreme than that of his companions. He detested slavery and was a rabid abolitionist; at the same time he was a Jacksonian Democrat, but as the debate over slavery and states' rights hotted up he moved to the right. In religion he developed a healthy scepticism, tolerant of all faiths yet finding flaws in those that were closest to his own upbringing. As Margaret Carnegie had no fixed views on the subject (beyond an interest in Unitarian writings), and did not hold with the Sabbatarianism then fashionable, young Andy was allowed, indeed encouraged, by her to go ice-skating on Sunday mornings while his pals were chafing under their starched collars in some church or other. At one stage he came under the spell of the local Presbyterian church, studiously avoiding the hellfire and damnation sermons of the Revd MacMillan, but regularly attending the midweek evening discussion groups at the manse presided over by the minister's comely wife, 'a born leader of the young'.

Carnegie was not long past his twentieth birthday when two events occurred that shaped his future life. On 22 February 1856 he attended the great national meeting in Pittsburgh at which the Republican Party formally came into being. Previously he had been an ardent Free Soil Democrat and, like many others, he had been unhappy with the mainstream of that party and its stand on slavery. Andy was still too young to vote, but already he was a political activist. Characteristically, this found firmest expression in his writings, and he took to firing off polemical letters on the subject of slavery and abolition to Horace Greeley's *New York Weekly Tribune*. When Greeley published some of these pieces, Andy organised a *Tribune* club among the railroad workers of Pittsburgh and enrolled over a hundred members. This became a debating society at which the burning issues of the day were hotly argued. Needless to say, the foremost debater in this club was its tiny chairman.

Shortly afterwards, he took his first flutter on the stockmarket. Early in 1856 the opportunity to acquire a block of ten shares in the freight and courier company Adams Express (forerunner of American Express) arose. They had belonged to William Reynolds, the station agent at Wilkinsburg, who had recently died. His widow had sold them to Mrs Ann Patrick for $600 but less than a month later she suddenly needed the money and approached Tom Scott, saying that she would be happy to sell them for what she had paid. Scott himself had a block of Adams stock and knew this to be a sound investment. He could have bought the Patrick shares for himself, but in a particularly generous moment he offered the deal to his assistant. Having just settled the last of the expenses on his father's funeral as well as the final payment to Andrew Hogan on the Rebecca Street property, Carnegie was strapped for cash, but without batting an eyelid he said that he thought he could manage the necessary sum. That evening he broached the matter with his mother.

The story goes that Margaret listened attentively as Andy explained that Adams was a blue-chip stock that paid the handsome dividend of 1 per cent per month. According to his *Autobiography*, Margaret told her son to accept Scott's offer, reckoning that she could raise the money by mortgaging the property. Early the following morning she boarded the steamer for East Liverpool, and that night put the proposition to her brother William, who was by that time one of the town's more prosperous citizens. William granted her a mortgage on her house and a day later she was back in Allegheny with $500, this being the sum which Andy thought was required. When he handed it over to his boss he was chagrined to discover that the total amount was actually $600. 'There was, unexpectedly, an additional hundred dollars to pay as a premium, but Mr Scott kindly said I could pay that when convenient, and this of course was an easy matter to do.'[18]

The truth belies this romantic tale of the indomitable heroine pledging her house in exchange for money from her brother. Carnegie's personal papers reveal that the transaction was much more prosaic. A document dated 17 May 1856 at Pittsburgh promises to pay to the order of Thomas A. Scott within six months $610 for value received. This note was endorsed 'Paid by cash, deposited in M&M Bank to credit. T.A. Scott, Nov. 1st'.[19] It is obvious that Tom Scott himself put up the cash for Andy to take advantage of Mrs Patrick's sale. As 1 November approached, when the note had to be settled, Andy had only managed to scrape together about $200. He raised the rest by borrowing $400 from a moneylender named George Smith, paying interest of 8 per cent per annum 'as long as it is held by me. It being understood that I have the privilege of retaining the principal longer than one year if required, but not for a shorter period.'[20] As security for the loan Carnegie lodged with Smith the block of Adams shares which the latter retained until the capital and interest had been repaid in full.

Andy made one payment of $100 plus interest on this loan in November 1857, and it was not until the spring of the following year (having diverted his savings into other investments in the interim) that he turned to his mother for help. It so happened that Margaret was in East Liverpool at the time, visiting William Morrison and his family and acting as nurse to the Bennett family next door, when she broached the subject with her brother. William then arranged for his sister to obtain a mortgage on her property from Richard Boyce, who advanced $500 on 27 March 1858, the sum plus interest to be repaid within twelve months.[21]

This complicated deal which, on the face of it, put the Carnegies deeper into debt, reveals a remarkable talent for juggling figures and notes; but within a month of the initial transaction, when he had the precious shares transferred to his name, Andy came to work one morning to find a white envelope on his desk, addressed to 'Andrew Carnegie Esquire'. The title tickled him inordinately as he studied the envelope:

> At one corner was seen the round stamp of Adams Express Company. I opened the envelope. All it contained was a check for ten dollars upon the Gold Exchange Bank of New York. I shall remember that check as long as I live . . . It gave me the first penny of revenue from capital – something that I had not worked for with the sweat of my brow. 'Eureka!' I cried. 'Here's the goose that lays the golden eggs.'[22]

That Sunday afternoon, when Andy and his chums were having a picnic in the countryside near Wood's Run, he produced the cheque and passed it round.

> The effect produced upon my companions was overwhelming. None of them had imagined such an investment possible. We resolved to save and to watch for the next opportunity for investment in which all of us would share, and for years afterwards we divided our trifling investments and worked together almost as partners.[23]

Towards the end of 1856 Tom Scott was promoted to general superintendent, to fill the post formerly held by Herman Lombaert. This required a move to the central offices in Altoona. In his wake went young Carnegie, now promoted to secretary with a salary of $50 a month. Carnegie was just turned twenty-one at the time and the upheaval from Pittsburgh, where he had spent the past eight years, was a major one. It was an even greater upheaval for Scott whose young wife had recently died, leaving him with two infants to rear. For the time being he entrusted the babies to his niece, Rebecca Stewart. Margaret Carnegie, whose immediate reaction was to accompany her son to Altoona, had to remain in Allegheny with young Tom until she could find someone willing to rent her property. For the time being, therefore, Tom Scott and Andy went alone to Altoona, and shared a room in a rather bleak hotel near the railway. 'At his desire I shared the same large bedroom with him. He seemed anxious always to have me near him.'[24]

They could not have arrived at a worse time. Scott was still grieving over the loss of his wife and, smarting at the resentment and jealousy surrounding his dramatic promotion, made little or no attempt to cultivate new friends in the grim little railroad town that was Altoona. Moreover, industrial relations were at breaking-point. Following months of sporadic stoppages and wildcat strikes among the freight-handlers, the trouble was now beginning to spread to the mechanics in the railway workshops. One night Andy was awakened by a junior official to be told that the freight-men had abandoned their trains at Mifflin and the single-track line was blocked on that account. Scott was sleeping soundly and Andy had not the heart to disturb him. Tom stirred in his sleep and half awoke as Andy was up and hastily dressing. The young man said that he would go and attend to the matter, to which Tom drowsily assented. While the boss went back to sleep, his secretary went down to the yards and argued the question with the strikers, and in Scott's name promised them a hearing the following day. As a result, the men agreed to resume normal working and get the trains moving again.

Andy's skill in man-management also saved the day when the men of the machine-shops decided to come out on strike. One evening, as he was walking back to his hotel in the dark, Andy became aware of the fact that he was being followed. Eventually the stranger caught up with him and whispered that he should not be seen talking to one of the bosses, but that Carnegie had done him a favour once and he owed him one in return. It seems that the man had once called at the Pittsburgh office seeking work as a blacksmith. There was no opening for a blacksmith at Pittsburgh at that time, but Andy had gone to a great deal of trouble to wire Altoona on the man's behalf and secure him employment. Now his informant told Andy that the shopmen had signed a paper pledging themselves to come out on strike the following Monday. Next morning Andy told Scott, who immediately had notices posted in the machine-shops stating that all men who had signed the strike paper were dismissed and that they should call at the office immediately to be paid off. Scott backed this by adding that he had acquired a list of all those who had signed the strike paper. Whether this was true or not, 'consternation followed and the threatened strike was broken'.[25]

Young Carnegie had come a long way in a short space of time, and the memory of how spies and informers were bitterly detested by the Chartists seems to have been completely erased. Mention of this incident with the blacksmith at Altoona provoked a moralising passage which would have had Old Tom Morrison turning in his grave:

> I have had many incidents, such as that of the blacksmith, in my life. Slight attentions or a kind word to the humble often bring back reward as great as it is unlooked for. No kind action is ever lost . . . I am indebted to these trifles for some of the happiest attentions and the most pleasing incidents of my life. And there is about such actions: they are disinterested, and the reward is sweet in proportion to the humbleness of the individual whom you have obliged. It counts many times more to do a kindness to a poor working man than to a millionaire, who may be able some day to repay the favor. How true Wordsworth's lines:
>
> > That best portion of a good man's life –
> > His little, nameless, unremembered acts
> > Of kindness and of love.[26]

In the spring of 1857 Margaret and Tom moved to Altoona. About the same time Rebecca Stewart brought Tom Scott's children to be reunited with their father. Instead of a shared hotel bedroom, Scott and Carnegie now had their own houses, nestling in the heights overlooking the railway town. Frame houses were very cheap there, and on his current salary Carnegie could comfortably afford one. By now the Pennsylvania Railroad's marshalling yards, freight depots and machine-shops had spread out in all directions, covering the valley bottom, so that when Altoona began to acquire residential districts, they had to be sited in the foothills, hemmed in by the sheer precipices of the surrounding mountains. Far from the din and dust of the valley, the Scotts and the Carnegies took up their abode. To Margaret, it seemed like heaven itself, after the stench and din, the muck and misery of Slabtown.

Not only did Margaret have a fine new house and garden, but Andy insisted that the time had come for her to take things easy. One of the most sugary passages in his *Autobiography*, occupying two pages, was devoted to the matter:

> There comes a time . . . when a grown son has to put his arms around his saint and kissing her tenderly try to explain to her that it would be much better were she to let him help her in some ways . . . Especially should the slaving mother live the life of ease hereafter, reading and visiting more and entertaining dear friends — in short, rising to her proper and deserved position as Her Ladyship.[27]

Margaret was to play the lady. True, Andy was not yet in the position to give her what she craved most, her own carriage, but a servant-girl was decidedly a step in the right direction, even if Margaret had great difficulty in adjusting to the idea of letting another woman attend to the household chores. Though he could not yet afford a carriage, Andy had acquired a horse and took up riding with the same manic intensity which he brought to all his activities. Now fully grown, he stood little more than five foot two in his stocking soles. Only on horseback could he look down on other men, and he revelled in it. He had a fine high-spirited stallion called Dash, and, mounted on this charger, he would ride off into the hills and canyons around the town. He got a terrific thrill out of feeling the power of the horse under his thighs, power that he controlled superbly with spur, whip and rein.

From time to time Tom Miller, Davy McCargo or Bob Pitcairn would visit Altoona, and then they would go riding together; but there is no mention of new friends in Altoona, other than Rebecca Stewart, Scott's niece and housekeeper.

> She played the part of elder sister to me to perfection, especially when Mr Scott was called to Philadelphia or elsewhere. We were much together, often driving in the afternoons through the woods . . . She

was not much beyond my own age, but always seemed a great deal older. Certainly she was more mature and quite capable of playing the elder sister's part. It was to her I looked up in those days as the perfect lady.[28]

Tom Miller would later recall how, on one of his visits to Altoona, he and Andy were invited to Scott's house for dinner. When Rebecca left the table to attend to the next course, Andy hastily picked up a cream pitcher and said, 'Real silver, Tom!'[29] A big sister and a perfect lady of such obvious refinement – this was Carnegie's ideal of female companionship, but romance never entered his head.

Undoubtedly the high point of Andy's two years at Altoona came about in 1858 when the Pennsylvania Railroad was threatened with litigation. When it appeared that Carnegie was about to be subpoenaed as the chief witness for the plaintiff, the company's lawyer, Niles Stokes, who was handling the defence, decided that it would be better for all concerned if Carnegie made himself scarce. It was therefore arranged for him to take a prolonged vacation with his friends Tom Miller and James Wilson, who were at that time employed by the Ohio and Pennsylvania Railroad at Crestline, Ohio. In his book *Triumphant Democracy*, Carnegie described a chance meeting that would transform his life. While seated on the end seat of the rear car, watching the line, he was approached by a stranger:

> . . . a tall, spare, farmer-looking kind of man . . . wished me to look at an invention he had made. With that he drew from a green bag (as if it were for lawyers' briefs) a small model of a sleeping berth for railway cars. He had not spoken a minute, before, like a flash, the whole range of discovery burst upon me. 'Yes,' I said, 'that is something which this continent must have' . . .
>
> I could not get that blessed sleeping-car out of my head. Upon my return I laid it before Mr Scott, declaring that it was one of the inventions of the age. He remarked: 'You are enthusiastic, young man, but you may ask the inventor to come and let me see it.' I did so, and arrangements were made to build two trial cars, and run them on the Pennsylvania Railroad. I was offered an interest in the venture, which, of course, I gladly accepted . . . A triumphant success was scored. And thus came sleeping-cars into the world.[30]

The story of the rustic inventor (with his crude model approaching the rising young business executive who immediately appreciated the sheer genius of the invention) would, much embellished, later find a prominent place in the *Autobiography*, despite the fact that when the tale was first unfolded in 1886 it provoked an immediate and very angry response from the inventor, Theodore T. Woodruff, who wrote to Carnegie:

> Your arrogance spurred you to make up the statements recorded in your book, which is misleading and so far from the true facts of the case and so damaging to your friend of old as to merit his rebuke. You must have known before you ever saw me that there were many sleeping-cars furnished with my pattern seats and couches running upon a number of railways, viz: B.E. & C. R.R., N.Y.C. R.R., M.C. R.R., C. and G. R.R., O. and M. R.R., C.C. and C. R.R., M.S. and N.I. R.R., together with my sample sleeping-car. In the aggregate there were twenty sleeping-cars running before my application had been made for the right to place them on the Pennsylvania Railroad.
>
> Now I will relate to you what transpired in connection with the introduction of sleeping-cars upon the Penn. R.R. Firstly, I met J. Edgar Thomson, at the Monongahela House in Pittsburgh, and gave him a letter of introduction from the then President of the O. and M. Rr. Co. (I cannot recall his name). Mr Thomson read the letter and requested me to give it to Mr Scott, who was then the general superintendent of the road, and was then in Pittsburgh. I asked Mr Thomson if he would call at the depot and see my sample car, which was standing there. He responded that his engagements were such that he could not then go to the depot, and that he was to take the early morning train to Philadelphia. Thinking, perhaps, that he might have time to drop in the car in the morning before the train left, I resolved to give him an opportunity to see the car, and accordingly had the interior properly arranged for his inspection with the car doors left open. It so happened that Mr Thomson's industrious habits led him to inspect the said sleeping-car, though it appeared not to have any attendant, and yet the porter was in the car when Mr Thomson and one other gentleman came in, inspected and commented on its merits, which was overheard by the said porter. In the meantime I had seen Mr Scott and on the following

evening Mr Scott and myself sat upon the same car and concluded
an arrangement for the operation of my patent sleeping-cars upon
the Pennsylvania Railroad before we reached Altoona. One of the
conditions of the said agreement was that a certain specified
interest therein should be held for another person, and represented
(so the talk ran) by a boy then in the superintendent's office at
Altoona; and that four cars should be immediately constructed
under my direction as the agent for the patent company.

When we came to consummate the agreement in a written form,
I learned that the boy alluded to was 'Andie Carnegie'. A contract
was entered into with Murphy and Allison, of Philadelphia, for the
construction of four sleeping-cars, which were built and placed
upon the Pennsylvania Rail R. Their rank in numerical order was
Nos. 22, 23, 24 and 25, the model of which was a full-sized car of the
finest construction . . . and a little too big for the said green bag in
use for lawyers' briefs, to which you allude in that fine spun
recollection of yours.[31]

The original of this letter has not survived among the copious
Carnegie archives of this period, and was presumably consigned to
the trash-can by the recipient. Three days later, however, he did
dash off a brief note to Woodruff, brushing the complaint aside
with:

> Your letter surprises me. Your error lies in the supposition that I
> intended to write a history on the 'rise and progress of sleeping-
> cars'. I only mention them incidentally . . . It is impossible to enter
> into details in one volume, which aims to give a history of the
> country as a whole. Please take the will for the deed.[32]

When he was fobbed off with such an unsatisfactory response from
Carnegie, far less a public apology, Woodruff sent a copy of his letter
to the *Philadelphia Sunday News* where it was published in full the
following November. With the decent passage of time, Carnegie
ignored this and stuck to his original version of the 'farmer-looking
man with a small green bag in his hand' when he wrote his
Autobiography.[33] In turn, it would be unquestioningly accepted by all
of Carnegie's early biographers.[34]

There is absolutely no reason to doubt any of Woodruff's statements. He did, in fact, obtain his first patents on 2 December 1856 and the first sleeping-cars were constructed by T.W. Watson of Springfield, Massachusetts, early in 1857. By the end of that year his sleeping-cars were running on the New York–Albany night express and other lines in the East and Midwest were operating these cars by the early months of 1858. Woodruff's contract with the Pennsylvania Railroad was signed on 15 September 1858.[35]

This only leaves the intriguing passage concerning the boy 'Andie Carnegie' and the circumstances surrounding his involvement in the project. Whereas Carnegie would have us believe that his eighth interest in the venture was in grateful recognition of his sterling role in bringing the bashful inventor before the commercial world, the facts give the lie to this. The truth seems to be found in Woodruff's statement that it was Scott who insisted that the 'boy then in the superintendent's office' should be cut in on the deal. This extremely generous gesture was entirely consistent with the many other kindly acts which Tom Scott performed for his youthful assistant. Of course, by sticking to his tale of the chance meeting with the man and the little green bag, Carnegie could conveniently neglect to pay any tribute to his employer's embarrassing generosity, so the specific reason why Scott insisted that his secretary be given a share of the deal (when, in fact, he does not appear to have been involved in any of the preliminaries at all) remains a mystery.

That this was an extremely important deal cannot be over-emphasised. Well might it be described as the start of Carnegie's fortune. Carnegie himself acknowledged as much when he wrote that 'the first considerable sum I ever made was from this source . . . Blessed be the man who invented sleep.'[36] Andy was allowed to pay for his shares in monthly instalments. When the first payment of $217.50 fell due, however, he did not have the cash. Rather than engage in a complicated arrangement such as financed his Adams Express purchase, he went straight to a local banker and asked for a loan.

> I explained the matter to him, and I remember that he put his great arm (he was six foot three or four) around me, saying, 'Why, of course I will lend it. You are all right, Andy.' And here I made my

89

first note, and actually got a banker to take it. A proud moment that
in a young man's career![37]

The loan was the only one he required in order to pay for his
interest in Woodruff's company. Thereafter, each monthly dividend
from the company was more than sufficient to pay for the instalment
due for his interest in the company. Within two years this initial
investment of $217.50 was bringing in an annual income of almost
$5,000 – more than three times his annual salary from the railroad.
'My boy Andy' was well on the way to fame and fortune.

FOUR

The Spoils of War

1859–65

For your poor friend, the Bard, afar
He sees and hears the distant war,
A cool spectator purely:
> Robert Burns, 'Election Ballad, 1790'

FIVE DAYS AFTER HIS TWENTY-FOURTH BIRTHDAY, ANDREW
Carnegie became superintendent of the Western Division. About a
month earlier he had first heard rumours that the Pennsylvania
Railroad, which had expanded out of all recognition during the
previous five years, was about to get a new vice-president, and the
likelihood that Tom Scott would get this coveted position became
more certain day by day. One jump ahead, Carnegie began to fear for
his own position. The prospect of accompanying his high-flying boss
to Philadelphia exhilarated him; but just as frequently he was
depressed by the thought that he might be left behind at Altoona to
serve some new man who might not be so indulgent, easy-going and
generous. For two days, while Scott was absent in Philadelphia
conferring with J. Edgar Thomson, Carnegie was on tenterhooks. His
worst fears seemed to be confirmed when Scott returned to Altoona
and asked him to come to his private study at home, rather than
discuss the matter in the office. Carnegie's heart was in his mouth as
Scott informed him that he had, in fact, been appointed vice-
president, and that Enoch Lewis, previously the superintendent of
the Eastern Division, was to succeed him as general superintendent
at Altoona. Then Tom dropped the bombshell: 'Now, about yourself.
Do you think you could manage the Pittsburgh Division?'

Carnegie's immediate reaction was characteristic: he was nettled to be asked a question that seemed to imply a lingering doubt as to his abilities. 'I was at an age when I thought I could manage anything. I knew nothing that I would not attempt.' And he nodded vigorously.

'Well,' said Scott. 'Mr Potts [the superintendent of the Western Division] is to be promoted to the transportation department in Philadelphia and I recommended you to the president as his successor. He agreed to give you a trial. What salary do you think you should have?'

'Salary,' replied Carnegie, quite offended. 'What do I care for salary? I do not want the salary; I want the position. It is glory enough to go back to the Pittsburgh Division in your former place. You can make my salary just what you please and you need not give me any more than what I am getting now.' Carnegie was now on $65 a month.

Scott pointed out that his own salary at Pittsburgh three years previously had been $1500 a year, and his successor, Potts, was currently getting $1800. Tom therefore considered that it would be reasonable to start Carnegie at $1500 and raise it to $1800 if he succeeded in the job. 'Would that be satisfactory?' he asked.

'Oh please,' said Andy, apparently embarrassed, 'don't speak to me of money!'[1] He could afford to take such an altruistic line, in view of the fact that the income from his interest in the sleeping-cars was already generating a great deal more than the proposed salary. What meant much more at this stage was the fact that, instead of signing orders 'T.A.S.', he would now be appending his own initials. 'That was glory enough for me.'

On 21 November 1859 Tom Scott published General Order No. 10 to all employees of the Western Division, notifying them that, with effect from 1 December, the Western Division from Pittsburgh to Conemaugh, including the Indiana Branch, 'will be under the superintendence of Andrew Carnegie, whose title will be Super-intendent of the Western Division. His office will be at Pittsburgh. Employees of the Company . . . will be under his charge.'[2]

Carnegie lost no time in making preparations for the return to 'dirty, smoky Pittsburgh'. Though he had enjoyed the spaciousness and pleasant life in the hilly suburbs of Altoona, the prospect of returning to his old haunts, and old friends, excited him. But there would be no going back to Slabtown; for Margaret there would be no return to cobbling for Henry Phipps. Now, the Carnegies were coming back in triumph to an entirely new life very far removed from the old.

The winter of 1859–60 soon proved to be one of the most severe in living memory and for the time being Margaret remained in Altoona while her sons went off without her. Tom, recently graduated from high school, was now his brother's secretary. Margaret sold her house in Rebecca Street and in the spring of 1860 moved into a rented house on Hancock Street (now Eighth Street) in the city centre, within walking distance of the Pennsylvania Railroad station.

This would be their home for more than a year. Clearly Carnegie chose it because it was so convenient for his office, especially as his duties meant that he was on call twenty-four hours a day, seven days a week; but it had its drawbacks:

> Any accurate description of Pittsburgh at that time would be set down as a piece of the grossest exaggeration. The smoke permeated and penetrated everything. If you placed your hand on the balustrade of the stair it came away black; if you washed face and hands they were as dirty as ever in an hour. The soot gathered in the hair and irritated the skin, and for a time after our return from the mountain atmosphere of Altoona, life was more or less miserable.[3]

David Stewart, Rebecca's brother who was the railroad's freight agent in Pittsburgh at the time, suggested a house next door to his own, in the outlying suburb of Homewood, some fifteen miles from the city centre. Carnegie and his mother went out to the Liberty Valley to inspect the property and immediately fell in love with it. The two-storey frame house was set in extensive lawns, screened by Norway spruce. The happiest years of Margaret's life would be spent here, amid her extensive flowerbeds and her chicken-run.

Homewood was a select district, where many of the wealthiest or most socially prominent families of Pittsburgh had their homes. The young railroad superintendent was clearly a coming man, to be cultivated, and Carnegie rose to the occasion. Soon he was being invited home by mothers who regarded him as a good catch for their daughters. Though small in stature, he was well proportioned and personable. His ready wit and jovial manner, with just sufficient trace of a Scottish accent remaining to guarantee his Old World credentials, made him socially acceptable everywhere. Although arrogant and cocksure with subordinates, Carnegie had the good sense to moderate these traits when in the company of his social superiors, though when discussion swung around to the burning political issues of the day he was never slow to voice his own firmly held opinions.

Tom Miller, one of Carnegie's bosom pals from the Slabtown days, was also back in Pittsburgh as a railroad official, and likewise purchased a house in Homewood, thus giving Carnegie a precious link with his boyhood. But there were many new friends to be made, and acquaintances to be cultivated. Chief among them were the Vandevort brothers, Benjamin and John, and the latter would become one of Carnegie's closest confidants and a regular travelling companion on jaunts round the world. David Stewart and his wife also became his close friends. Both Stewart and John 'Vandy' Vandevort would later become partners in the various Carnegie enterprises.

Doyen of Homewood's aristocracy was Judge William Wilkins, who had at one time owned all the land in the Liberty Valley where Homewood was situated. Immensely wealthy and now in his eightieth year, he continued to preside over Homewood society like some grand seigneur. His vast mansion in the centre of the suburb was the mecca of Homewood society and, in due course, the young railroad executive secured an invitation to meet the great man. To Carnegie, Wilkins was a piece of living history. Born during the War of Independence, he had been appointed a Federal judge for western Pennsylvania by President John Quincy Adams. In 1828 he had become a Jacksonian Democrat and among important posts held subsequently were American Minister to Russia and Secretary of War in John Tyler's cabinet. His wife was the daughter of George W. Dallas, who had been Vice-President of the United States. The Judge, tall, slender and handsome, had 'the most wonderful store of knowledge and reminiscence of any man I had yet been privileged to meet', and his conversation was peppered with casual remarks about what President Jackson had said to him, or what he had told the Duke of Wellington or the Tsar of Russia.

Though Carnegie was unduly impressed by all this name-dropping, when it came to politics he and the Wilkins family differed radically.

They were strong Democrats with leanings towards the South, so it was inevitable that the ardent young abolitionist would clash with their views. When Mrs Wilkins complained about northern Negroes being admitted as cadets to West Point military academy where her darling grandson Dallas was obliged to sit next to one of them, Carnegie remarked drily that there was something even worse: 'I understand that some of them have been admitted to heaven!' There was a silence that could be felt.

Then Mrs Wilkins said gravely, 'That is a different matter, Mr Carnegie.'[4]

Although he could hold his own in polite society, Carnegie was now acutely aware of the shortcomings and deficiencies in his own education. There was just so much that he could pick up from books, but now he required to give his manners and diction a polish. Fortunately there was yet another new friend to take him in hand. Leila Anderson was the daughter of a Dr Addison who had recently died. Her mother hailed from Edinburgh and 'the wee drap o' Scotch bluid atween us' became a strong bond. Thomas Carlyle had been Mrs Addison's tutor for a time, and both she and her daughters had been educated in Europe and spoke French, Spanish and Italian as well as impeccable English. Leila became a special friend, who undertook to polish this rough diamond. 'She was my best friend, because my severest critic. I began to pay strict attention to my language, and to the English classics, which I now read with great avidity.'[5] She never hesitated to correct any Scotticisms or errors in his speech; but she also taught him to read music and listen appreciatively to the works of the great classical composers. Most important of all, she gave direction to his reading, where previously he had indiscriminately read anything that came to hand. Self-deprecatingly, he says that she was also instrumental in making him pay closer attention to his dress and manners:

> I began also to notice how much better it was to be gentle in tone and manner, polite and courteous to all – in short, better behaved. Up to this time I had been, perhaps, careless in dress and rather affected it . . . Anything that could be labeled foppish was looked upon with contempt.[6]

Outwardly, Carnegie acquired the trappings of the gentleman, but he retained his blunt, Scottish personality, realising that it was his best asset. He was also shrewd enough to appreciate that his elders and betters might often patronise him, as a rather amusing little Johnny-come-lately, but they could not ignore him.

Carnegie's *Autobiography* dwells rather heavily on the new social milieu to which he was now admitted, and devotes comparatively little space to a description of his duties as divisional super-intendent, though he commented on the fact that the line was poorly constructed and totally inadequate for the business that was crowding upon it. The rails were laid on huge stone blocks and secured with chairs of cast-iron rather than steel. Consequently, fractures occurred frequently, and on one night alone Carnegie recorded forty-seven breakdowns as a result of this design fault. Although he had a telegraph line laid to his house at Homewood, so that he could run the trains (especially at night) from the comfort of his own home, the superintendent was expected to go out and remove all wrecks and personally see to it that the lines were kept open.

> At one time for eight days I was constantly upon the line, day and night, at one wreck or obstruction after another. I was probably the most inconsiderate superintendent that ever was entrusted with the management of a great property, for, never knowing fatigue myself, I overworked the men and was not careful enough in considering the limits of human endurance.[7]

Certainly no consideration was given even to those who had claims to Carnegie's friendship. George Alexander, another of his chums from Rebecca Street, was hired by Carnegie as a conductor on the Altoona–Pittsburgh passenger service. Although there was an enormous gap between the superintendent and a humble train-conductor, they remained on close terms socially. One Sunday George joined Carnegie and his mother on a jaunt to visit the Forrester family, old friends who had left Allegheny and now resided some miles to the west, along the line of the Pittsburgh, Fort Wayne and Chicago Railroad. Many years later, George Alexander recalled this occasion:

The weavers' cottage in Dunfermline, at the corner of Moodie Street and Priory Lane, in which Andrew Carnegie was born, 25 November 1835

Carnegie's beloved mother, Margaret Morrison Carnegie, was the most important person in her son's life. Their triumphant return to Scotland, in a coach-and-four, was the realisation of a long-cherished dream

Thomas Morrison (the 'Bailie') and George Lauder (above) were two of the most important formative influences on the young Andrew Carnegie

Carnegie and his younger brother Tom were very close throughout their lives. Above: *Andrew at sixteen with Tom;* opposite: *the two men in their twenties*

Andrew Carnegie about 1878, already a very wealthy businessman

The day was as beautiful as could be, and I well remember that we had to wade through dust up to our shoe tops for about a mile and one half to get from the station to the house. We had a delightful time until about 10 o'clock when there came up a terrible wind and rain storm. It simply poured. I was a passenger conductor at the time and my train left the depot at two o'clock A.M. I knew there was no train for me to get to Pittsburgh on, and I did not fancy much the idea of having to get there for that train, so I approached the Supt. (A.C.) and asked him how about my getting to town to take out my train. He replied, 'Well, George, you know that train goes out at two o'clock and it can't very well go without a conductor.' That is all the satisfaction I got and there was nothing left me but to foot it through all the storm and I arrived at the depot just in time to get on the train, though soaked to the skin.[8]

In fairness to Carnegie, it is difficult to see what else he could have said. As superintendent, he was now exposed to the rough and tumble of railway life, and in ensuring that wrecks and other obstructions did not keep his beloved trains from running to schedule he had no qualms about getting his hands dirty, or getting soaked to the skin, if need be. He led from the front, and pitched in as valiantly as any ganger. The teenager who had been affronted by the coarseness of the railmen had now shed his aversion to rough company, and shared their primitive conditions and appalling food, clad in the same heavy boots and rough clothing, when out on the job. The difference now was that he could associate with them as their employer and not as an equal, and this invisible barrier set him apart, even when they slept together in filthy freight-cars. It was at this period that someone coined the nickname 'Little Boss' which would follow Carnegie through all his enterprises, to the end of his life.

His slight build and tiny stature seldom caused embarrassment, but there was one occasion which George Alexander would recall with relish. Not long after Carnegie had been appointed superintendent there was a serious accident when several freight-cars were derailed. Carnegie was rapidly on the scene, barking orders for a temporary track to be laid around the derailment so that the traffic could be kept flowing. He was everywhere at once, and in his frenzy to get the work done he kept getting in the way of the men carrying the rails to be laid. In the end a giant of an Irish navvy, exasperated by the little man's antics, seized him by the scruff of the neck and put him down at one side with the words: 'Get out of my way, you brat of a boy. You're eternally getting in the way of the men who are trying to do their job.'[9] Later Carnegie would relish telling this story, particularly when he got to the punch-line and described the big Irishman's discomfiture on discovering the identity of the 'brat of a boy' he had so roughly manhandled. But it is probably significant that, shortly after this incident, he began sprouting a thin wisp of a beard. This straggly fringe on his otherwise clean-shaven pink face made him look like a youthful garden gnome and, if anything, underlined his boyish appearance.

Just as Carnegie had been Tom Scott's personal telegraph operator and confidential clerk, so too Tom Carnegie, just turned sixteen, served his brother. Lest Carnegie lay himself open to a charge of nepotism, he was harder on young Tom than he would have been on an employee who was not related to him. Tom, who had learned telegraphy at the railroad office in Altoona under his brother's tuition, proved to be well up to the job and a valuable asset. Every bit as competent and energetic as his elder brother, he lacked the latter's overweening confidence and ambition and therefore did not cut corners. He seems to have inherited the traits of his late father: quiet and reserved, almost diffident in manner but utterly dependable, he was tactful and discreet in every way, both in business and in personal matters, and Carnegie could rely on him completely.

Tom did not raise eyebrows as another of Carnegie's appointees did. His cousin Maria Hogan, whom he employed in the freight department, was the first woman telegraphist anywhere in the United States and eventually she trained many other girls for what had hitherto been regarded as a male preserve. Carnegie soon afterwards secured for his old friend Davy McCargo the appointment as general superintendent of the telegraph department. Henceforward he could rely on the communications system, upon which the railroad depended so completely. It was a valuable lesson in business organisation that he was to apply, over and over again, in his many later enterprises.

★

Blunt and bumptious, Carnegie frequently spoke out of turn. He recalled a Sunday spent at the Greensburg home of Niles Stokes just after South Carolina had seceded from the Union. Carnegie 'was all aflame for the flag' but Stokes, a Democrat of the old school, argued that the North had no right to coerce any state to return to the Union.

> He gave vent to sentiments which caused me to lose my self-control, and I exclaimed: 'Mr Stokes, we shall be hanging men like you in less than six weeks.'
>
> I hear his laugh as I write, and his voice calling to his wife in the adjoining room: 'Nancy, Nancy, listen to this young Scotch devil. He says they will be hanging men like me in less than six weeks.'[10]

Other people than Mrs Wilkins or Niles Stokes might have been less tolerant or good-humoured about Carnegie's ill-judged remarks. We may be certain that there were many who reacted more violently to opinions so freely expressed, but Carnegie would have brushed them aside, and never recorded them in his *Autobiography*. Confident at the time that he had morality on his side, he could later look back on those stirring times and feel that history had proved him right. A confirmed Republican who voted enthusiastically for Lincoln in 1860, Carnegie saw in his new party a combination of the radical idealism of the Chartists and the entrepreneurial spirit of America. Lincoln, born in a humble log-cabin, the log-splitter turned lawyer, a homespun philosopher turned politician, was just the sort of man with whom Carnegie could identify.

Carnegie's lifelong pacifism was sorely tried in those dark days of 1860–61 as the country slid inexorably into war. While many of his business associates held out for peace at any price, and even his old hero Horace Greeley disappointed him with his *Tribune* editorials urging Washington to let 'erring sisters go in peace', Carnegie strenuously advocated a policy of coercion to bring the seceding states back into the Union. If Greeley had proved a broken reed, Carnegie had a new hero. Edwin M. Stanton, the Pittsburgh lawyer whose telegrams he had once delivered, had become Attorney-General in the closing months of James Buchanan's outgoing administration. Vacillating and ineffectual, Buchanan had belatedly shaken up his moribund administration with a cabinet reshuffle in December 1860 which brought to prominence a powerful triumvirate, consisting of the new Attorney-General, Joseph Holt as Secretary of War, and Jeremiah Black as Secretary of State. Now they cajoled the unhappy President into making a stand on the issue of Fort Sumter, a Federal military base which was under siege by Confederate troops. When Stanton publicly declaimed that its surrender by the Federal government 'would be a crime equal to that of Arnold' (whose treachery in the War of Independence was proverbial), Carnegie was one of his staunchest supporters. Henceforeward, the rather sinister figure of Edwin Stanton, who made a remarkable transition from one administration to the next and later emerged as Lincoln's Secretary of War, would be, in Carnegie's shining eyes, 'destined to live in American history as one whose service to the republic in her darkest hour ranks in value with those of the foremost early fathers: Franklin, Hamilton, Adams, Jefferson, Jackson, and Lincoln. No lower place can be assigned him than in that circle.'[11]

By the time of Lincoln's inauguration in March 1861, the garrison at Fort Sumter was desperately short of provisions. So far, not a shot had been fired, the forces of South Carolina being content to blockade the fort in the hope of starving its defenders into surrender. At first Lincoln sat back and did nothing, hoping that the crisis would merely blow over, and then he dithered between evacuating the garrison and standing firm. When he wired Governor Pickens of South Carolina, informing him that he proposed to send a supply ship, but no reinforcements or ammunition, he was trying to maintain the correct protocol. When the South responded foolishly on 12 April by firing on Fort Sumter, however, the die was cast. The rebels had fired on the flag, and that was sufficient to galvanise the North into action. 'The Union and Old Glory!' wrote Carnegie. 'That was all the people cared for, but that was enough.'[12] When Major Robert Anderson was forced to surrender the fort two days later, the North was in an uproar. Old doubts and sympathies vanished overnight. At the Pittsburgh Theatre that evening the performance was interrupted by a newspaperman rushing on stage to report the fall of Fort Sumter. This provoked one of the audience to leap to his feet shouting, 'I'm a Democrat! But three cheers for Major

Anderson!'[13] Paradoxically, the gallant loser was regarded as a national hero.

The following morning Carnegie boarded his commuter train to go downtown:

> . . . the cars resembled a disturbed beehive. Men could not sit still or control themselves. One of the leading Democrats who had the previous evening assured me that the people would never approve the use of force against their southern brethren, nor would he, came forward greatly excited, and I am sorry to say, some of his words were unquotable. 'What's wrong with you?' I asked. 'Didn't I tell you last night what the Secessionists intended?' In less than a week I saw my friend one morning drilling to be ready as captain of a company to revenge the unpardonable crime. So with others of like view the night before. Stanton was right: the Union was stronger than all its foes.[14]

Men like Niles Stokes swallowed their principles and clamoured to join the coming conflict. Ironically, Carnegie would subsequently pull strings to secure a commission for Stokes as a major of volunteers. Even Judge Wilkins, who had been an outspoken critic of Republican agitation against the South, now headed the citizens' committee recruiting volunteer companies in the Pittsburgh area. Despite his age, he worked tirelessly to convert the municipal fairgrounds into the vast military base which was named Camp Wilkins in his honour. Day by day, fresh-faced farmboys poured into the city, bound for the training camp. The trains were filled to capacity with raw recruits, and peacetime freight gave way to arms and ammunition as Pennsylvania prepared for war. Enthusiastic for the North, Carnegie himself did not rush to the colours, but soon he would be in the very thick of the action.

Barely a week after the fall of Fort Sumter, Thomas Scott was recruited by Simon Cameron, Lincoln's original Secretary of War, to leave the Pennsylvania Railroad for the duration of hostilities and come to Washington. There, he was appointed Assistant Secretary of War with overall command of military transportation. The Civil War would become the first major conflict in which the railways played a vital role, and the success of the Union forces in rapid deployment over vast areas was due in no small measure to Tom Scott's organising genius. At the very outset, he had to contend with overwhelming problems due to the outmoded system of raising state militias in time of war which had to be tailored to the present crisis. Thousands of men hurried to enlist in Massachusetts, New York and Pennsylvania, but by the time they could be mobilised Washington itself might fall to the enemy.

The first Northern troops to be rushed to the nation's threatened capital were the men of the Sixth Massachusetts regiment. On their way from Boston to Washington, however, they had been attacked by Southern sympathisers in Baltimore. Although the troops managed to struggle through to their destination, the Baltimore mobs went on the rampage, tore up the railway tracks and prepared to ambush any further Federal units sent south. Thomas Hicks, Governor of Maryland, telegraphed Lincoln urging him to 'send no more troops here' and instructed his police chief, Marshal George P. Kane, to destroy all the railway bridges north of Baltimore. Kane, a rabid Secessionist who had been involved in the recent conspiracy to assassinate the President-Elect on his way to Washington,[15] needed no second bidding. During the night of 20 April the four main bridges north of the city were blown up on Kane's orders. By the time Tom Scott got to Washington he discovered that the communications with which Simon Cameron had entrusted him were virtually non-existent. Washington was in an uproar; panic and confusion reigned supreme. Businessmen and government officials alike were convinced that the rebels from Virginia would arrive at any moment, and everywhere there was frenzied activity as people tried to get away from the doomed capital.

By contrast, Tom Scott acted with his customary businesslike manner and immediately got down to establishing the nerve-centre of his communications network. Before leaving Philadelphia he had swiftly drawn up his staff plans. The first name on his list was Andrew Carnegie whom he recruited as his right-hand man. Given temporary leave of absence by the railroad, and a free hand to select a team of élite railwaymen, Carnegie arrived in Philadelphia on 20 April, to be greeted with the news that Baltimore was in the hands of the Secessionists and that the direct route to Washington had been cut. The only way to proceed south was to take a train as far as

Perryville in Maryland. At this little seaport on Chesapeake Bay Carnegie's hand-picked corps would board a steamer bound for Annapolis – but there they found that the branch line to Annapolis Junction had been destroyed by rebel sympathisers. Somehow they managed to get to the junction with the Baltimore and Ohio main line south to Washington. At the junction depot they found some coaches and freight trucks but no locomotive. The troops of General Ben 'the Beast' Butler's Eighth Massachusetts Infantry were already held up at Annapolis, and the New York Seventh were expected at any moment. It was imperative that rail communications be restored as rapidly as possible.

Carnegie detailed his railwaymen to re-lay the track, with the assistance of Butler's troops, while he scoured the depot at Annapolis. By chance, he found a partly dismantled locomotive in one of the repair sheds. Carnegie's mechanics worked feverishly to reassemble it and get it fully operational. By the time the New York Seventh disembarked at Annapolis on 25 April the line was open and the locomotive had steam up, ready for the hazardous journey to Washington. General Butler and his staff occupied the leading coach while the officers and men of the Eighth Massachusetts perched on the freight-cars as best they could. In their wake, the New York Seventh had to march the ten miles to Annapolis Junction where there were additional coaches and a more powerful locomotive. Carnegie himself rode the footplate alongside the driver and fireman, keeping a sharp lookout for ambushes and obstructions. When he spotted telegraph wires which had been pinned to the ground with stakes to earth them and immobilise the line, he leapt from the cab and pulled up the stakes. The wires, suddenly released, recoiled and hit him in the face, slicing open his cheek. With his face covered in blood, he remounted the cab and ordered the engineer to drive on. He was still a gory sight when he rode triumphantly into Washington, bringing the first Federal troops to break the Secessionist blockade.

> With the exception of one or two soldiers, wounded a few days previously in passing through the streets of Baltimore, I can justly claim that I 'shed my blood for my country' among the first of its defenders. I gloried in being useful to the land that had done so

much for me, and worked, I can truly say, night and day, to open communication to the South.[16]

While the Yankee soldiers disembarked and paraded before a delighted President Lincoln, Carnegie reported to Tom Scott at the War Department. Tom's orders were brief and to the point: Carnegie would be responsible for organising railroad and telegraphic communications south from Washington into Virginia, vital to the Federal objective of capturing Richmond less than ninety miles from Washington. Richmond had no military or strategic value, but as the rebel capital it was a symbol for all that the South represented, and no one worked harder or more diligently than Andrew Carnegie, the Chartist radical turned ardent Republican. Over the ensuing four years, a vast fortune in arms and *matériel*, to say nothing of countless thousands of lives, would be expended in one side trying to take the other's capital, and though the war ranged far and wide, these narrow objectives remained at the core of the conflict.

Carnegie wired Davy McCargo to send him a squad of his best telegraphists from Pittsburgh. This élite band formed the nucleus of the Military Telegraph Corps whose services in maintaining communications were subsequently recognised by the government which erected a bronze plaque in Pittsburgh bearing the portraits of all the original telegraphists. Carnegie's portrait appeared in the centre at the top.

Carnegie's immediate task was to re-establish the ferry across the Potomac to Alexandria and to extend the Baltimore and Ohio track from the old depot in Washington, along Maryland Avenue to the river and thence across Long Bridge which had been partially demolished by the rebels. In the remarkably short period of seven days, 'all hands, from Carnegie down, worked day and night to accomplish the task'.[17] Carnegie established his headquarters in Alexandria, and was there when news reached him that rebel forces had routed McDowell's army at Bull Run. At first, he could not comprehend the extent of the defeat, but soon it became evident that every locomotive and car would have to be rushed to the battlefront, to evacuate the defeated forces. The closest point to the battle was Burke station. Carnegie immediately went there and personally supervised the loading of the trains with the wounded. Carnegie and his telegraphist were the last to leave Burke when rebel forces advanced on the station. Back at Alexandria, he found total panic, but noted smugly that, while a few conductors and engineers had fled by boat across the Potomac, his telegraphists were standing firm despite the closeness of the gunfire. Grimly he watched the long lines of Union soldiers as they straggled back across the bridge into Washington, before dashing off a brief despatch to his local newspaper, the *Pittsburgh Chronicle*:

> After our forces had full possession of the Bull Run batteries last night. Gen. Johnson [*sic*] with twenty thousand men came up and forced them to retire. Our forces are now forming at Alexandria, and will attack the enemy again shortly.[18]

This up-beat message belied the true state of affairs. There would be no regrouping at Alexandria, far less a counter-attack in the immediate future. More soberly, he wrote to a friend four days later:

> Depend upon it, the recent defeat is a blessing in disguise. We shall now begin in earnest. Knowing our foe, the necessary means will be applied to ensure their overthrow . . . What might have been half work, a mere scotching of the snake, will now be thorough & complete. You shall at no distant time be able to proclaim in New Orleans that God has made all men free and equal and that slavery is the sum of all villanies.
>
> Alexandrians are now getting used to the utterance of some strange sentiments. We wanted a gang of laborers the other day. Sam Barr, one of our best boys from Pgh, was delegated to organize it – the first question – boys are you all free? – Yes all but one – Why ain't you free? 'Cause Massa owns me Sar' – Why don't you go and tell him you now owns yourself & if he say you don't – show him you do by knocking him down – you can't work with Free Negroes unless you do – That gave the Colored population something to think over.
>
> I am delighted with my occupation here – hard work, but how gratifying to lie down at night & think By George you are clearer for those who come hereafter as well as maintaining the position that humanity has, after laborious efforts, succeeded in reaching.[19]

Carnegie, who once claimed that he knew no fatigue, drove himself beyond the limit. That summer was the hottest on record and one day, while supervising the repair of a bridge, he collapsed. He was badly sunburned and suffering sunstroke, and was obliged to return to Washington for several days' complete rest. With his very fair complexion he was unduly sensitive to the sun, and ever afterwards took very good care to avoid exposure if he could help it.

When he had recovered, he settled in at the old War Building under his former boss, who, early in August 1861, was formally appointed Assistant Secretary of War with the rank of colonel. Tom Scott asked him to remain in Washington as his assistant. Carnegie's office adjoined that of Colonel Scott and became the communications centre where all incoming field despatches were processed. William Seward (Secretary of State), Simon Cameron, and later his successor Stanton, were frequent visitors to Carnegie's office; but from time to time the President himself would come in and wait while a particularly important despatch was being transmitted. He would loll against Carnegie's desk, half-sitting, half-leaning, chatting away with his young communications chief. Carnegie would remember him as 'one of the most homely men I ever saw when his features were in repose'. But what impressed him most of all was the way Lincoln's face lit up when talking animatedly:

> When excited or telling a story, intellect shone through his eyes and illuminated his face to a degree which I have seldom or never seen in any other . . . His charm lay in the total absence of manner. It was not so much, perhaps, what he said as the way in which he said it that never failed to win one. I have often regretted that I did not write down carefully at the time some of his curious sayings, for he said even common things in an original way. I never met a great man who so thoroughly made himself one with all men as Mr Lincoln.[20]

When the Confederate agents Mason and Slidell were arrested by Federal officers on boarding the *Trent*, a British ship, feelings ran high in Britain where sympathies lay with the Confederacy. Carnegie, better than most, appreciated British sensitivity about her naval autonomy being challenged in this way, and impressed on Scott the necessity of liberating the prisoners as soon as possible. Scott was summoned to a Cabinet meeting in the absence of Secretary Cameron and, while he was at first inclined to ignore Carnegie's advice, he later reported that Seward had also advocated this prudent action. The meeting was postponed until Cameron could be present, but Seward asked Scott to explain the case fully to the Secretary of War, especially as Cameron was regarded as a diehard who would wish to hold the captives. At any rate, Scott used all his powers of persuasion and in due course Cameron fell into line.

Most of Carnegie's criticism was reserved for the seventy-five-year-old Commander-in-Chief, Lieutenant-General Winfield Scott. As far back as 1852 Carnegie had been aware of this 'old warrior' when he had been standing as a presidential candidate. Less than a decade later, General Scott was doddery and senile. 'He was an old, decrepit man, paralyzed not only in body, but in mind; and it was upon this noble relic of the past that the organization of the forces of the Republic depended.' No more effectual or competent was General Scott's chief of staff, General Taylor. Carnegie had nothing but contempt for these men – 'martinets who had passed the age of usefulness'. Long years of peace had atrophied and fossilised the high command, and someone as active and impetuous as Carnegie often chafed at the inordinate length of time taken by the general staff in coming to even the most trivial decision. Fortunately, the political head of the military machine, Simon Cameron, bypassed the generals and gave Colonel Scott *carte blanche* to do whatever was necessary to keep communications and transportation of men and supplies operating as smoothly as possible. Cameron, who liked to be addressed as Lochiel, was a second-generation American-Scot. Before the war he was the political boss of Pennsylvania and had a reputation as being one of the wiliest manipulators in politics, but in Edwin Stanton he had met his match, and would eventually be ousted by him. But during the summer of 1861 he got to know young Carnegie very well and the two became lifelong friends. In his ninetieth year 'Lochiel' paid a visit to the land of his forefathers as Carnegie's guest and travelling companion and was overcome by the grandeur of the Highland glens.

Initially it had been considered that the business of putting down the Southern rebellion would be over within a matter of weeks, but after the first battle of Bull Run it seemed that General Scott's absurd prophecy of a three-year war might be true after all. The traditional manner of raising militia levies from each state to serve for ninety days was soon replaced by the Military Act of 1861 which provided a more definitive mobilisation for a three-year period. At the same time, younger officers such as Major-General George McClellan were brought to the fore, and talented men like Tom Scott and Carnegie, briefly seconded by their companies, were replaced by permanent officials. Such was the power of the Pennsylvania Railroad that it succeeded in retrieving its key men after a few months. By late September Tom Scott returned to his vice-presidential suite in Philadelphia, while Carnegie went back to Pittsburgh.

War fever was at its height, and Carnegie was flattered to discover that a company of Pennsylvania railwaymen had been organised into a militia unit named in his honour by John B. Dailey and Captain William Mills. Raised originally for home defence, the Carnegie Corps was subsequently drafted to Washington to join McClellan's great Army of the Potomac. More importantly, however, the Little Boss was back where he belonged, issuing orders which he knew would be instantly obeyed, rather than subjected to the bureaucratic delays which he had found so exasperating in Washington. The railroad was stretched to the very limit by the exigencies of war, and soon Carnegie was firing off impatient memos to superintendent Enoch Lewis requesting that the telegraph lines be manned all round the clock, demanding that the railway line between Altoona and Pittsburgh be upgraded to twin-tracking operations, and insisting that additional sites west of Pittsburgh be acquired for new marshalling yards and freight depots.[21] When the newly opened Pittsburgh and Connellsville Railroad offered stiff competition in the suburban network, Carnegie urged Lewis to cut the passenger fares by five cents, and recoup the difference by making the railwaymen work shifts of thirteen hours instead of ten, arguing, 'I do not regard 13 hours Train service as more exhaustive than ten hours manual labor — We have never found the efficiency of the force impaired by the amount of service required from the crews referred to.'[22] Drive and expand, minimise costs and maximise profits; those were precepts that Carnegie would turn to time and time again in later years.

While getting the maximum out of the railroad, and justifying his recent increase in salary to $1800 per annum, Carnegie was continuing to look for other ways of feathering his own nest. The income from the Woodruff sleeping-cars was piling up almost faster than he could invest it; almost, but not quite, for in the winter of 1861–62 Carnegie diversified his investments. But now an opportunity came up which seemed to promise even greater wealth. In 1859 mineral oil had been discovered at Titusville in western Pennsylvania. Carnegie had been impervious to the oil fever of that time and had refused to invest in this new industry; but as new fields were discovered and came on stream in September 1861, at a time when oil was daily becoming more and more vital to the war effort, Carnegie had second thoughts.

One of his Homewood neighbours was William Coleman, an ironmaster for whose business acumen Carnegie had great respect. When Coleman formed the Columbia Oil Company, with an option to buy the strategically placed Storey Farm on the west branch of Oil Creek for $40,000, he approached Carnegie to see whether he might be persuaded to join in this venture. The canny Scot wanted to see the farm for himself before investing a dollar, and late in 1861 he and Coleman travelled up the Allegheny River by steamboat to the oilfields. From Oil City at the mouth of Oil Creek they made an uncomfortable journey by wagon over dirt tracks. Fighting back the nausea from the frightful stench, Carnegie viewed the incredible scene. Amid the crudest shacks imaginable stood a forest of roughly fashioned derricks from which spouted the black viscous substance. It lay in vile puddles everywhere and the smell clung to clothes and hair. There was a frenzied atmosphere, but the good humour of the roughnecks surprised him:

> It was a vast picnic, full of amusing incidents. Everybody was in high glee; fortunes were supposedly within reach; everything was booming. On the tops of the derricks floated flags on which strange mottoes were displayed. I remember looking down toward the river and seeing two men working their treadles boring for oil upon the banks of the stream, and inscribed upon their flag was 'Hell or China'. They were going down, no matter how far.[23]

Carnegie was immediately smitten by the oil bug. By the time he and Coleman had returned to Pittsburgh, he had made his plans to take a share in the Columbia Oil Company. The initial share capital was $200,000 but the $100 shares were sold to investors at $10 a share. Using his sleeping-cars income, Carnegie bought a thousand Columbia shares. His outlay of about $11,000 netted him $17,868.67 in dividends in the first year alone.[24] When supply exceeded demand and the market price of oil dropped from $5 to 10c a barrel, Carnegie persuaded Coleman to stockpile the raw material. As a result a huge hole was excavated into which the surplus oil, over 100,000 barrels of it, was pumped. Natural seepage was balanced by the daily output of the surrounding wells. Thus the company created a vast reservoir of oil and when the wells dried up, as assuredly they would, the price of crude would recover and might even double to $10. Then they would start to offload their surplus. That, at least, was the theory; but when the wells showed no signs of exhaustion and other oilfields were discovered, driving the price of crude oil down even further, the gamble with the huge black pond proved disastrous. Meanwhile seepage was costing the company thousands of barrels of oil. This sorry state of affairs could not go on indefinitely, and after several months Carnegie, Coleman and their partners cut their losses and aborted the reservoir project.

The situation improved somewhat when, in October 1862, the railway from Corry was extended to Titusville. By now the company had begun to realise that the price of crude oil would never recover, and that profitability would only return when more efficient ways of refining the oil were devised. Hand in hand with this was a policy of securing the best workforce that money could buy – no easy task in an industry where every man jack with a hundred bucks could buy the tools to set up on his own. Not only did the Columbia Oil Company pay top dollar to its drillers and roustabouts, but it provided proper housing, the best-equipped machine-shops, and a whole host of recreational facilities, including the Columbia Cornet band, the first musical organisation in the oilfields, and (significantly) a good library. It would be Carnegie's first exercise in practical philanthropy, but he was by no means altruistic. The Storey Farm oilfield rapidly acquired a reputation in the industry as the best-paying and most efficient. Profits rose sharply as production methods were streamlined and improved. Soon the débâcle over the oil pond was a distant memory, and in the second year of operations the company paid out more than a million dollars to the shareholders. In total, the men who had laid out that initial $40,000 eventually made over five million out of the venture. At the age of twenty-seven, Andrew Carnegie was well on the way to becoming a millionaire.

Meanwhile, there were other irons in the fire – quite literally this time. Andrew Kloman, an immigrant blacksmith from Trier in Prussia, had started with a modest forge at Girty's Run in Millvale, a suburb of Pittsburgh. A mechanical genius, he had invented a method of forging axles by twisting strands of iron to produce a remarkably strong and resilient product. This came to the notice of Tom Miller who, by 1859, had become the purchasing agent for the Pittsburgh, Fort Wayne and Chicago Railway. When Kloman casually mentioned that if only he could afford a second trip-hammer he could double output and make a small fortune, Miller chipped in with $1600 of his own money which gave him a one-third interest in the Kloman forge. Apprehensive about profiting from a business in which his railroad was a customer, Miller sought a dummy partner whom he could trust. In this manner Henry Phipps, younger son of the Rebecca Street cobbler and another old friend from the Bottom Hooshiers gang, was brought into the deal, acquiring a half of Miller's share for $800 (which Miller very obligingly lent him). As part of the arrangement Phipps, then employed as a book-keeper with Dilworth and Bidwell in Pittsburgh, agreed to act as Kloman's part-time book-keeper so that Miller could keep a close watch on his investment. For two years Kloman's business progressed steadily if unspectacularly; but then came the war and the price of axles leaped from two to twelve cents a pound. The Kloman forge was working flat out day and night, and the original plant at Girty's Run soon gave way to a huge new mill in the heart of Pittsburgh, with the grandiose title of the Iron City Forge. New articles of association for this venture, drawn up on 1 January 1862 to run for five years, gave Andrew Kloman and his brother Anton a third share apiece, while Phipps and Miller had a sixth share each. Under the energetic management of Andrew Kloman and Henry Phipps, the new venture prospered beyond their wildest dreams. Miller continued as a railroad executive but, like his buddy Andrew Carnegie, his official salary was now only a fraction of his income.

Carnegie himself was finding that the task of balancing his expanding business interests with the exacting duties of a divisional superintendent was more than he could cope with. Frequent but extremely uncomfortable trips to Storey Farm, on top of the rigours of the railroad, inevitably took their toll on a constitution that had never fully recovered from the privations of the previous summer. By March 1862 Carnegie was seriously ill and his doctors ordered complete rest for several months. By May, a gravely debilitated Carnegie gave way and applied for a three-month leave of absence. Alarmed at his poor shape, J. Edgar Thomson readily granted him his wish. It was Carnegie's first holiday since that morning, fourteen years previously, when he had gone to work at Blackstock's cotton mill, and he felt he had earned not so much a rest, but a vacation that would fulfil his wildest dreams. On the very day he received notification of leave, he dashed off a letter to cousin Dod giving the great news. He would shortly be visiting Scotland: 'Uncles, Aunts and Cousins – all are to be greeted again.' He reminisced for a couple of pages about old haunts he longed to see again.

At New York on 28 June 1862, Carnegie, with his mother and Tom Miller, boarded the luxury steamer *Aetna*, flagship of the Inman Line. The suite of staterooms provided an infinitely more comfortable and luxurious voyage than the ordeal on the *Wiscasset* fourteen years earlier.

On disembarking at Liverpool, the Carnegie party immediately caught the train north. As they headed for Carlisle and the border, Carnegie's heart beat faster:

> Every mile that brought us nearer to Scotland increased the intensity of my feelings. My mother was equally moved, and I remember, when her eyes first caught sight of the familiar yellow bush, she exclaimed: 'Oh! there's the broom, the broom!'[25]

And she dissolved in tears. Carnegie, trying to soothe and comfort her, was overcome by emotion himself. When the train crossed the Sark, Carnegie would have leaped out of the carriage to kiss the sacred native soil if he could. Excitement mounted as they drew closer and closer to their destination, but Carnegie was puzzled to note how small everything was compared with what he had imagined. At Dunfermline station the clan was assembled on the platform: Bailie Morrison, Uncle George Lauder, Dod and Aunt Charlotte Drysdale. The jubilant party moved swiftly to Uncle Lauder's shop and, as he stood in the poky little grocery, Carnegie exclaimed, 'You are all here; everything is just as I left it, but you are now all playing with toys.'

Everything about Dunfermline seemed much smaller than he had remembered. 'Here was a city of the Lilliputians,' was his rueful comment, adding that: 'What I felt on a later occasion on a visit to Japan, with its small toy houses, was something like a repetition of the impression my old home made upon me.'[26] Only 'the glorious old Abbey and its Glen' did not disappoint him, and he was comforted to hear the sonorous bell again. His relatives proved to be just as disappointing as the town, with their small minds and blinkered outlook. Aunt Charlotte epitomised their attitudes when she exclaimed exultantly, 'Oh, you will just be coming back here some day and *keep a shop in the High Street.*' This, to her, was the very acme of success; to the budding millionaire, however, it seemed a pitifully limited goal.

Carnegie was even more disconcerted to discover, at a very early stage, that the people of Dunfermline were Southern sympathisers, almost to a man. This was a very complex attitude which Carnegie could never comprehend, a blend of romanticism and sentimentality which tended to see the Old South as the reincarnation of the Scotland of the Jacobites, coupled with the more immediate economic realities: a war which had almost destroyed the British textile industry as well as the sugar and tobacco trade with the Southern states, and brought widespread unemployment and destitution in its wake, was hardly likely to be popular. Sympathy for the plight of the slaves, evoked in *Uncle Tom's Cabin*, vanished when Harriet Beecher Stowe subsequently wrote a book entitled *Sunny Memories of Foreign Lands* extolling the land policy of the Duchess of Sutherland who had evicted her Highland tenants to make way for sheep. This book provoked a savagely satirical rejoinder from Donald McLeod whose *Gloomy Memories in the Highlands*, in condemning Harriet Beecher Stowe, cast serious doubts on her evidence against slavery. Compared with the landless cotters cast adrift to starve, the lot of the Southern slaves seemed a happy one.

Carnegie had furious arguments over the relative merits of North and South with Uncle Tom Morrison, but the Bailie won, as he did every argument, by blustering and shouting down his adversary. Only in Uncle George Lauder did Carnegie find a kindred spirit, a man whose unswerving loyalty to the abolitionist principles made him extremely unpopular in the town. Carnegie would later remember him with special affection:

> He had not shrunk, no one could fill his place. We had our walks and talks constantly and I was 'Naig' again to him . . . My dear, dear uncle, and more, much more than uncle to me.[27]

Later Uncle George remitted a substantial sum in gold, asking Carnegie to invest the cash in Federal bonds as a token of his support for the Union. His faith was handsomely repaid when the bonds doubled in value.

What with all the excitement of his homecoming and his generally rundown state, Carnegie caught a cold which rapidly developed into pneumonia. For six weeks he lay in his uncle's house in a critical condition, exacerbated by the drastic medical practice of bleeding him with leeches. 'My thin American blood was so depleted that when I was pronounced convalescent it was long before I could stand upon my feet.' Only when he had fled these doubtful ministrations and withdrawn to a lodge in Loch Leven did he slowly begin to recover. This setback put paid to his plans to tour Britain and the Continent, and as soon as he was fit enough he and his mother sailed for America. Saddened and disillusioned at the shattering of childhood memories, Carnegie soon recovered his equilibrium on the ocean voyage. By the time the ship docked at New York he was fighting fit and anxious to resume work. He was heartened when the train heading for Pittsburgh entered the eastern end of his division and he saw the men of the Carnegie Corps drawn up in uniform, around a cannon with which they fired a salvo in greeting.

> This was perhaps the first occasion upon which my subordinates had an opportunity of making me the subject of any demonstration, and their reception made a lasting impression. I knew how much I

cared for them and it was pleasing to know that they reciprocated
my feelings. Working men always do reciprocate kindly feeling. If we
truly care for others we need not be anxious about their feelings for
us. Like draws to like.[28]

During the voyage back to America, Carnegie and Tom Miller had
many long discussions. It may be assumed that, rather than reminisce
about the Scottish scenery, they discussed the progress of the war
and the seemingly endless business opportunities which it was
creating. While Carnegie was now earning a salary of $2400 a year
from the Pennsylvania Railroad, the revenue from his investments
was many times that amount. When income tax was introduced in
1863 by the Federal government as a wartime expedient, Carnegie
filed his first tax return, revealing an investment income of almost
$40,000 per annum, drawn from an astonishing variety of sources.
Even so, he was not satisfied, but had set his heart on achieving an
annual investment income of at least $50,000. Consequently, he was
always on the lookout for ways of reinvesting an income that was far
in excess of his modest requirements.

At this period Carnegie's sights were set mainly on oil, the interest
in the Columbia Oil Company providing over half of his annual
income; but he also made substantial investments in the Pit Hole
oilfield and the East Sandy Oil Company. A joint venture with William
Coleman in the Brick House heavy lubricating oil business, however,
proved unprofitable, as did a joint venture with Bob Pitcairn to mine
coal from the bed of the Monongahela River. Shortly after their return
to Pennsylvania, Carnegie and Miller were involved in a number of
projects. Together they purchased stock in the Pennsylvania Oil
Company and the Western Union Telegraph Company which (from
his experience in Washington) Carnegie shrewdly suspected would
emerge as the communications giant of America. Together they
helped in the foundation of the Third National Bank of Pittsburgh,
and Miller drew his friend into participation in the Iron City Forge.

In view of the fact that his investments were now yielding almost
twenty times his salary, it may be wondered why Carnegie continued
to labour so long in a job that produced such a relatively small return;
but he considered it his contribution to the war effort to remain at his
post as divisional superintendent. Nevertheless, by 1864 the war must

have seemed remote when suddenly, with terrifying abruptness, the reality of it was brought home to him. The previous year a hard-pressed government had introduced the Conscription Act, and now the twenty-eight-year-old bachelor found himself on the receiving end of a draft notice. The *Autobiography* is silent on the matter, but doubtless Carnegie felt that he had already shed blood for his country and his health had suffered grievously on active (if civilian) service. Furthermore, the work of the divisional superintendent of one of the country's busiest railroads was vital to the efficient conduct of the war. But the only way he could escape becoming blue-coated cannon fodder was to pay $300 to the Federal government, or find someone willing to go in his place. To Carnegie, the payment of $300 was not the honourable solution. Instead, he contacted H.M. Butler, a Pittsburgh draft agent, and he in turn procured John Lindew, newly arrived in America from Ireland. This alternative cost Carnegie $850, but as a result he was granted a certificate of non-liability for military service, valid for three years, with effect from 19 July 1864.[29]

On 28 March 1865, as General Ulysses S. Grant's army was poised in the suburbs of Richmond for the final assault on the Confederate capital, Andrew Carnegie drafted a letter to all the officers and employees of the Western Division:

> Gentlemen:
>
> I cannot allow my connection with you to cease without some expression of the deep regret felt at parting. Twelve years of pleasant association have served to inspire feelings of personal regard for those who have so faithfully labored with me in the service of the Company. The coming change is painful only as I reflect that in consequence thereof, I am not to be in the future, as in the past, intimately associated with you . . . who have become my personal friends . . .
>
> Thanking you most sincerely for . . . your most zealous efforts made at all times to meet my wishes . . . I bid you all Farewell.[30]

The finality of this letter, which followed on his resignation from the Pennsylvania Railroad, implies a break with the past as Carnegie faced the future. In fact, though he was to be no longer a salaried official of the railroad, Carnegie would be inextricably linked to railways for the rest of his active business life.

FIVE

Many Fingers, Many Pies

1865–73

There centum per centum, the cit with his purse
Robert Burns, 'No Churchman am I'

THE YEAR THAT WITNESSED THE END OF THE CIVIL WAR WAS A major turning point in Andrew Carnegie's life. Not only did he leave the Pennsylvania Railroad, exchanging the role of paid employee for that of fully fledged capitalist, but he also changed direction in terms of his business interests. Hitherto oil had been the dominant factor, but bad experiences such as the Storey Farm oil pond and the Monongahela riverbed project had soured him off mineral exploitation as the key to rapid wealth.

This change of direction had, in fact, been heralded several years earlier through the friendship which had developed between Carnegie and John L. Piper. They had met at Altoona in 1858 when Piper was the engineer in charge of bridge-building on the railroad, and their mutual passion for fine horses drew them close together. Up to that time railroads spanned river gorges by means of colossal wooden trestles, but Piper argued that the job could be done more efficiently and durably by using iron which, unlike timber, was impervious to flood and fire. This view was shared by J.H. Linville, the Pennsylvania Railroad's chief engineer, and in 1859 they were authorised to build a small iron bridge as a replacement for one of the wooden bridges on the line. The success of this bridge made an immediate convert of Aaron Shiffler, the railroad's general bridge supervisor, who was convinced that sooner or later all rail bridges would be made of iron.

When Carnegie was given the task of rebuilding Long Bridge linking Washington and Alexandria, it was to his old friend Colonel Piper that he turned immediately for practical assistance. On his return to Pittsburgh he had suggested to Piper, Linville and Shiffler that they should set up an independent company for bridge-building. The Piper and Shiffler Company was established in February 1862 and Carnegie got a one-fifth interest for $1250. When he filed his first tax return at the end of 1863, he was already earning $7500 from this business. After the Columbia Oil Company, it was his most valuable source of revenue. Throughout the remainder of the war this business continued to expand steadily, but that was as nothing compared with the boom in bridge-building which came in the immediate post-war years as railroads grew exponentially across the continent. That one-fifth interest would give Carnegie an important foothold in heavy engineering and secure his entry into the iron and steel industry. Within a month of leaving his employment with the railroad in 1865, he had reorganised this concern as the Keystone Bridge Company, under the management of Piper and Shiffler. The small iron bridges erected since 1859 were but toys compared with the huge structures required to span the mighty Ohio, Mississippi and Missouri rivers, and a hefty injection of capital was required to give the new company the capacity to take on such major projects. Nominally Carnegie held all of the $80,000 stock, but put up only a fraction of the cash himself. About half came from J. Edgar Thomson (who scrupulously registered his shares in his wife's name) and six other railroad executives, but the rest of the money came from Carnegie's old boss Tom Scott. Though denied voting rights in the company, the easy-going Scott trusted his old subordinate and was content to sit back and reap the dividends from his half share of the investment.

Carnegie's direct involvement in the iron industry came about in a most unusual and dramatic manner, however. On the afternoon of 20 August 1863 an extremely angry Tom Miller had burst into Carnegie's office brandishing a copy of the *Pittsburgh Evening Chronicle*.

'Look what that damned Dutchman has done!' he yelled. 'Just look at this!' He thrust the paper under the startled superintendent's eyes.

There, on the front page, was an advertisement in heavy bold type from Kloman and Company intimating that Thomas N. Miller was 'not a member of our firm, nor has he any authority to transact business on our account'.

The previous autumn, the Iron City Forge had been given a thorough shake-up. There had been a rift between Andrew Kloman and his brother Anton; the latter was too fond of the bottle and no longer pulling his weight in the organisation. Andrew had then consulted Henry Phipps and Tom Miller and, as a result, Anton was persuaded to part with his one-third interest in the business to Miller for $20,000. An endorsement on the original articles of partnership, dated 13 June 1863, named Miller as a partner for the first time. Too late, however, it dawned on Andrew Kloman that control of the business had passed to Miller who now owned half of it outright and, of course, could presumably always rely on Phipps for his unstinted support. Miller tried to placate Kloman by immediately selling him sufficient stock to give him exactly 50 per cent of the business, but still Kloman was not satisfied and demanded that Miller or Phipps should sell out to him completely. He accused Miller of sharp practice and hard bargaining over orders placed with the Forge on behalf of the Fort Wayne Railroad. Miller retaliated by holding up the settlement of the railroad account, a drastic move that led to Phipps siding with Kloman against his old chum. In desperation Miller proposed bringing Andrew Carnegie into the business as a disinterested outsider, but Kloman would have none of it, even though he respected Carnegie as an increasingly influential figure in the murky world of business. When the *Evening Chronicle* printed a squib stating that Kloman & Co. would henceforward be styled Kloman & Miller, the irascible Kloman erupted. He consulted his lawyer, Ludwig Koethen (he who had once rapped the knuckles of choirboy Carnegie for singing out of tune). Koethen's advice was that Kloman should immediately publish a disclaimer in the same newspaper.

Had Miller foreseen the consequences of his actions that hot August afternoon he would never have appealed to Carnegie for help. As he sat at his desk trying to soothe his angry friend, Carnegie was already considering the potential benefit to himself from acting as mediator in the squabble. Over the ensuing days he had meetings with Kloman, Phipps and Miller, both individually and together. When the dust had settled on the quarrel, Miller found to his chagrin that he had been ousted from the company. His place was now taken by young Tom Carnegie whose partnership was purchased by his wily brother. Exactly how Carnegie pulled off this masterstroke is not known, especially as he somehow contrived to retain Miller's friendship.

This coup was achieved by stages. The first was the creation, on 1 September 1863, of a new concern, Kloman and Phipps, with a capitalisation of $60,000. In this venture Miller remained a 'special partner' in respect of his original one-sixth interest. This agreement was to run until 1 January 1870, but it contained a curious clause:

> But if at any time during the term aforesaid the said Kloman and
> Phipps shall desire to terminate the same as the said special partner,
> then upon the said Kloman and Phipps giving to the said Thomas N.
> Miller sixty days notice in writing, and jointly signed, of their
> desire to that effect, the interest of him, the said Thomas N. Miller,
> shall at the end of said sixty days, and upon the payment to him of
> the capital invested by him and share of profits coming to him, or,
> in case of loss, of the total amount of capital still remaining due to
> him, retire from said firm, and his interest therein shall at that time
> wholly cease, and the same shall in such case accrue to the said
> Henry Phipps, Jr., as having a pre-emption right thereto, upon his
> paying in the capital for the purchase thereof.[1]

A separate and private agreement provided that, in the event of Miller's removal, one half of his interest should go to Tom Carnegie. Not long afterwards the ever-suspicious and irascible Kloman again quarrelled with Miller, who was duly notified that the ejecture clause would be enforced. Andrew Carnegie's role in the matter is understandably shadowy. He subsequently drafted a memorandum justifying his own course of action in the squabble. In this, he conveyed the impression that he was solely motivated by a desire to protect the good name of his friend Miller 'as enemies were not wanting who began circulating slanderous reports about his clandestine arrangement with Klowman [sic] while acting as agent of the Fort Wayne Road'.[2]

In a freewheeling era when all major railroad executives, from Edgar Thomson and Tom Scott downwards, had hidden interests in the manufacturing and engineering companies to whom they awarded contracts, this concern for Miller's good name seems rather specious. But clearly Miller himself accepted this explanation for the usurpation of his special partnership, and any lingering doubts were swept aside when, only months later, Carnegie invited Miller to join him in an entirely new venture, the Cyclops Iron Company. In getting Miller to accept the *fait accompli*, Carnegie insinuated that the real cause of Miller's ejectment was Henry Phipps, the very man that Miller had brought into the Kloman company. Miller was stung by this betrayal by his old chum from Rebecca Street and fellow choirboy. While Miller vowed that he would never forgive Phipps for breaking his solemn trust, Carnegie aggressively suggested a practical means of getting revenge, and lining his own pocket at the same time. Thus Cyclops would be established as a rival to Kloman. Miller had a site in mind, a field barely half a mile up the Allegheny River from the Kloman foundry, and the first call on their capital was the $400 which Carnegie and Miller paid to a market-gardener named Cummings to take over the lease of his cabbage-patch.

Cyclops formally came into being on 14 October 1864, Miller having a controlling interest while Carnegie, John Piper and J.H. Linville (Carnegie's associates in the bridge-building enterprise) held the remainder of the stock. From the outset, Cyclops was perceived in the business community as the direct rival of Kloman, and the fact that these deadly rivals each had a Carnegie brother on its board of directors added fuel to the speculation. While Tom Carnegie resigned from the Pennsylvania Railroad to devote himself wholeheartedly to the Kloman–Phipps enterprise, brother Andrew pressed ahead with his plans for Cyclops. Neither Carnegie nor Miller had any practical experience of the foundry business, so the day-to-day running of the mill was in the hands of John C. Matthews. When it commenced operations in the spring of 1865, there were numerous snags and teething troubles, all of which earned the luckless Matthews the vociferous criticism of Carnegie and Miller. Matthews stood his ground, however, and bluntly told the partners: 'The trouble with you fellows is that you wanted a $400,000 mill for $100,000.'[3]

It was small consolation to Carnegie that while Cyclops was running into unforeseen problems, the revitalised Kloman mill was reaping spectacular profits, much of which, of course, would find its way indirectly into his hands. Tom Carnegie was turning out to be one of Kloman's best assets, having a happy knack of handling the short-tempered German. He had his brother's charm without Andrew's cockiness, and his modest manner, relieved by a quiet sense of humour and low-key persuasive skills, brought to the Kloman partnership a new sense of unity and solidarity.

On the advice of John Matthews, Andrew Carnegie planned to increase the capitalisation of Cyclops. At the same time, the Kloman mill increased its capital from $60,000 to $150,000. Tom Carnegie discussed the matter with his brother and proposed the unthinkable: why not combine Cyclops with Kloman in one big company with the general management in the hands of Andrew Kloman, who knew more about iron than all the Cyclops partners would ever know. The upshot was that Tom Carnegie was given a free hand to persuade Phipps and Kloman, while brother Andrew undertook to bring the unforgiving Miller round to this way of thinking. Getting Kloman and Miller to bury their differences was a superhuman task, but the combined talents of the Carnegie brothers eventually broke down the mutual resentment, anger and hostility. 'Money talks', and Kloman was won round with a quarter share of the combined companies and a hefty increase in salary. Miller, the implacable enemy of Phipps and hellbent on driving Kloman into bankruptcy, was a tougher nut to crack, but eventually he too capitulated, though he drove a very hard bargain and ended up with the largest share of the business – larger than Kloman's, larger even than the combined shares of Tom Carnegie and Henry Phipps. Miller also insisted that he have absolutely nothing to do with Phipps, and this was agreed, even though it created the idiotic situation of the largest shareholder refusing to attend board meetings or take any active part in the company's management.

As a result of this agreement, Andrew Carnegie and Tom Miller surrendered the Cyclops Mill, with a cash adjustment of $50,000, to Kloman and his partners, receiving in exchange 49 per cent of the shares in a new concern, which was to be known as the Union Iron Mills Company. This combine, with a capitalisation of $500,000, came into existence on 1 May 1865. Henceforward, the Iron City

Forge became the Lower Union Mill and the Cyclops plant the Upper Union Mill. Just as Carnegie's Keystone Bridge Company had derived its name from Pennsylvania's nickname as the Keystone State, so too the new combine reflected the rebirth of the Union, with the re-admission of the Confederate States. Thus, within a matter of months, Carnegie had created a major engineering concern that relied heavily on the mechanical genius and trusting nature of John Piper, and an equally powerful concern which gave him control of the raw materials. The Lower Union Mill and the Keystone plant were conveniently located side by side, and over the coming years Tom Carnegie and John Piper would become close friends. To Tom is due the credit for developing the close working relationship between the two firms.

Having completed the practical organisation of the two businesses, Carnegie took himself off to Europe with his old friend John Vandevort. At the last moment they were joined by Henry Phipps, invited by Carnegie as a conciliatory gesture. Phipps, still smarting over the recent breach with Miller, got to know Carnegie much better during this trip, and was utterly charmed by him. Carnegie and Vandevort had been reading Bayard Taylor's *Views Afoot* and this gave Carnegie the notion of a hiking trip of his own. At Liverpool they were joined by John Franks, a cousin of Phipps, who kept a journal of the tour. For five months the quartet wandered on foot, knapsacks on their backs, through France, Germany, Switzerland and Italy. The Franks journal has frequent and copious references to Andy: 'He is full of liveliness, fun and frolic . . . Andy is so overflowing that it is extremely difficult to keep him within reasonable bounds, to restrain him within the limits of moderately orderly behavior – he is so con-tinually mischievous and so exuberantly joyous.'[4] Franks revealed that Carnegie had a rough and ready fluency in French which proved very useful time and again; and also that the dapper and debonair little Scot was quite the ladies' man, whether chucking a barmaid under the chin or engaging in a flirtation with a passing lady of the evening. His more timid companions were awed by his amorous conquests. This dalliance was, of course, quite ephemeral, the hard-headed tourist taking good care to avoid the slightest hint of commitment.

That Carnegie should go off on an extended foreign trip at a crucial time in his business career might seem unwise, but it was to be characteristic. He had supreme confidence in the men he had left behind to run the twin businesses. Kloman, Piper, Miller and Tom Carnegie were much abler men than Andrew Carnegie in their own particular fields; his genius lay in bringing together such men and in delegating responsibility to them. Throughout the rest of his life, in fact, he would seldom devote more than six months in any year to his multifarious business interests; the rest of the time would be spent in travelling the world and cultivating his mind. Needless to say, having created a superb organisation, Carnegie maintained close contact with it while abroad. While Vandy and Phipps exchanged letters with their brother and sister respectively, Carnegie was in constant communication with his business associates. While he wrote regularly to Tom, and received lengthy reports from him in return, Carnegie also found time to fire off long articles, based on his experiences, to the editor of the *Pittsburgh Commercial*.

John Franks recorded that: 'The boys are elated by glorious news in their letters of continued advances in prices, of stocks advancing, of their mills working double turns, of large orders pouring in, of new patents obtained and of still greater successes looming in the future.' These glowing reports, however, were not confirmed when Carnegie returned to Pittsburgh early in 1866. To his dismay, he found that the Union Iron Mills were not doing as much business as he had been led to believe. In vain, his brother tried to explain that there was a general downturn in business throughout the country, the inevitable result of the struggle to adjust to peacetime conditions. Carnegie would brook no excuses: there was always business to be had even in hard times – you just had to hustle harder to get it. What made matters worse was the fact that the poor showing of the Union Iron Mills was responsible for Keystone failing to secure certain vital contracts.

Suspecting that Miller's continuing intransigence lay at the heart of Union's troubles, Carnegie got to work on him and urged him to let bygones be bygones. When Miller would not budge, Carnegie was forced to take drastic measures. Phipps was persuaded to resign from the board of directors, though he remained a partner in the firm. This face-saving device enabled Miller to take his place on the board, and for fifteen months all was sweetness and light at the Union Mills. But Tom Carnegie was unhappy at what he regarded as the unfair treatment of Henry Phipps and continually stuck up for him. And, when it emerged that Miller was not as sound a businessman as Phipps, Andrew came round to his brother's way of thinking. When a vacancy on the board arose in 1867 he invited Phipps to fill it. Unfortunately neither of the Carnegie brothers thought to inform Miller of this. The first he knew of this development was when he arrived for the next board meeting and saw Phipps already seated at the table. Miller was livid, and demanded to know where 'that man' had come from.

'Oh come, Tom, don't act like a child,' soothed Carnegie. 'Come back, shake hands with Harry and be friends once more.'

Miller made no reply, but grabbed his coat and hat and slammed the door loudly as he charged out of the boardroom.[5]

Carnegie's memorandum of this angry scene concluded: 'I found reconciliation impossible between him and his two partners, hard as I tried to secure it. Finally Tom asked me to buy his interest and named a figure. I reluctantly bought it — no other course possible.' Matters were not quite as simple as that. On 3 June 1867 Miller wrote a letter of resignation, and this provoked an instantaneous response:

> When you know how we are placed I think instead of embarrassing
> us by resigning you should put your shoulder to the wheel with us.
> We never needed the efforts of all more urgently than now.[6]

When Miller remained adamant, there was considerable haggling over the price. Carnegie talked down the value of the stock, and said that as he was anxious to divest himself of the Union Mills interest he would probably be selling his own shares shortly, and therefore was not too keen on having to buy Miller out. The most he could offer, in the circumstances, was $27.40 a share. Miller held out for more, and in the end Carnegie was compelled to pay him $32.75 for each of his 2203 shares. Miller thus sold out his majority interest for $71,362, though he would live to see that interest multiply two-thousand-fold. Miller was ever afterwards quite philosophical about it: his honour meant much more to him than the chance to become a multi-millionaire. Almost forty years later he would recall this incident, in a letter to Carnegie:

You say in your precious note, 'It was a pity, a foolish quarrel between you and your pards' – truly it was – in a *commercial* sense – in me a folly, but, do you know, I never regret that day! I could not stand the stink of such treachery as his conduct had been in 1863 – indeed after 40 years, while I have forgiven him, I cannot meet him comfortably. As to yourself, what you did then was wise, you had no quarrel with Henry Phipps, you advised me well to 'Let bygones be bygones' – and I loved you then Andy, as I have *ever* loved you, but Phipps had stabbed me at a critical time in my life – but why weary you with dirty linen of the past –[7]

A few months after that letter was written, Miller reiterated the main points in a letter to the *Pittsburgh Leader*, adding a shrewd comment on his old friend:

The only fault I found, and in the business world it is rarely deemed a fault, was that to Andy, Napoleon that he was in business, blunder was worse than a crime. He could forgive the one; he could never excuse the other, and we parted as business associates on this line.[8]

When the partnership was dissolved, Union Mills was renamed Carnegie, Kloman and Company, although it continued to be popularly known by the original name. Carnegie personally purchased 1656 of Miller's shares. At the same time, he purchased shares from his brother as well as Phipps and Linville, bringing his own holding up to 3000 shares. In this manner he acquired the controlling interest in the company, and over the ensuing thirty-three years he would add considerably to his share of the business. Nevertheless, Carnegie subscribed to the old adage of not keeping all his eggs in one basket. In addition to his shares in a wide range of businesses, he was actually at this time more preoccupied with his investment in the American Steeled Rail Company. During the European trip he had met Thomas Dodd, and reported jubilantly to brother Tom that he had acquired the American rights in a process of steel-faced rails invented by Dodd. Later, however, he learned that Dodd had naïvely granted patent rights in America to other individuals. Carnegie himself was ignorant of the pitfalls of patent law. The matter was still pending when the Dodd brothers lost control of their own mill in Sheffield. Carnegie continued negotiations with the Dodd creditors for a further three years, without success. In the meantime Carnegie was cutting corners again, producing 'Doddized' rails at the American Steeled Rail Company without legal authority, and spending an inordinate amount of time and money in trying to persuade the American railroads to use these rails. It soon transpired, however, that the steel-shod rails rapidly wore out, provoking an angry response from the railroad companies who soon reverted to the traditional iron rails.

In the end, J. Edgar Thomson, who had taken a small consignment of Doddized rails, advised Carnegie to abort this operation and abandon his attempt to gain the American patent, saying that the experiments made in relation to the strength of the Doddized rails 'had so much impaired my confidence in the process that I didn't feel at liberty to increase our order . . . Unless you can overcome this difficulty − which I fear is impracticable − the process is not a success'.[9] Despite this, Carnegie persisted with his sales drive, even using the Pennsylvania's single (and minute) order as an advertisement for their success: 'Mr Thomson's report estimates the process to extend the life of the Rail three fold,' he wrote brazenly the very same day to W.B. Ogden, the president of the Chicago and Northwestern.[10] Only when cancelled orders came in thick and fast, and rumours of the poor performance of the Dodd rails circulated widely, did Carnegie admit defeat.

He failed to learn a lesson from this episode, for soon he was negotiating with another English firm to secure the American rights to *their* process of rerolling iron rails with steel heads. This, the Webb process, however, would prove no better than the Dodd system, and this disappointment left Carnegie wary of similar schemes. When Tom Scott approached him in 1869 with an improved process for chromed steel, Carnegie was quite negative about it. Later in life he would propound his famous dictum 'Pioneering don't pay', taking the view that once a product or process was proven, then was the time to invest in it − and not before. But in those crucial years of the late 1860s Carnegie frequently gambled on untried projects that seemed to promise untold riches.

A good example was his experiments with Bessemer steel. Early biographies put Carnegie's interest in Sir Henry Bessemer's steel process as being kindled in the spring of 1872, during a visit to the Bessemer plant at Derby. In fact, he had been experimenting with the Bessemer process at least six years earlier, when he began converting the Freedom Iron Company (which he and Miller had formed in 1861) into a steel plant. He intended to use the renamed Freedom Iron and Steel Company to manufacture Webb rails faced with Bessemer steel. By the spring of 1868 this plant was in operation, producing steel for the ill-fated Webb rails as well as a small quantity of rails made entirely of Bessemer steel. When the Dodd and Webb rails failed, Carnegie tentatively offered dissatisfied customers these Bessemer rails, but the price was too high and he found very few takers. The plain truth of the matter was that the quality of pig-iron then available in America was inadequate for the production of Bessemer steel in any quantity. As a result, pure steel rails were expensive to produce, hence all those futile experiments with steel-faced rails. The fundamental problem was that the iron ores of America had a high phosphorus content which made for very friable steel. Bessemer himself learned this the hard way, but once he began using ores from Wales and Sweden which had a very low phosphorus content he could produce the finest steel. Later discoveries of similar high-grade ores in Scotland and Spain produced Bessemer steel in vast quantities and much of this was exported to the United States until the American iron producers persuaded Congress in 1869 to impose a high tariff on imported iron and steel products. The settlement of a patent dispute, and the timely discovery of phosphorus-free ores in Michigan, enabled Bessemer to establish steelmaking facilities in the United States, thus getting around the tariff barrier. By the time Carnegie went to England in 1872 he had already taken steps to expand his own production of Bessemer steel. Contrary to the long-established myth about Carnegie's sudden and dramatic conversion to steel in 1872, all that the visit to the Bessemer plant at Derby achieved was to show Carnegie that his plans for expanding the Freedom Iron and Steel Company were not ambitious enough. Subsequent visits to the steel mills of Sheffield and Birmingham convinced him that he must enlarge his plans. Suddenly, the dazzling prospect of revolutionising the American iron and steel industry struck him.

Up to that time, however, Carnegie had always regarded steelmaking as subsidiary to bridge-building. In the late 1860s, as more and more wooden bridges were replaced, first by iron structures and then by steel, Carnegie concentrated his energies on bigger and stronger bridges. At length, only America's mightiest rivers, the Mississippi and the Missouri, had yet to be spanned, and Carnegie was determined that Keystone should do it.

In 1867 the Union Iron Mills were hit by industrial unrest. The Sons of Vulcan, the puddlers' trade union, came out on strike throughout the Pittsburgh area to resist an attempt by the employers to reduce wages. The iron companies retaliated by bringing in immigrant workers. One of those labourers, whom Kloman hired more or less straight off the boat, was a young German named Johann Zimmer who had previously worked in a plate mill in Prussia. When Zimmer described, from memory, a rolling-machine which produced plates with finished rolled edges, Kloman was very excited. Kloman, who had already invented a saw that would cut cold iron into precise lengths, as well as a machine for making bridge lengths, put all his ingenuity and inventiveness into the problem of making the first universal rolling-mill in America. The Zimmer–Kloman universal mill would, literally, give the Union Mills the edge in competing for engineering contracts. The plates and girders produced by the Union Mills were utilised by Keystone in erecting the great bridges that ultimately spanned the last natural barriers to transcontinental transport, and, in turn, gave Carnegie a major influence in railroad development from 1868 onwards. His bridges determined the routes of the new railways, for which he would ultimately supply the rails and chairs, as well as the axles, wheels and boilers of the locomotives and rolling-stock. The vast profits from steelmaking and heavy engineering could be diverted into investment in the railroads which expanded out of all recognition in the 1870s and 1880s.

Carnegie's ultimate goal was the bridge across the Mississippi at St Louis. This had been the dream of many engineers since the 1840s but the first man to produce what appeared to be a workable plan was Captain James B. Eads who was appointed engineer-in-chief to the St Louis and Illinois Bridge Company which had been formed in 1864. Carnegie was determined to get the contract for the bridge's superstructure and used the good offices of his friends Edgar Thomson and Tom Scott to see that this lucrative contract was awarded to

Keystone. As the Pennsylvania Railroad would be one of the principal users of the bridge, Thomson and Scott persuaded the Bridge Company to hire J.H. Linville as chief consultant to Eads. Linville, of course, was a director of Keystone, and while advising Eads he was in an excellent position to pass vital information back to his co-directors. In due course, the contract was awarded to Keystone, though not without tough opposition from the American Bridge Company of Chicago. Carnegie, however, clinched the deal by telling Eads confidentially that, in addition to the financial support of Thomson and Scott, he was prepared to offer his services as a bond salesman. He would travel to New York to negotiate the necessary capital for the project. Carnegie's prize for selling $4,000,000 of first mortgage bonds would be commission of $50,000.

To this end Carnegie, with his mother in tow, moved from Pittsburgh in October 1867 and took up residence in the St Nicholas Hotel, on Broadway between Broome and Spring Streets in lower Manhattan. The St Nicholas, opened in 1853, was New York's most opulent hotel and its glittering marble façade one of the wonders of the city. This move coincided with the marriage of Tom Carnegie to Lucy Coleman, daughter of Andrew's partner in the Columbia Oil Company. Andrew and Margaret gave Tom the Homewood mansion as a wedding present. As Margaret eyed herself in the huge gilded mirror in her bedroom at the St Nicholas, she must often have marvelled at the transformation wrought in the two decades since she had first landed in New York as a penniless immigrant. Carnegie himself was too busy going places to reflect on this contrast. He opened an office in Broad Street, in the very heart of the financial district, and on the glass door was the bold inscription in gold lettering: 'Andrew Carnegie, Investments'. Later he would boast of having sold $30,000,000 worth of railroad bonds within his first three years in New York, though he omitted to mention that some of these bonds turned out to be worthless. This was the age of the wildcat, when fortunes were made – and lost – in all manner of get-rich-quick schemes. Carnegie's spectacular success may be attributed to his unerring instinct for a good proposition and a sixth sense that warned him off those that were not so sound. As he acquired a reputation for sound judgement he came to be highly regarded by investors and big business alike.

One evening, about a year after moving to New York, Carnegie drew up a list of his assets, using a blunt pencil on the back of an envelope retrieved from the wastepaper basket in the office. In the first column he noted the sixteen companies in which he had an interest. Characteristically, Keystone, 'his pet', headed the list. His 1170 shares, then worth $70 each, produced an annual income of $15,000. This was surpassed only by Union Mills in which he had 2873 shares at $40, yielding about $20,000 per annum. The second column listed the number and price of shares, the third the net worth of each shareholding (a total of $400,000), and the final column the income, which had now risen to $56,100 a year. All this had started with $817 of borrowed money thirteen years previously.

As he sat at his desk and perused this list, his initial satisfaction gave way to nagging doubt. All his mentors and role models, like Edgar Thomson and Tom Scott, William Orton of Western Union or Jay Gould the railroad magnate, had one goal in life – money; and only one talent – the successful pursuit of money. They were wealthy men in purely material terms, but intellectually and culturally they were paupers compared with Tom Morrison and George Lauder, or even Carnegie's own late lamented father William. These men might be scant of cash, but they could quote Burns and Shakespeare, and could discourse on matters as disparate as religion and politics, literature and economics, history and philosophy. In other ways, Carnegie differed radically from his fellow tycoons. Money was the be-all and end-all of their existence and they devoted their time and energy wholeheartedly in its pursuit, but Carnegie, for all his greed and ambition, had no desire to allow money to take him over completely. The plain fact was that he easily tired of the cut and thrust of business. He was at his most energetic in organising businesses, but once they were up and running he preferred to delegate the management and operation to talented executives. In the same way, he was content to invest his money in businesses where other men had the task of making that money grow.

Always at the back of his mind was a hankering to see more of the world. Originally his ambition had been confined to making a triumphant return to the land of his birth, and to this end he tried, through Tom Scott, to get appointed as United States Consul in Glasgow. At the time Carnegie was about to leave the Pennsylvania

Railroad in the spring of 1865, Tom Scott had written to his old wartime political master Simon Cameron (now returned to his former role as political boss of Pennsylvania) in the hope that Cameron would be able to do something to bring this about, but Cameron seems to have done nothing, and in the end Carnegie had had to make the five-month trip to Europe at his own expense. Seeing the wonders of Rome, Venice, Paris and Berlin on that extended tour whetted his appetite. In London he had attended the Handel anniversary concert at the Crystal Palace and felt the power and majesty of great music for the first time. 'At Rome the Pope's choir and the celebrations in the churches at Christmas and Easter furnished, as it were, a grand climax to the whole.'[11]

One evening in December 1868 he sat in his hotel room and wrote a memo to himself, arising out of the statement of assets and income compiled shortly before. Unlike the previous document, this was neatly written in pen and ink:

> Thirty-three and an income of 50,000$ per annum.
>
> By this time two years I can so arrange all my business as to secure at least 50,000 per annum. Beyond this never earn — make no effort to increase fortune, but spend the surplus each year for benovelent [sic] purposes. Cast aside business forever except for others.
>
> Settle in Oxford & get a thorough education making the acquaintance of literary men — this will take three years active work — pay especial attention to speaking in public.
>
> Settle then in London & purchase a controlling interest in some newspaper or live review & give the general management of it attention, taking a part in public matters especially those connected with education & improvement of the poorer classes.
>
> Man must have an idol — The amassing of wealth is one of the worst species of idolitary [sic]. No idol more debasing than the worship of money. Whatever I engage in I must push inordinately therefor should I be careful to choose that life which will be the most elevating in its character. To continue much longer overwhelmed by business cares and with most of my thoughts wholly upon the way to make more money in the shortest time, must degrade me beyond hope of permanent recovery.

I will resign business at Thirty five, but during the ensuing two
years, I wish to spend the afternoons in securing instruction, and in
reading systematically.[12]

This was an amazingly self-revelatory document, which finds no
parallel in anything written by Ford, Morgan, Rockefeller or any of
the other great magnates of the period. Indeed, none of these men
could have penned such a personal memo, nor understood the man
who did. This note was written by Carnegie solely for his own
enlightenment; it was certainly never intended for publication and
found no echo in any of his published writings. Ironically, it has
probably been more widely quoted and disseminated since his death
than anything else he ever wrote.

The promise made to himself, however, was soon broken. In 1869 he
crossed the Atlantic again, not to Oxford but to the London offices of
Junius Spencer Morgan (the father of J. Pierpoint Morgan), who was
a partner of the great New York financier George Peabody. Through
finance houses such as Morgan and Baring Brothers in London, Drexel
Harjes in Paris and Sulzbach Brothers in Frankfurt, Carnegie
successfully negotiated the sale of the St Louis Bridge bonds and
many other issues. There were occasional misses, to be sure, and he
never got over his chagrin at failing to clinch a deal with Barings,
involving $5,000,000 of Philadelphia and Erie Railroad stock, largely
due to the outbreak of the Franco-German War in 1870, when
Chancellor Bismarck had frozen hundreds of millions of pounds'
worth of banking business in Magdeburg and thus triggered off a
Europe-wide panic. Carnegie calculated that he let a cool half-million
dollars in lost commissions slip through his fingers as a result.

By the time of his thirty-fifth birthday, in 1870, Carnegie was not
only fully committed to the sale of bonds and the building of
bridges, but was developing other interests. One that had now
assumed increasing importance was the Pullman Palace Car
Company, destined to become a household name all over the world,
or at least in those parts where luxury rail travel was established. It
will be recalled that Carnegie had been granted a one-eighth interest
in Theodore Woodruff's sleeping-cars. What had begun as a tiny
share of the business, arising out of a generous and altruistic gesture
by Tom Scott, would become the grain of sand in the oyster's shell,

133

a minor irritation that would lead eventually to a pearl of great price. When Woodruff was granted the franchise to place his sleeping-cars on the Pennsylvania Railroad in 1862 he needed a hefty cash injection to expand his business. It was then that the most junior of junior partners, the energetic young superintendent of the Western Division, had drafted the reorganisation and capitalisation of the business which emerged as the Central Transportation Company in which Woodruff found himself elbowed aside to make way for young Carnegie and his cronies. Now Carnegie repaid a good turn by bringing in Tom Scott as a major partner, along with Edgar Thomson, Springer Harbaugh, John Childs and L.B. Franciscus. Of course, the ever-scrupulous Thomson concealed his major share-holding by having his stock registered in the name of R.D. Barclay, his personal secretary. The ever-trusting Scott, however, registered his shares in the name of 'my boy Andy'. This gave Carnegie majority control.

At first Theodore Woodruff and his brother Jonah had no complaints. The company chairman was well connected not only within the Pennsylvania Railroad but miraculously in rival lines, with the result that he secured a tremendous amount of business. Carnegie, in turn, constantly nagged the Woodruff brothers to improve their models and guard against infringements of their patents by rival firms. Carnegie's ultimate goal was to secure the infinitely lucrative contract to provide the sleeping-cars for the Union Pacific which would, in 1869, finally provide coast-to-coast rail communication. In a journey that would take up to six days to accomplish, the provision of sleeping-cars was of vital importance. This was a mighty project, as grandiose in its way as Carnegie's ambitions to span the Missouri and Mississippi rivers, and his plans were laid long and carefully. Realising the limitations of the Woodruff brothers, Carnegie brought in other men active in the same field, first William Knight of Knight Cars, and then George Mortimer Pullman. Unlike Theodore Woodruff, Pullman was no inventor, but he had tremendous entrepreneurial flair and boundless energy. Though he had trained as a cabinetmaker, his early sleeping-cars, modelled on the Woodruff pattern, were crude by comparison. Not surprisingly, they were unsuccessful; and Pullman gave up the idea, going off instead to the Colorado goldfields to open a general store.

Having made a fortune in this venture, he returned to Chicago in 1863, more determined than ever to try his hand at sleeping-cars. This time he had learned his lesson; his sleeping-cars, though still imitating Woodruff models, would be the last word in luxury and comfort. The Pullman car was a palace by comparison, and significantly this was a keyword in the name of Pullman's company. At first railway officials doubted whether customers would pay the two-dollar premium for the privilege of using Pullman 'rolling palaces', but they were soon proved wrong. The Pullman Palace Car Company was incorporated in 1867 and soon the luxury cars were in operation on a number of lines in the North and West. Later that year Pullman gained entry to the New York Central, and this brought him into direct competition with Carnegie's Central Transportation Company.

Carnegie immediately saw Pullman as his most serious rival for the Union Pacific contract: 'a lion in the path' is how he himself described his opponent. In many ways the two men were very much alike: aggressive, ruthless, possessed of limitless self-confidence, and often blind, to the point of utter recklessness, regarding the legal niceties of patents. However, it took one to know one, and Carnegie swiftly perceived that Pullman had blatantly infringed the Woodruff patents. What held him back from rushing to litigation was the fear of legal costs and, more importantly, protracted delays in getting the courts to uphold the Woodruff patents. In the meantime, Pullman might even yet snatch away the Union Pacific contract under Carnegie's nose, and any court victory thereafter would be quite hollow.

Instead, Carnegie tried a more subtle tactic. If he could not beat Pullman, then Pullman must somehow be persuaded to join him. By an interesting coincidence, George Pullman himself was a long-term resident of the St Nicholas Hotel. One evening, therefore, Carnegie contrived to bump into his rival on the main staircase. Carnegie's version of this historic encounter would be recounted many years later:

> 'Good evening, Mr Pullman! Here we are together, and are we not making a nice couple of fools of ourselves?'
>
> He was not disposed to admit anything and said: 'What do you mean?'

135

I explained the situation to him. We were destroying by our rival positions the very advantages we desired to obtain.

'Well,' he said, 'what do you propose to do about it?'

'Unite,' I said. 'Make a joint proposition to the Union Pacific, your party and mine, and organize a company.'

'What would you call it?' he asked.

'The Pullman Pacific Car Company,' I replied.

This suited him exactly; and it suited me equally well.

'Come into my room and talk it over,' said the great sleeping-car man.[13]

It was merely the application of the same concept as the naming of those rabbits in Dunfermline; ever since that time, Carnegie had never underestimated the importance that people placed on their own name. Nevertheless, the merger was not as dramatic, nor as easily accomplished, as the above exchange implies. When Carnegie broached the subject with his fellow-directors the following morning some were against the proposal, arguing that the Central Transportation Company could secure the contract without such a drastic measure. Carnegie had to pull out all the stops to persuade, cajole or browbeat his partners into accepting the merger. Moreover, Pullman himself, having slept on the idea, was now having second thoughts. Not surprisingly, he was having grave doubts concerning Carnegie's motives, and was insisting that his company be given the controlling interest in the planned merger. Carnegie dug his heels in and threatened to initiate immediate legal proceedings against Pullman for infringement of the Woodruff patents. Pullman eventually caved in, and in June 1867 Carnegie moved swiftly, drawing up a simple contract which he submitted to the Union Pacific. This document named Carnegie and Pullman as partners in the project to furnish sleeping-cars for the line and to 'keep up the upholstery, bedding clean, and furnish one porter per car'. In return, the Union Pacific was expected 'at its own expense to furnish fuel for the stoves and lights and keep the cars in good running order'.[14]

This opened the door to the Union Pacific, but several months of wrangling between all of the interested parties were required before a definitive contract, satisfactory to all concerned, was finally drafted. It took all of Carnegie's skills as a diplomat and salesman and consummate manipulator of men, to pull off this masterstroke. In November 1867 the Pullman Pacific Car Company was formed with a capital of $500,000 in $100 shares. Of these, 2600 shares went to Oliver Ames in trust for the Union Pacific stockholders, 1200 went to Pullman and 1200 to Carnegie and his associates, on condition that all of the patents held by the Central Transportation Company should be sold to the new company for $20,000. As regards the sale of patent rights, Carnegie had a tough battle with his associates, who would only agree to this aspect of the deal provided Carnegie agreed to sell to them part of his interest in the Pullman Pacific Car Company. In March 1868 Carnegie confided to Pullman how his partners had demanded compensation for selling their patents for such a low sum: 'I have had to augment it considerably out of my own stock, but I am always willing to share with my associates & do not regret having given away a portion to make all satisfactory.'[15] Even in this magnanimous gesture Carnegie made a handsome profit, selling to his associates for $45 a share the stock which he and Pullman had allocated to themselves at $25 a share. The profit of almost 100 per cent realised on this deal was more than adequate to cover the first instalment of $10 a share on his total subscription of 1200 shares in the company. Yet again, Carnegie had demonstrated his uncanny ability to invest in a business without having to put up any of his own money.

Pullman soon proved to be a much tougher nut to crack than Carnegie had originally anticipated. There was protracted wrangling over the $20,000 which Pullman was obliged to pay for the Woodruff patents. Understandably, however, Pullman was more concerned with raising the cash to construct as many sleeping-cars as he could, in anticipation of the completion of the transcontinental railroad. Far from Carnegie and his associates wheedling the $20,000 out of Pullman, Carnegie was obliged to pay up a further $6400 as a second instalment on his shares in March 1869, though he complained querulously at having to inject so much cash into what now seemed a risky venture. Two months later, though, the line was opened from coast to coast, and Carnegie's earlier fears were soon dispelled. Although Pullman Pacific soon proved a very profitable undertaking, Carnegie was shrewd enough not to let the Central Transportation Company be elbowed out. Indeed, throughout 1868 and 1869 he continued to expand that organisation and strengthen its hold over the lines of the eastern states. This paid off when Central's own profits continued to soar, and by September 1869 it was paying a dividend of almost 20 per cent, substantially more than Pullman Pacific was able to pay to its shareholders.

This fact was not lost on George Pullman, who began to adopt a more conciliatory approach. As a result, a new contract between Central and Pullman was negotiated in January 1870. Central would henceforward lease its entire business to the Pullman Palace Car Company in exchange for an annual rent of $264,000, to be divided in quarterly instalments among the Central shareholders. Once more Carnegie had succeeded in reconciling two great rivals and creating a merger than would eventually be much stronger than the two had they continued to operate separately.

Having set up the deal he now turned to other matters. He would continue to negotiate contracts with many railroad companies on behalf of Pullman, though the latter often felt that Carnegie had other priorities. This arrangement survived until 1874. He continued as vice-president of Central, although this organisation likewise had less of his attention as the years passed. In 1877 when J.F. Cottringer, now president of Central, went to court to break the contract with Pullman, on the grounds that he had not kept his end of the bargain, Carnegie studiously avoided involvement. Cottringer won the case, but by that time Pullman was so dominant in the field of sleeping-cars that it never profited Central, now relegated to the minor league. Carnegie had, in the meantime, been quietly selling off his shares in Central. Shortly after he disposed of his last ninety-four shares in 1884, the company went into voluntary liquidation, paying the remaining stockholders $30 a share.

Carnegie's other major interest in the late 1860s was far more predictable than his almost casual entry into the realm of sleeping-cars. The Western Union Telegraph Company had been formed in 1856 with capital of $500,000, and by the outbreak of the Civil War it had swallowed up numerous smaller companies, to become the largest operator in the eastern states, with ambitions to extend from coast to coast. During the war, Western Union forged ahead, as telegraphic communications became vital to the conduct of military operations on such a vast scale. By 1864 its capital had grown to more than $10,000,000, and it was paying massive dividends – 100 per cent in March 1863, with a further 33 per cent only nine months later. Carnegie, who could claim to have been at the cutting edge of this industry almost since its birth, was more aware than most of the potential growth of telegraphy. In April 1867 he formed the Keystone Telegraph Company with a capitalisation of $50,000, under charter from the state of Pennsylvania. From the outset, this company had the right to erect two wires along the Pennsylvania Railroad, utilising the railway telegraph poles. This concession cost a mere $4 a mile per annum; but before the first wire had been strung, Carnegie was already negotiating with the Pacific and Atlantic Telegraph Company, Western Union's main rival. This led to a merger of the Keystone Company with Pacific and Atlantic five months later. As part of the deal the entire thousand shares in Keystone, worth $50,000, were exchanged for 6000 shares in Pacific and Atlantic, then valued at $150,000. In less than six months, therefore, Carnegie had trebled the value of Keystone without a single telegram being transmitted.

Furthermore, Carnegie now controlled almost a third of the Pacific and Atlantic stock, and using this as his power base he now prepared to take on the might of Western Union. By November 1867 he had worked out detailed plans for the expansion of Pacific and Atlantic to Chicago, Cleveland and St Louis. Soon, the company would be living up to its name. In this enterprise Carnegie relied on David Brooks, his former supervisor at the O'Reilly telegraph office. A contract was negotiated with George H. Thurston, president of the company, giving Carnegie and Brooks $3 in company stock for every dollar they spent on laying wire. With this powerful inducement, it is small wonder that the lines between Philadelphia and Pittsburgh were erected in record time. Carnegie also secured for his old chum Davy McCargo the position as general superintendent. With close friends ensconced in the highest echelons of the company, and with a lucrative contract and a substantial block of shares in his pocket, Carnegie was ready for the fray.

He used his connections with Edgar Thomson, Tom Scott and other railroad executives to expand Pacific and Atlantic's network. By the spring of 1869 the lines stretched from New York to St Louis and New Orleans, and shareholders got a dividend of 37.5 per cent.

Hopes of beating Western Union, however, faded when the latter anticipated every move, and outbid Pacific in obtaining railroad contracts. At the same time Western Union undercut Pacific's rates, with the result that the latter was brought to its knees. No dividends were paid after December 1872. McCargo blamed the decline in Pacific and Atlantic's fortunes on Thurston and the company secretary Edward Allen, and persuaded Carnegie to join with him in a bid to wrest control of the company from them. In the ensuing boardroom battle Thurston retired, but effectively blocked his opponents from appointing the president of their choice, General Thomas J. Wood. Instead, the post went to W.G. Johnston who had the thankless task of winding up the company.

Since the end of 1872, however, Carnegie had been hedging his bets, secretly negotiating with Western Union to exchange six Pacific shares for each Western share. Such was the depreciation in the value of Pacific shares by that time that this arrangement actually represented an immediate profit of $13 per Western share. Carnegie confided in McCargo and Johnston, and these three quietly sold their stock to Western Union. At the same time, they were buying up all the Pacific shares they could lay their hands on, through several confidential brokers – and promptly selling them on to Western at a handsome profit. Inevitably word of this activity leaked out and Pacific shares suddenly rallied. At this point Carnegie stopped buying and began pestering William Orton, boss of Western Union, to take the Pacific stock off his hands as they had agreed. By now Western Union had tumbled Carnegie's little ploy and Orton was understandably reluctant to purchase any more of what was virtually worthless stock. There was no point in buying out an organisation that was heading for bankruptcy anyway. Yet again, Carnegie had to summon up all his resources as a negotiator in order to persuade Orton to honour his end of the bargain.

The fact of the matter was that Western Union had gobbled up so many of its major rivals in recent years that a period of consolidation was required before further expansion. Carnegie would not push Orton too hard in any case, once he had offloaded his own personal shareholding. Besides, having acquired 983 Western shares in exchange for his 5898 Pacific shares, Carnegie had a vested interest in protecting Western Union from the importunings of his friends and fellow Pacific stockholders. The situation was exacerbated by the panic of September 1873, in which the value of all shares plummeted after a period of boom. Western Union's shares likewise fell sharply, and made any further exchange for Pacific shares impractical. The smaller investors lost heavily as a result, but Carnegie, Scott, Thomson and other fat cats had, by that time, got rid of their shares at a handsome profit. In the end, Western Union took over Pacific's contracts, leases and property and undertook in return to pay off the latter's creditors.[16]

Ironically, an indirect result of this episode was that Western Union missed the opportunity to take over another company, with a confusingly similar name. The Atlantic and Pacific Telegraph Company had major franchises with the Union Pacific and Central Pacific railroads and in the long run Orton's failure to grasp this plum when it was there for the plucking in 1873 would cost him over $20,000,000 — twice what it would have cost at the time. By his own speculative activities, therefore, Carnegie had unwittingly helped Atlantic's supremo, Jay Gould, to double his fortune. There is not the slightest evidence to suggest that Carnegie and Gould were acting in concert, but it would not be the last time by any means that Carnegie would render valuable service to the sinister figure later known as the Mephistopheles of the stockmarket.

In this early part of his business career, Carnegie had more than his fair share of luck. As the size of the deals rose astronomically, his audacity became greater and greater, overweening self-confidence being compounded by risk-taking that was as foolhardy as it was dangerous at times. Yet Carnegie's gambles nearly always paid off, and very handsomely at that. One exploit, however, that had serious consequences, had its origins in 1871 when Carnegie learned, through George Pullman, that the Union Pacific had a cashflow problem and urgently needed $600,000 to tide it over. Immediately, Carnegie saw an opportunity for the Pennsylvania Railroad to gain control of the Union Pacific so he hurriedly consulted Edgar Thomson. The two men had come a very long way since Thomson had first encountered Scott's Andy, and the quondam telegraphist now exercised an almost hypnotic control over the older man. Carnegie proposed that if the Pennsylvania were to entrust him with sufficient securities on which $600,000 could be raised, he would guarantee practical control of Union Pacific. The Pennsylvania Railroad could not lose, for it would have Union Pacific stock as security for the loan.

Thomson readily assented, and the deal was struck. As a result, Carnegie and Pullman became directors of Union Pacific, while Tom Scott became president. These three, as trustees, were given custody of $3,000,000 in Union Pacific shares which were placed in a bank vault by Carnegie on the understanding that they would remain there until the $600,000 loan was repaid. When Wall Street got wind of the fact that the Pennsylvania was backing Union Pacific, the latter's stock rose sharply. In some way (which has never been explained) large blocks of the Union Pacific stock were spirited out of that bank vault and sold at a vast profit. The Union Pacific board regarded this as a gross breach of faith and promptly dismissed Carnegie, Pullman and Scott. Pullman reinvested his profits in Union Pacific but neither Carnegie nor Scott followed his example.

This humiliating experience drove a wedge between Carnegie and Scott. The latter was always an honourable man, and his only fault seems to have been that he was too naïve, too trusting, where his boy Andy was concerned. He was embittered by the manner in which he was ejected from the presidency of Union Pacific, but soon turned to a project to build a railway across Texas. On the capitalisation of the Texas Pacific Railroad he naturally turned to Carnegie for help; but while Carnegie was happy to purchase shares in the project he refused to endorse its notes in connection with a loan from Junius Morgan, which would fall due for repayment within sixty days. When Scott upbraided him for his ingratitude, Carnegie coolly retorted: 'No. I merely won't go in to wade where the water is too deep. I made it a rule long ago not to put my name to any paper that I knew I couldn't pay when it came due.' Carnegie justified his course of action on the grounds that it was not the loan itself that bothered him, but the half-dozen other loans that would be required thereafter. 'This marked another step in the total business separation which had come between Mr Scott and myself. It gave more pain than all the financial trials to which I had been subjected up to that time.'[17] Such pains would become chronic, but Carnegie's stout heart would survive them surprisingly well.

Furthermore, Carnegie had the advantage of hindsight when he wrote his *Autobiography*. 'It was not long after this meeting that the disaster came and the country was startled by the failure of those whom it regarded as its strongest men. I fear Mr Scott's premature death can measurably be attributed to the humiliation which he had to bear.' In fact Tom Scott did not die until 21 May 1881, but Carnegie was undoubtedly correct in saying that his death, at the relatively early age of fifty-eight, was hastened by financial troubles. Carnegie, who owed his first break to Scott's generosity, stood by and did nothing to help him.

Much has been made by previous biographers of an affair of the heart, as the chief reason for the rift between Carnegie and Scott. The oft-repeated story goes that Carnegie introduced the wealthy widower Scott to Anne Dike Riddle, a girl on whom the dapper little Scotsman had set his heart. Anne and Tom fell head over heels in love, and Carnegie's 'best girl' soon became the second Mrs Scott. Carnegie, however, was philosophical about this, telling Tom Miller, 'If anybody else in the world can win her, I don't want her!'[18] Carnegie, in fact, gave the happy couple his benison, probably only too relieved at having extricated himself from a relationship that had no place in his plans at that time.

Carnegie's refusal to get entangled with Scott's Texas venture may actually have been underscored by the fact that, at that time, he was coming to the attention of Jay Gould, impressed by Carnegie's ruthless handling of the Union Pacific stock-selling episode. Gould, who had little or no sense of what was moral or ethical, clearly considered that he had found a kindred spirit, and consequently approached Carnegie directly one morning at the Windsor Hotel, New York, with a breathtaking proposition. He would buy the Pennsylvania Railroad and give Carnegie half of the profits if he would manage the railroad for him. Shortly after the failure of the Texas project, Tom Scott had been elected president of the Pennsylvania. Carnegie thanked Gould for his interest, but told him that, although he and Scott had parted company in business matters he 'would never raise [his] hand against him'.[19]

By September 1873 Tom Scott was in a desperate situation. He turned to Edgar Thomson, urging him to use his influence with Carnegie to secure his co-operation in the Texas and Pacific Railroad. Thomson obligingly wrote to Carnegie: 'You, of all others, should lend your helping hand when you run no risk – if you cannot go further.'

And he added a postscript that he himself would be glad to extricate himself from the Texas matter 'with a loss of three times your subscription'.[20] Again Carnegie ignored the plea, prudently as it turned out, for Thomson himself was by now in financial difficulties, as well as being on the receiving end of a costly lawsuit that dragged on long after his death in 1875. Rumours that Thomson and Scott were heading for disaster did nothing to reassure the banking sector, already jittery as the market panic deepened. Carnegie himself was peremptorily summoned back from New York to Pittsburgh to face a rigorous cross-examination by the directors of the Exchange Bank from whom he had borrowed heavily for the erection of his new steel plant at Braddock.

Carnegie faced the music resolutely and forthrightly. He answered every question quietly and self-righteously. Questioned closely about his involvement with Scott and Thomson, he could say with hand on heart that the sum total of his commitment to the Texas and Pacific Railroad was $250,000 cash invested in shares. He stood to lose that, but it was his alone to lose. Besides, he considered that the investment would work out well in the long run, for Texas was a vast and potentially profitable area for future railroad development. He ended up by delivering the astounded bankers a homily on American business and his abiding faith in it to weather the current panic. He emphatically denied that he had endorsed any of Scott's loans. At the end of the cross-examination Carnegie rose from his chair, in the words of one biographer,

> A new man – new, at least, in the estimation of his own community. The steelmaker whom the bankers had regarded as the weakest and most likely to collapse with hard times suddenly appeared as practically the only one who could successfully ride the storm.[21]

One might have added that Carnegie had learned a valuable lesson. Hitherto he had concentrated on speculation, playing the stock-market, manipulating shares and selling short on the exchange. Henceforward he would spurn such doubtful and devious practices. Instead he would concentrate on heavy engineering and the manufacture of steel.

SIX

Man of Steel

1873–81

See these hands, ne'er stretch'd to save,
Hands that took, but never gave.
Keeper of Mammon's iron chest
Robert Burns, 'Ode, Sacred to the Memory of Mrs Oswald of Auchencruive'

ANDREW CARNEGIE'S CONVERSION FROM SPECULATION TO MANU-
facturing, from iron to steel, was a gradual process, but his interest
in steel came long before his visit to the Bessemer works in 1872. In
fact, almost two years previously, he had been the instigator of the
decision, foisted on Kloman and Phipps, to erect a blast furnace so
that they could produce their own pig-iron, essential to the
manufacture of steel. In the spring of 1871 a site was obtained at
Fifty-first Street in Pittsburgh and construction of the blast furnace
began. By the summer of 1872 it was ready for operation. The plant
was named the Lucy Furnace, after Carnegie's sister-in-law, and
within a year it was producing almost 600 tons of pig-iron a week. By
October 1874 it was producing over 100 tons a day, seven days a week,
an output without precedent anywhere in the world at that time. The
drive to produce more and more pig-iron was powered by intense
rivalry with a neighbouring plant, known as the Isabella Furnace,
which lagged not far behind.

The Lucy Furnace was not without its teething troubles, but
Carnegie got rid of the original manager and installed Henry M.
Curry, a young shipping clerk who had come to his attention. His confidence was fully justified as, under Curry's able and efficient management, the production of pig-iron went ahead by leaps and bounds.

On his return from England in 1872, however, Carnegie determined to enlarge his output of Bessemer steel, and to this end he acquired an entirely new site on the outskirts of Pittsburgh. In this venture he had the enthusiastic backing of William Coleman, Tom Carnegie's father-in-law, who had in the previous year toured all the Bessemer plants in the United States. He, too, was convinced that iron was a thing of the past, and that henceforth steel would dominate heavy engineering. It was Coleman who secured the option on 100 acres of farm land, twelve miles beyond the city boundary, on the banks of the Monongahela at a place known as Braddock's Field, where General Edward Braddock's expeditionary force had been cut to pieces by the French and their Indian allies a century before.

Carnegie's partners in the Union Mills did not share his enthusiasm for steel, however. Kloman and Phipps – even Carnegie's brother Tom – were firmly wedded to iron and viewed the latest proposals unfavourably. Carnegie swept their objections aside, telling them bluntly that they were free to join him in this venture if they wished, but that he would go ahead anyway, with or without their backing. To this end he turned to other men and soon secured the support he required. David Stewart, Tom Scott's nephew and now president of the Columbia Oil Company, was one. David McCandless, a fellow-Scot whose friendship dated right back to the time when the Carnegies had settled in Slabtown, was another. McCandless had founded the Swedenborgian Church in Allegheny along with William Carnegie and Annie Aitken, and had since prospered as a businessman in a moderate way. Though not a wealthy man by Carnegie's standards, McCandless had one invaluable asset: he was widely respected and trusted by Pittsburgh's banking community, and his support for the venture gave Carnegie the vital financial backing he needed. As a result, Carnegie named the new enterprise McCandless & Company, formally incorporated on 5 November 1872 with capital of $700,000. Carnegie chipped in with $250,000, much of this cash coming from the recent commission on bond sales alone. With more than a third of the total capital, Carnegie had the controlling interest. William Coleman, who was the next largest investor, put in $100,000. Stewart and McCandless contributed $50,000 each, as did the banker John Scott and William P. Shinn, vice-president of the Allegheny Valley Railroad. In the end,

Kloman, Phipps and Tom Carnegie also came in with $50,000 apiece, though with considerable reservations.

Carnegie sold on a few of his shares to Tom Scott and Edgar Thomson, partly to offset the distance that seemed to be growing between Carnegie and his old business associates, and partly from a reluctance to embark on any venture without at least their nominal support. Their connection with the project was brief, however, owing to Scott's problems with the Texas Pacific Railroad. When Carnegie refused to endorse Scott's notes, both Scott and Thomson sold their shares in the steel business back to Carnegie. Writing to Shinn, who had been appointed secretary-treasurer of the company, Carnegie commented waspishly: 'Mr Scott was alarmed at the danger of becoming a partner & I relieved him of that. I only hope he will never be involved in anything worse.'[1] Although Thomson had also sold his shares back to Carnegie, he still had a useful service to perform. Carnegie needed a name for the new steelworks and wrote a very flattering letter to Thomson on 30 October 1872 proposing to name the works after him as a tribute to his 'exalted character & career'. Thomson replied guardedly, agreeing to his name being used so long as it was clearly understood that he should bear no responsibility for the management of the business. He stated that he had no funds available for investment in the company, though he tentatively offered some bridge bonds in exchange. Carnegie, who was anxious to retain Thomson's goodwill, as well as his influence with the Pennsylvania Railroad, was content with his old employer's name; it was the business with the rabbits and Pullman all over again. In due course the Edgar Thomson Steel Works came into being, though it was usually known simply by its initials, as ET.

By the time ET was established, American steelmaking had made rapid strides. Already several giants were emerging, and the Cambria, Lackawanna and Troy steel plants had a formidable head start. Fortunately, Alexander Holley, who had built the Cambria steel plant, had approached Coleman, offering his services, and he was snapped up with alacrity. Small wonder, for Holley was the golden boy of the steel industry. Still in his thirties, he was as handsome as a Greek god, with the brain of an engineer, the heart of a hero and the soul of a poet. Far and away the most charismatic figure in American heavy industry in his heyday, he had been employed as consultant engineer by most of the great steel companies, singlehandedly transforming what was virtually a cottage industry into a colossus that dominated world output. It was Holley who made the Bessemer process both practical and economical; but he was much, much more than an engineer. He was a genius, a visionary, a master strategist who led and inspired and organised and instilled efficiency, brought order out of chaos and streamlined production.

Holley recruited Captain William Jones who had been chief assistant to the general superintendent at the Cambria Iron Company, but had recently been passed over for promotion. Four years Carnegie's junior, Jones had been born in Catasauqua, Pennsylvania, one of the meanest, most squalid, little iron towns in the country. The ironmaster there was David Thomas and most of the workforce were Welshmen. Bill Jones' father was a patternmaker by day, but by night and at weekends he was the spiritual and cultural leader of the Welsh community, as noted for his fiery preaching as for his library – he possessed more than a hundred books. Bill was articulate and well read, and could quote Shakespeare as readily as Carnegie himself. At ten he was a handyman in the Crane ironworks. At eighteen he had run away from home, wandered the length and breadth of the States, met a girl in Chattanooga and married her, and settled at Johnstown as a mechanic on two dollars a day. When the Civil War erupted he enlisted as a private but bravery in action won him a commission and he ended the war as a captain, a title he wore proudly for the rest of his life. Returning to Johnstown, he became a foreman at the Cambria works under Daniel J. Morrell and rose swiftly through the ranks, as he had done during the recent conflict. When George Fritz, the Cambria works manager, died, all the men at the works hoped that Bill Jones would be selected to fill his place. Instead, Morrell gave the appointment to another Catasauqua Welshman, Daniel N. Jones, and Captain Bill decided that it was time to move on.

On Holley's recommendation, Bill Jones was appointed by Carnegie as general superintendent at ET. Over the ensuing years Jones got his revenge on Dan Morrell; as Morrell cut the wages of his workforce, Jones lured them away to ET, picking and choosing the best men for his new team. At one stroke, therefore, Carnegie obtained skilled men who had served their long and costly apprenticeship in steelmaking at Cambria's expense. Eventually, over two hundred of Cambria's key workers, including all of the departmental superintendents, followed Jones to the new plant. Among others, Jones recruited Captain Thomas H. Lapsley, superintendent of the rail mill; John Rinard, superintendent of the converting works; Thomas James, superintendent of machinery; Thomas Addenbrook, head furnace-builder; F.L. Bridges, superintendent of transportation; and C.C. Teeter, the chief clerk. It is hardly to be wondered at, that relations between Cambria and ET were strained, especially as the former company began to go downhill as ET's fortunes prospered. Morrell would eventually comment on his misfortune that he had promoted the wrong Jones.

Jones was not only a mechanical wizard but also a shrewd judge of men, though not without his prejudices. In a memorandum concerning the type and calibre of men he sought, he wrote:

> We must steer clear, as far as we can, of Englishmen, who are great sticklers for high wages, small production and strikes. My experience has shown that Germans, Irish, Swedes and what I denominate Buckwheats – young American country boys – judiciously mixed, make the most effective and tractable force you can find. Scotchmen do very well, are honest and faithful. Welsh can be used in limited numbers. But mark me, Englishmen have been the worst class of men I have had anything to do with.[2]

Holley and Jones were arguably the most important, most valuable men who ever served Carnegie (with the possible exception of Henry Clay Frick, whom he would meet in 1882). Yet, incredibly, Carnegie's *Autobiography* contains no mention of Holley at all, and dismisses Jones in half a dozen fleeting references which do not even give his first name. This cavalier treatment of Bill Jones may have derived from the fact that the Pennsylvania Welshman actually turned down the offer of a partnership which would have made him a millionaire. Carnegie was fond of dangling this tempting prospect in front of his more promising executives, and he was taken aback when Jones, the preacher's son, said that he did not want to have his thoughts running on business. Carnegie was not accustomed to having his Faustian overtures rejected, and was baffled whenever someone showed such altruism and independence of mind.[3]

By September 1873 the construction of the giant converters at the ET plant was under way. With Holley, Jones and other hand-picked steelmen in place, Carnegie could afford to take things easy. On 18 September he was relaxing on the veranda of Braemar Cottage, the Gothic extravaganza he had bought for his mother at Cresson Springs in the Allegheny Mountains, when he received word that the great New York banking house of Jay Cooke and Company had failed. Jay Cooke was the doyen of American bankers, the man who had raised the money with which the North had fought the Civil War. His bank funded the Northern Pacific Railroad and many other major projects; hundreds of thousands of investors, large and small, had put their faith as well as their money in the bank. Carnegie bade Margaret a hasty farewell and caught the first train back to Pittsburgh. To his amazement, he found that his partners and other business associates were unconcerned by the bank failure, shrugging it off as nothing more than a 'Wall Street flurry'. They had no relations with Cooke or his railroad projects and assumed that the crash would pass them by. But the Cooke failure had a disturbing domino effect, and as banks and financial institutions which had done business with Cooke were sucked into the vortex, panic spread like wildfire, shares plummeted and the New York Exchange closed. This was swiftly followed by a run on the savings banks, then the railroads and bridge companies aborted construction projects and defaulted on bills as they fell due. Orders for coal and iron dried up, and by the end of the year the country was in the grip of the worst depression in its history up to that time.

This was a terrible time for everyone, and Carnegie and his partners were badly affected by the panic. The construction of the steel plant was halted and men at the Union Mills and other Carnegie concerns were laid off or put on short-time working. There were those, especially among the older, more conservative businessmen in Pennsylvania, who thought smugly that cocky young Carnegie had had his comeuppance at last. Carnegie himself would later recall the day he was walking down the street and overheard old John Moorhead, the richest man in Pittsburgh, pointing him out to a friend and saying sourly: 'There goes a foolish young man. He has bitten off more than he can chew. He wasn't satisfied to do a small, safe business like the rest of us. He had to launch out. Mark my words – he'll come to grief yet.' A number of prominent businessmen had invested in ET but were unable to meet their payments when instalments fell due. 'I was compelled to take over their interests, repaying the full cost to all,' wrote Carnegie. 'In that way control of the company came into my hands.'[4]

Luckily for Carnegie his partners backed him to the hilt and kept the nascent steel business going by dipping heavily into their own coffers. In particular William Coleman proved a staunch supporter, contributing heavily not only to the steel business but also to Carnegie's other enterprises. 'How the grand old man comes before me as I write!' Carnegie would exclaim emotionally in his *Autobiography* more than four decades later. A few pages later, however, he mentioned casually how Coleman 'became dissatisfied with the management of a railway official who had come to us with a great and deserved reputation for method and ability. I had, therefore, to take over Mr Coleman's interest.'[5] In this manner Carnegie glossed over the bitter quarrel in 1876 which led to him forcing the 'grand old man' out of the highly lucrative steel business just as it turned the corner. The former 'railway official' was William P. Shinn who, prior to joining the company, had been the auditor, and later vice-president, of the Allegheny Railroad. Considering how close Carnegie and Shinn became, for a time at least, it is remarkable that Shinn is nowhere mentioned by name in Carnegie's rather selective *Autobiography*. Coleman and Shinn soon crossed swords over the sweeping innovations which the latter effected in book-keeping. The dispute was petty and trifling, and might readily have been resolved; Carnegie, however, not only took Shinn's side, but did so in such a way that Coleman felt personally humiliated. Moreover, he hinted to a third party (knowing that it would get back to Coleman) that the old man was no longer pulling his weight in the organisation. Coleman was very fond of his son-in-law Tom, but increasingly had little time for Tom's arrogant, overbearing elder brother.

During the cyclone of 1873 Carnegie used every trick in the book to keep his creditors at bay. At the same time, no one was more assiduous at chasing up debtors. The Fort Wayne Railroad was heavily indebted to the Union Mills, so Carnegie broached the matter with William Thaw, the executive vice-president. Thaw bluntly told him that the company was paying no bills that were not protestable.

'All right,' replied Carnegie. 'Your freight bills are in that category and we shall follow your excellent example. Now I am going to order that we do not pay you one dollar for freight.'

The two men glowered at each other. 'If you do that,' said Thaw, bringing a fist down on his desk, 'we will stop your freight.'

Carnegie merely smiled. 'We'll risk that,' was his parting shot as he walked out of Thaw's office. His gamble proved correct, and for some time afterwards he got away without paying the freight bills. It was simply impossible for the manufacturers of Pittsburgh to pay their accruing liabilities when their customers stopped payment. Thaw had witnessed the dramatic rise of Carnegie from his telegraph days, and even in the depths of the depression he was confident that the energetic little Scotsman would survive.

One of the victims of the 1873 crash was Andrew Kloman. He had invested heavily in two independent smelting and mining businesses, the Escanaba Furnace Company and the Cascade Iron Company. Both enterprises crashed spectacularly, dragging down the stockholders who were personally liable. In the aftermath of the panic, limited liability companies were authorised by the Pennsylvania legislature, but that safeguard came too late to save Andrew Kloman. In desperation and teetering on the verge of bankruptcy, he went to Carnegie for help. The latter was furious. He had known nothing of Kloman's extracurricular activities, and was immediately concerned lest Kloman's collapse would drag down his partners. As a result, he compelled Kloman to assign his various interests to him and to secure a judicial discharge, promising in writing that he would restore Kloman to full partnership when business picked up again. Carnegie took charge of Kloman's affairs and settled the claims of creditors at fifty cents in the dollar. Once more Carnegie had not only kept outside creditors from getting a toehold in his empire but also, at the same time, consolidated his control. Kloman was no longer a partner, but his expertise was too valuable to lose; he now found himself as an employee of the company he had created, on a salary of $5000 per annum.

Two years later, when Kloman was discharged from bankruptcy and once more legally entitled to hold property, he asked Carnegie to honour his written promise and restore his partnership. Carnegie bluntly refused, pointing out that his letter did not constitute a binding contract. Kloman could stay with the company, so long as he devoted all of his time to manufacturing and ceased outside ventures. As a sop, Carnegie offered him an interest of $100,000, to be paid out of profits. The stiff-necked Kloman, suspicious and intractable as ever, refused and stalked off in a fury. Thus he parted company with Carnegie who paid him off with $40,000, a relatively paltry sum. With this cash, Kloman took a lease of the Superior, a rival steel mill in Allegheny. In due course he used this as a pawn with which to bargain his way into the Pittsburgh Bessemer Steel Company which was building a new steelworks at Homestead, but he died before this plant became operational. He left to his sons nothing but a small interest in this company, and an unfulfilled desire for revenge against the wily Scot who had brought him down.

Undoubtedly, Carnegie treated Kloman unfairly. In his *Autobiography*, however, Carnegie put his own interpretation on the episode, saying of Kloman that 'notwithstanding the most urgent appeals on my part, and that of my colleagues, he persisted in the determination to start a new rival concern with his sons as business managers. The result was failure and premature death.'[6] There then ensued one of the most hypocritical passages in the entire volume:

> How foolish we are not to recognize what we are best fitted for and can perform, not only with ease but with pleasure, as masters of the craft . . . I never regretted parting with any man so much as Mr Kloman. His was a good heart, a great mechanical brain, and had he been left to himself I believe he would have been glad to remain with us. Offers of capital from others – offers which failed when needed – turned his head, and the great mechanic soon proved the poor man of affairs.

The man whose genius had created the company at the core of the Carnegie empire deserved better treatment than was meted out to him. Kloman was the first partner to be ejected but by no means the last. Never again would any partner jeopardise Carnegie's business by indulging in private speculation; he would take good care to ensure that such outside ventures were strictly forbidden.

Ironically, the man who replaced Kloman was William Borntraeger, a distant cousin whom Kloman had encouraged to emigrate from Prussia. Kloman had taken him into the business and taught him everything he knew. Borntraeger proved an apt and willing pupil. Moreover, he had qualities lacking in Kloman, being companionable and, above all, tractable. These qualities endeared him to Carnegie who appointed him manager of the Union Mills. He would end his career as a junior partner on $50,000 a year. Borntraeger had not a word of English when he came to America, and to the end of his days his command of the language was idiosyncratic. Carnegie, a born mimic, often regaled his associates with Borntraeger's strange Teutonic utterances. Once, when he was delivering a pep talk to his colleagues, William concluded: 'What we haf to do, shentlemens, is to get brices up and costs down and efery man stand on his own bottom.'[7]

While Holley and Jones were making good progress with the construction of the plant, the indefatigable Carnegie himself was in New York, going the rounds of the railroads and construction companies trying to drum up business. The country was still recovering from the 1873 panic and the railroads were spending as little as possible. Steel rails were selling for $120 a ton, but manufacturers would only take gold; paper was out of fashion. Carnegie and his mother were now ensconced in the new Windsor Hotel, then regarded as the place for the smart set. The Carnegies threw lavish dinner parties and were, in turn, entertained in the homes of the great and good of New York. The dumpy old lady (now in her late sixties) proved to be a surprisingly good asset. Plain in speech as well as looks, she was something of a novelty to New York's high society but people warmed to her, even when they found her son's vanity and arrogance off-putting. It was Margaret, in fact, who secured entrée to the most sophisticated salons, and gradually people thawed out as they found her cocky son to be quite amusing, actually. Carnegie loved an audience and honed his anecdotal techniques. Hostesses first tolerated him, then courted him. Many of the prominent citizens whom Carnegie encountered casually at dinner parties would rather disconcertingly find him in their offices the following morning, pressing his claim on their goodwill and support in furthering his sales drive. This brash technique, however, paid handsome dividends, and William Shinn was inundated with lucrative orders, even before the first ounce of steel was produced.

Late in August 1875 the Edgar Thomson Steel Works were completed. Carnegie and his associates congregated there on 1 September, flags flying and bands playing, as Bill Jones rolled out the first rail.

From the outset ET was a howling success. In the first four months of operations alone, Captain Jones and his dedicated workforce produced double the amount of steel ever manufactured with similar plant previously. Furthermore, William Shinn operated an accountancy system that kept a very tight control of costs and profits; Shinn's nit-picking approach to accounts might have been a source of friction with the easy-going Coleman, but week on week the figures were itemised down to the last cent. At the end of December 1875 Shinn could show Carnegie a net profit of $41,970 and 96 cents. This was immensely satisfying, but Carnegie demanded 'Mair! Mair!' and Bill Jones responded to the challenge. Soon he and his splendid team were turning out more steel rails in a day than most plants produced in a week. The Captain led his men from the front, constantly on the move, never out of the shops, encouraging here, cursing there. In his office he hung a huge broom, symbolising his attitude to ancient methods and obsolete working practices. He was a dictator, but he tempered hard-driving with benevolence. He knew every man on the floor by his first name, and knew every detail of his domestic situation. When one employee died suddenly, leaving a wife and five young children, Jones sent a workmate to the widow with a 'piece of paper', a casual reference to a high-denomination dollar bill which came out of his own pocket. Jones cared little for money, continuing to live relatively modestly; but cash was liberally dispensed to those that needed a sub.

By the end of August 1876 and the completion of the first full year in operation, ET earned a net profit of $181,007.18. Carnegie's share of the proceeds was substantial, but he was not satisfied. In April that year, when Shinn delivered the first half-yearly statement, Carnegie's reaction was to write back: 'I want to buy Mr Coleman out & hope to do so.' At this time Kloman had not yet been discharged from bankruptcy, and was therefore effectively out of the partnership for the time being. Now Carnegie showed his hand to Shinn:

> Kloman will have to give up his interest, these divided between
> Tom, Harry [Phipps], you and I would make the concern a closed
> corporation – Mr [John] Scott's loan is no doubt in some banker's
> hands and may also be dealt with after a little, then we are right and
> have only to watch the Bond conversions which will not be great as
> our foreign friends will want to stick to the sure thing I think.[8]

At first Carnegie offered Coleman $100,000 for his interest in the business. Coleman, who had supported Carnegie so loyally when the panic was at its worst, was still recovering from the severe drain on his financial resources and Carnegie's offer must have been tempting. But Coleman realised that ET was the best venture he had got into, and was not minded to lose such lucrative long-term prospects. He declined the offer. Then came the quarrel with Shinn over his accountancy methods, a quarrel that seems to have been deliberately engineered by Carnegie (much as he had caused Phipps and Miller to fall out some years earlier). Coleman, boxed into a corner, finally gave way. Using his son-in-law Tom Carnegie as intermediary, Coleman finally accepted the offer on 1 May 1876 and departed the scene, saddened and disillusioned. While Carnegie's slice of the pie got larger, the pie itself expanded out of all proportion; but still the greedy little man was not satisfied. One year later he wrote to Shinn again:

> There are possible Combinations in the future. It isn't likely
> McCandless, Scott & Stewart will remain with us – I scarcely think
> they can. I know Harry & Tom have agreed with me that you out of
> the entire lot would be wanted as a future partner & I think we will
> one day make it a partnership Lucy F Co., U Mills, ET &c, &c, &
> go it on that basis the largest Concern in the country.[9]

David McCandless, first chairman of the steel company, earned Carnegie's displeasure as a result of an unfortunate flutter on the stockmarket. Angered at this 'miserable conduct', Carnegie was scheming to oust the old man when McCandless died in the winter of 1878. Even as Carnegie wrote to his associates on their sad loss –

> It does seem hard to bear, but we must bite the lip & go forward I
> suppose assuming indifference, but I am sure none of us can ever

efface from our memories the image of our dear, generous, gentle &
unselfish friend . . . Let us try to be as kind and devoted to each
other as he was to us. He was a model for all of us to follow. One
thing more we can do – attend to his affairs & get them right that
Mrs McCandless & Helen may be provided for – I know you will all
be looking after this & you know how anxious I shall be to co-
operate with you.

– he was scheming to acquire the McCandless stock from the widow
and daughter who got face value, no more. His son, Gardiner
McCandless, however, refused to sell a small holding of bonds which
had been converted into ET stock and continued for a brief time
with the company. With the elder McCandless out of the way,
Carnegie seized the opportunity to consolidate his iron and steel
businesses according to the plan outlined to Shinn. The immediate
reason for this move was the long-standing bickering between the
Lucy Furnace Company and ET over the price of pig-iron charged
by the one to the other. The argument was personalised, with Tom
Carnegie and William Shinn at loggerheads. It has been argued that
Carnegie obeyed the Roman dictum of 'divide and rule' and
deliberately set partners and senior executives against each other, in
order to control them more effectively; but in truth he disliked
squabbles of this kind, especially where money was concerned. Some
rationalisation of the various iron and steel concerns was inevitable.
When Kloman left the Union Iron Mills, the company changed its
name from Carnegie, Kloman and Company to Carnegie Brothers,
with a capitalisation of $507,629, of which Carnegie held just under
50 per cent. When Coleman sold out to Carnegie in 1876, the firm
of Carnegie, McCandless & Company was dissolved and a new firm,
known as the Edgar Thomson Steel Company, was created with a
capitalisation of a million dollars. Two years later the share capital
was increased to $1,250,000, Carnegie taking the entire $250,000
increase for himself. The increase in capitalisation was wholly
justified by the net profits which that year passed the $300,000
mark, almost a quarter of the capitalisation of the company; but at
one stroke Carnegie gained unassailable control of the company, and
was now in a position to impose the terms for consolidation and
reorganisation.

By October 1878 this amalgamation was completed and Carnegie was well satisfied with the way things had worked out. He could now afford to take time out for a trip round the world, something he had long cherished. On the eve of his departure, he wrote expansively to Shinn:

> I feel so perfectly satisfied to leave E.T. in your hands. This absolute confidence is worth everything & I daily congratulate myself that I have met you & got such a man bound in the closest manner to our party. Your fortune is secured that I do know.[10]

Carnegie was rarely as fulsome as this, but Shinn was invariably the bearer of good news about percentages and profits. Even in 1878, when prices were falling, Shinn's cost-cutting and cheese-paring tactics ensured that the healthy profit margin of 20 per cent was maintained.

On his global travels Carnegie took along his docile companion John Vandevort. They were in Sorrento when Carnegie received Shinn's report that the profits for November 1878 alone had topped $52,000. That night the two travellers celebrated in fine style. Acknowledging the report, Carnegie wrote back to the company treasurer: 'Tell Capt. Jones there was a proud little stout man who gave a wild hurrah when he saw ET ahead.' These and other close confidences, together with the fulsome praise of the valedictory letter, planted in Shinn's mind the idea that he could do a lot better for himself in the company, that his true worth had not yet been fully recognised. Carnegie was in India when McCandless died, leaving the chairmanship vacant. Now Shinn saw his opportunity and wrote to Carnegie applying for the position. Carnegie was taken by surprise and replied immediately: 'It never occurred to me that you would prefer to be called chairman rather than genl. manager, on the contrary the latter was your own choice.' Then he went on, soothingly: 'Let the matter rest until my return & I am sure our happy family will remain one. Tom cares as little for names as I do, I think, and that is simply nothing – it's the prosperity of the work we seek. *That's our pride.*'[11] Now Carnegie began to entertain second thoughts about Shinn. Six months previously Shinn had asked for, and got, a raise in salary to $8000 per annum. Now Carnegie discovered that Shinn had not only granted himself another raise (of $2000 this time) but he had hired an assistant at a generous salary. Shinn was getting above himself. Carnegie mulled over the problem before writing from Rome to the banker and shareholder John Scott:

> I think Mr Shinn might have spared me his long letter of complaint. It has of course cut my holiday short & made me uneasy. Surely he couldn't expect me to act on such a matter until my return. What use then in annoying me. I would not have done it to him had he been away. You have increased his salary to 10,000$. I consented to 8000$ reluctantly explaining to him I had doubled his interest from my own stock expressly to compensate him . . . His action after what I have done for him seems to me ungracious. Then he has gone into a damned gambling operation contracting for 45,000 tons low-priced rails without first covering with Pig-Iron. I can't trust such speculative people as you & he appear to me to be. Gas Mills, Old Blast Furnaces &c. Why can't you try to reform & make yourselves respectable manufacturers in which hope your friend Andrew will offer up today in St Peter's a solemn prayer.[12]

When he returned to America in the middle of 1879 Carnegie was confronted with even more disquieting signs of Shinn's ambition. The demand for an exalted title was bad enough, though that had been neatly scotched by Harry Phipps and the other partners who had appointed Tom Carnegie temporary chairman. On returning to Pittsburgh, Carnegie's first act was to confirm his brother's appointment. But Carnegie soon discovered that his ambitious general manager had been engaging in a private venture. Using information that had come to him from the company's metallurgist concerning a low-phosphor limestone in the Pittsburgh area, Shinn had kept this to himself and clandestinely formed a separate firm, the Peerless Lime Company, which bought up a substantial portion of the limestone beds. Shinn had then sold the lime to ET at a thumping profit to himself. Shinn was actually suspected of planning a similar deal over iron ore.

These disagreeable matters were laid before Carnegie by his partners. It is obvious that they did not relish Shinn becoming their chairman, but the latter had provided them with ample ammunition to block his elevation. Carnegie backed his partners and had a showdown with the unrepentant general manager. Shinn dug in his heels; if he did not become chairman he would resign. He alone knew the intricacies of the company's accounts and his position was impregnable. Carnegie coolly faced him down and told him that if he wished to make an issue of the chairmanship then the board would have to accept his resignation. When Shinn tried to effect a compromise, Carnegie was adamant. If Shinn could not be content with his role as general manager, then he must go, adding, 'If you go, go. Sell out & try another party. We want no drones in E.T. if we can help it.'[13] In fairness to Carnegie it should be pointed out that he did not seek this quarrel, but dealing on the side was a cardinal sin which he would never forgive – in other people, of course; this golden rule did not apply to himself. Shinn, of course, made the mistake of thinking himself to be indispensable. Moreover, at the time Carnegie was advising Shinn to try another party, the latter was already negotiating with the Vulcan Iron Company to become its general manager at a salary of $10,000, plus an interest in the company of $120,000 to be paid out of future dividends. Vulcan even offered Shinn a hefty bonus if he could bring the legendary Captain Jones with him as plant superintendent.

When Carnegie learned that, far from being on vacation in the St Lawrence River valley as he had stated, Shinn had actually been down in St Louis talking to the Vulcan partners, his anger knew no bounds. When word of the bonus to lure Bill Jones away from ET also leaked out, Carnegie exploded with wrath. Many years later, when he reflected that he had known of only one rotten apple in his thirty years in business, it was Shinn he had in mind. When the general manager resigned, Carnegie offered him the book value of his stock. This led to a bitter and increasingly abusive wrangle which eventually, in 1880, ended in the courts. When it came to litigation Shinn proved more than a match for Carnegie, obtaining a court order for the production of ET's books. Shinn knew only too well that the company accounts would reveal the vast profits made in recent years, especially 1880 when steel production at ET outstripped all its competitors. Carnegie's lawyers begged a brief adjournment to consider the order, and thirty minutes later announced that they had arranged to settle the matter out of court.

Above: *two portraits of Louise Whitfield Carnegie, whom Andrew married on 22 April 1887;* below: *the Carnegies with their daughter Margaret, on her twenty-first birthday*

Skibo Castle in Sutherland in the north of Scotland was Andrew Carnegie's sanctuary from the world of business. He and his family (left) returned there year after year

Tom Scott (above) *and Henry Clay Frick were major figures in Carnegie's success. The former set him on the road to riches with his first share deal, while the latter helped consolidate his millions in the steel industry*

Friends, enemies, allies and rivals: Carnegie would never let old friendships come before a good business deal. Top row: *Harry Phipps, Tom Miller, J. Edgar Thomson and Charlie Schwab;* bottom row: *Tom Carnegie, David McCargo, Junius Pierpont Morgan and John Pierpont Morgan*

Andrew Carnegie, tycoon and philanthropist

Shinn not only got the book value of his stock, but $200,000 on top. It is small wonder that William Shinn, the only man to get the better of Andrew Carnegie, should have incurred the little man's especial venom.

While the quarrel with the combative Shinn was dragging on, Carnegie turned for solace to a pet project. During his lengthy world tour in 1878–79 he had soaked up information, data and knowledge like a sponge. His hyperactive mind eagerly sought eternal truths. In China he read Confucius, in India he studied Buddha and the Hindu sacred texts. Mingling with the Parsees in Bombay, he had studied the writings of Zoroaster. In the end he concluded that there was good and bad in all religions; henceforward he would be tolerant of all faiths while accepting no formal religious code of his own. During the trip he made copious notes which formed the core of his first attempt at full-scale authorship. In his second book, *Round the World* (1884), he expounded his philosophy of evolutionary progress. Interestingly, this wordy tome was dedicated to 'my brother Tom and trusty associates, who toiled at home that I might spend abroad'. The text itself was a curious mixture of pawky humour, simplistic platitudes and, above all, outspoken opinions. Far from broadening the mind, travel had only served to confirm Carnegie's prejudices on a wide range of subjects. Here and there, however, one encounters lyrical passages, such as Carnegie's impressions of the Taj Mahal:

> Till the day I die, amid mountain streams or moonlight strolls in the forest, wherever and whenever the mood comes, when all that is most sacred, most elevating, and most pure recur to shed their radiance upon the tranquil mind, there will be found among my treasures the memory of that lovely charm – the Taj . . . I wandered around many hours, gazing at every turn, deliciously, not joyously happy; there was no disposition to croon over a melody, nor any bracing quality in my thoughts – not a trace of the heroic – but I was filled with happiness which seemed to fall upon me gently as the snowflakes fall, as the zephyr comes when laden with sweet odors.[14]

In one respect Shinn failed; he was unable to persuade Bill Jones to leave ET and join him at Vulcan. Perhaps Carnegie had hitherto tended to take his Welsh steelmaker for granted. Now Jones, sensing his opportunity, wrote fully and frankly to Carnegie, affirming his loyalty to the company, and extolling the merits of Tom Carnegie – 'a far more sagacious business man than the late Gen. Man. It is a pleasure to be associated with him' – but, at the same time, hinting that, on his present salary he could never expect 'to accumulate a competency' for himself or his family.[15] Carnegie took the hint and replied immediately: 'I like yours of the 5th much, – always be frank with us . . . Tom & I appreciate you I believe more than you do yourself. All you have to do is say what you want & *don't put it low either* . . . Tell me confidentially what would not only satisfy you – but *gratify* you as well.'[16]

Carnegie would have made Jones a partner but the Captain expressed a preference for 'a hell of a big salary'. When Carnegie asked him to name his figure, Jones pointed out that the general manager at Bethlehem Steel got $20,000 a year and added, 'I am egotistical enough to say that I can walk right around him on all points connected with a work of this kind.' Then he backed down and said that he would be satisfied with less than $15,000. For once in his life, however, Carnegie broke his golden rule regarding salaries for top executives; Jones was worth as much as the President of the United States and henceforward he must get the same salary – $25,000. The Captain's response was immediate and characteristic: 'We will lather the very devil out of Cambria in 1881. Give us the material is all we ask. You let little Tom attend to this and then look out for 1881. Maybe you would like to bet on 1881. If so, name your bet.'[17] Carnegie lost the bet but won the race; in the first four months of 1881 Cambria produced 34,443 tons of rails, while ET produced 42,071 tons.

This would be Carnegie's *annus mirabilis* in more ways than one. With the Shinn dispute resolved, the way was now clear to complete that process of consolidation begun after the 1873 panic. On 1 April 1881 the firm of Carnegie Brothers & Company Limited was formally instituted. The shareholders included the two Carnegie brothers, Henry Phipps, David Stewart, John Scott and Gardiner McCandless. The company was capitalised at $5,000,000. Carnegie's long-term travelling companion John Vandevort was rewarded with an interest of $50,000. McCandless held $105,191 of stock, while Stewart and Scott each had $175,318. Phipps and Tom Carnegie held $878,096 apiece; but the lion's share – $2,737,977 – went to Andrew

Carnegie. Each of the partners then contributed a slice to provide an interest for Carnegie's cousin George 'Dod' Lauder who, having taken a degree in metallurgy, had now been persuaded to cross the Atlantic and join the firm. The new enterprise embraced not only the Union Mills, Lucy Furnace Company and Edgar Thomson Steel Works but also sundry coalmines, the Unity coke ovens and a four-fifths interest in the Lorimer Coke Works. Tom Carnegie was appointed chairman; brother Andrew had no official title, but with 55 per cent of the stock in his pocket a title was meaningless to him anyway. At the close of the first year's business Carnegie Brothers cleared a profit of $2,000,000, of which almost half went to Andrew Carnegie himself. With such a vast income from steel, the one commodity for which there was a seemingly insatiable demand, Carnegie was now on the road to riches of such a magnitude that even he could never have imagined.

As soon as the company had been reorganised, Carnegie bethought himself of another holiday. Never was a vacation so well earned, but this was to be the trip of a lifetime. Remembering his oft-repeated promise to his mother when times were hard during his boyhood, he now sprang a surprise on her. One evening at the Windsor Hotel he interrupted the old lady's game of cribbage with the news. With a specially selected party of close friends, they would embark on the Cunard liner *Bothnia* on 1 June. On arrival in England they would embark on a trip, the climax of which would the triumphant entry of Margaret and her devoted son, in a coach-and-four, into Dunfermline. On 17 June the Carnegies and nine friends set out from the Grand Hotel in Brighton and arrived at Inverness seven weeks later. Along the way Carnegie indulged his passion for horseplay and practical jokes, flirting outrageously and exercising his skills as a raconteur. At Windsor on 19 June he presented the Queen Dowager (as he styled his mother) with a magnificent loving cup on her seventy-first birthday. When they crossed the Sark on 16 July and entered Scotland, Carnegie was moved to write in his diary:

> It is God's mercy I was born a Scotchman, for I do not see how I could ever have been contented to be anything else. The little plucky dour deevil, set in her own ways and getting them too, level-headed and shrewd, with an eye to the main chance always and yet

so lovingly weak, so fond, so led away by song or story, so easily
touched to fine issues, so leal, so true! Ah! you suit me, Scotia, and
proud am I that I am your son.[18]

The triumphal return to Dunfermline was the highlight of the
entire trip and Carnegie carefully stagemanaged it. He had previously
given the town its swimming-baths, for which he had received the first
of his fifty-seven civic freedoms. Now he promised his natal city a fine
free public library and the citizens dutifully rejoiced at his
munificence. Schoolchildren had a day off to line the roadway and wave
British and American flags, as Carnegie, with the reins in his tiny
hands, drove his coach into the town. At his side sat Margaret, grandly
bedecked in a new gown of black silk, positively bursting out of her
corsets with pride. To her fell the honour of laying the foundation
stone of the world's first Carnegie library. Later there would be the
Lauder Technical College, named by Carnegie after his favourite uncle.

The entire trip was a personal triumph, out of which Carnegie
would distil his second book. Once more, he used this medium to
preach and proselytise, but whereas his first volume had concentrated
on religion, this time he tilted at the British windmills of title and
privilege, attacking the institution of monarchy as well as inherited
wealth and status. His forthright opinions, expressed as pithily as ever,
were increasingly peppered with maxims, saws and quotations from
the English poets as well as his favourite bard, Robert Burns.

The Carnegie entourage broke up on disembarkation at New York
in August. Andrew and his mother dined alone at the St Nicholas
Hotel, and suddenly he felt depressed. He had revelled in the trip
where he had been the centre of attention, surrounded by his closest
friends and admirers. Now there seemed an emptiness in his life, as he
contemplated the return to the cut and thrust of business. Voicing
these thoughts over dinner, he was comforted by Margaret's words,
'Never mind, Andra, you still have one left that sticks to you.'
Carnegie responded by reciting a verse:

> The good book tells of one
> Who sticks closer than a brother;
> But who will dare to say there's one
> Sticks closer than a mother!

SEVEN

The Rise of Henry Clay Frick

1881–92

Princes and lords are but the breath of kings,
An honest man's the noblest work of God.
                Robert Burns, 'The Cotter's Saturday Night'

BACK IN NEW YORK IN THE WINTER OF 1881, THERE WAS ONE
particularly cold, blustery day when Carnegie did not feel inclined to
go down to his office in Broad Street. Never a man to sit idly
twiddling his thumbs, he dug out the twopenny notebooks in which
he had jotted down his impressions during the coaching trip. Perhaps
he might be able to knock out an article for some magazine. He sat at
his desk and began writing. The narrative flowed so freely that by
dinnertime he had produced between three and four thousand words.
Over the ensuing weeks, at weekends and on days when it was
unnecessary for him to visit his office, he wrote his account of the
trip in exactly twenty sittings. When the task was completed he took
the sheaf of manuscript to Scribner's and asked them to print a few
hundred copies for private circulation. The book duly appeared in
1882 under the title of *Our Coaching Trip, Brighton to Inverness*. A copy
was foisted on everyone Carnegie could think of, not only relatives,
friends, acquaintances and business associates but also prominent
figures whom doubtless he hoped to impress. It was vanity publishing, pure and simple, and Carnegie had no thought of it as a commercial venture; but Charles Scribner himself read a copy and
shrewdly considered that there might be some mileage in a book
written by a millionaire. In the early 1880s there were few men who
could claim that epithet, and Scribner judged that the public would

be curious to read between the lines and figure out what made this man tick. An approach was made to the author, with an offer of a royalty on sales, and in 1883 an edited version, entitled *An American Four-in-Hand in Great Britain*, was published. Carnegie was proud of the fact that, with all his millions, Scribner's were still paying him royalties on this book thirty years later. General publication brought forth a spate of fan mail from delighted readers. Carnegie had the letters bound into a scrapbook, topped up over the years as further letters of appreciation continued to come in from time to time.

Writing the book occupied only a fraction of his time. While his partners were slaving away in Pittsburgh, Carnegie was living the good life at the Windsor Hotel, though he would often be away on business trips that took him all over the country. Margaret preferred the hotel to having a home of her own. Waited on hand and foot, without the trouble and responsibility of servants, she had her own social life. But when Carnegie was in town, he entered into the social whirl with manic zest. He kept a high profile, being seen often at fashionable gatherings, the theatre, concerts, receptions and banquets. Now in his late forties, he was putting on weight which, due to his lack of height, gave him a rolypoly appearance. Realising the need to take exercise, he purchased a horse and went riding in Central Park early in the morning or late in the afternoon. The millionaire bachelor might not be particularly prepossessing in physical characteristics, but he was witty and charming. Mothers sought him out, and Carnegie delighted in the company of young ladies. He would often be seen riding with some fair charmer alongside. If Margaret were aware of this, she said and did nothing. She knew her son too well, and was supremely confident that *she* was the only woman in his life.

Carnegie joined the Nineteenth Century Club which Mr and Mrs Courtland Palmer conducted in their drawing-room overlooking Gramercy Park. As this informal gathering grew in popularity with the cream of New York's intelligentsia, it moved its monthly meetings to premises in the American Art Galleries on Twenty-third Street and Broadway. Here the fashionable rubbed shoulders with the intellectual. It was the ideal terrain for the predatory Carnegie to stalk quarry that might prove useful to him in his multifarious business interests. Unlike his partners in Carnegie Brothers, there were no restrictions on *his* wheeling and dealing. It was here that he met Colonel Robert G. Ingersoll, a brilliant, generous free-thinker who kept open house at his mansion on Murray Hill every Sunday afternoon. Soon Carnegie was joining Ingersoll and his intimates at these congenial gatherings. Unlike the Nineteenth Century Club, where upwards of five hundred people would crowd uncomfortably to hear lectures by leading artists and writers, the atmosphere at Colonel Bob's was relaxed. In the Ingersoll drawing-room Carnegie met such widely assorted individuals as John W. Mackay, one of the first Western pioneers to make a million, and his no less talented son Clarence; John D. Crimmins, the leading Catholic layman; the celebrated actor Maurice Barrymore and the humorist Marshall P. Wilder. Visiting celebrities included the English writer Matthew Arnold. A real live poet – now here was someone worth cultivating! Carnegie courted him assiduously and they became lifelong friends. Through Arnold, moreover, Carnegie obtained entrée to intellectual and politically liberal circles in England, and eventually such prominent figures as William Ewart Gladstone and John Morley were added to Carnegie's bag.

Carnegie revelled in the intellectual atmosphere of New York, but he never lost his grip on the steel business back in Pittsburgh. It was in this period that the myth developed that Carnegie, who made his millions from steel, was blithely ignorant of the processes and techniques which produced the magic metal. This may have been inspired by Carnegie's occasional descent on the ET works with prominent personages in tow, and the inevitable gaggle of pressmen covering the event. Carnegie might address a simple, even naïve, question to one of his workmen, and thus convey the impression that he knew next to nothing about the business; but his departmental superintendents knew better, and often dreaded the close questioning which they received, in private, at the end of these visits. Carnegie kept abreast of the latest technical developments by studying all of the relevant technical literature. Furthermore, on his increasingly frequent trips to Europe, he never missed an opportunity to tour blast furnaces and steel mills, observing the latest plant, machinery and working practices and reporting back to Pittsburgh in minute detail.

Sometimes he was able to mix business with pleasure, as when, early in 1882, he entertained a rather aloof, self-possessed young man of thirty-two and his beautiful bride to lunch at the Windsor. Carnegie had never met the newly-weds before, but he treated them with the utmost cordiality, and at the end of the meal he raised his glass to toast his latest partner, Henry Clay Frick. Margaret Carnegie, of course, was present and after a momentary pause queried this in her customary blunt manner: 'Surely, Andra, that will be a fine thing for Mr Frick, but what will be the gain for us?' But not even Carnegie himself could have envisaged the astronomical gain in his fortune which would result from this partnership.

What brought Carnegie and Frick together could be summed up in a single word – coke. The three essential ingredients of steelmaking were iron ore, limestone and coke. Of limestone there was a great abundance in and around the Pittsburgh area, while iron ore, suitable for steelmaking had to be imported; but what gave Pittsburgh the edge as a centre of steel manufacturing was the limitless supplies of soft, bituminous fuel in the vast coalfields of western Pennsylvania. This had to be baked in special ovens to burn away the sulphur and phosphorus and produce the coal cake which could be mixed with iron ore and lime in the blast furnace. Under intense heat the unwanted elements in the ore fused with the lime to produce slag, leaving the pure molten iron which could be converted by the Bessemer process into high-grade steel. Considerable improvements had been wrought in the techniques of smelting and refining over the course of a single decade. In 1871, for example, it had taken a ton and a half of coke to produce a ton of pig-iron; by 1881 the amount of coke had been reduced to two-thirds of a ton. Prior to the 1860s, however, American steelmakers had used wood charcoal. Bessemer's process changed all that and suddenly the coalfield of Connellsville on the western slopes of the Allegheny Mountains leapt to wealth and fame. Most of that wealth and fame reposed in the hands of one man.

Henry Clay Frick was born in 1849 on the farm of his maternal grandfather Abraham Overholt, a Mennonite farmer who was reputed to be the richest man in Westmoreland County.[1] Overholt's riches came not from crops and cattle but from the whisky he distilled on the farm. In 1847 Overholt's daughter Elizabeth married a handsome but penniless young farmer named John Frick. The old man was not happy at this match, but grudgingly he gave the young couple the old spring house at the rear of the farmyard. In this humble cottage Elizabeth gave birth to a son who was named after her father's political idol, Henry Clay. Clay, as he was familiarly known, was a delicate child, prone to sickness and illness; but he had inherited his grandfather's indomitable will as well as a ruthlessness which would stand him in good stead later in life. Grandfather was reputedly worth half a million; well then, he, young Clay Frick, would have a million before he died. Grandfather saw to it that the boy got a good education, though the only aptitude he had was for mathematics. At seventeen he left school and went to work as a clerk in a store run by his Uncle Martin in Mount Pleasant. Here he blossomed as a salesman. His drive, industry, initiative and flair transformed the sickly youth into a dynamic, thrusting young businessman. Though he almost died from typhoid, he pulled through, and went to work in his grandfather's distillery as book-keeper, on a salary of $1000 a year.

He might have remained there for many years, had it not been for a casual conversation with his much older cousin Abraham Overholt Tinstman who had joined with Joseph Rist in an unwise gamble, purchasing 600 acres of coalfield and sinking their savings in a venture to produce coke. Unfortunately for Tinstman and Rist, there was very little demand for coke at the time. Frick begged to join them, and Tinstman, desperate for capital to keep his precarious business going, readily assented. Frick's solution was a bold and drastic one; instead of trying to dispose of the near-worthless coalfield, he urged expansion. Tinstman and Frick formed a new company and bought a further 123 acres with $52,995 of borrowed money. Tinstman and Rist were extremely doubtful of this venture and would not lend their names to the company which was duly incorporated under the name of the Henry C. Frick Coke Company of Broadford, Pennsylvania.

Having begged money from his relatives and friends to fuel his obsession for more and more coalfields, more and more ovens and coking plant, Frick went cap in hand to the Pittsburgh banker Judge Thomas Mellon. The twenty-one-year-old Frick, with remarkable aplomb, told the conservative banker that Connellsville coal produced the best coke in the world, and that he could sell every pound of coke he could produce. All he needed was $10,000 for six months at 10 per cent to build a further fifty coke ovens. The Judge liked the look of this earnest youth and advanced the cash. That meeting in the spring of 1871 cemented a relationship between Frick and the Mellons which lasted for almost fifty years and proved of immeasurable advantage to both parties.

Before the fifty ovens were completed, however, Frick was back in Mellon's office seeking a further $10,000. The cautious banker temporised, but sent one of his executives out to Broadford to investigate the Frick enterprise. This official reported back unfavourably: the young man was still working as the distillery book-keeper and only giving part of his attention to the coke business. The boy's business premises were 'half office and half living-room in a clapboard shack' strewn with prints and sketches, some of his own composition. Mellon decided that a more detailed report was required, so he sent his mining partner, James B. Corey, to look over the Frick project. Corey reported laconically: 'Lands good, ovens well built; manager on job all day, keeps books evenings, may be a little too enthusiastic about pictures but not enough to hurt; knows his business down to the ground; advise making loan.'[2] Frick got that second $10,000, and a great deal more. Even during the dark days of the 1873 depression Mellon continued to have faith in him.

By the end of that year things looked bleak for Frick as the demand for coke dwindled to vanishing point. Nothing daunted, he opened a sales office in Pittsburgh (on borrowed cash, of course) and for most of the ensuing year he 'got up at six, looked over the ovens and set things going, took the train for Pittsburgh at seven, reached his office at ten, legged it from factory to factory soliciting orders till three, reached home at about six, and attended to the details of mining till bedtime.'[3] Tinstman and Rist were appalled that Frick would actually spend more and borrow more during such hard times. They panicked and cut their losses, selling out their interest to Frick for peanuts. Having thus gained total control of the company that bore his name, Frick cast around to buy out his equally frightened competitors. With coke selling at 90c a ton, discouraged rivals were only too eager to quit the business. It needed nerves of steel to carry on when everyone else was getting out, but Frick's faith in coke never wavered.

The depression bottomed out eventually, and then gradually prices began to climb as steel production returned to normal. By 1877 the price of coke had trebled, then peaked at $5 a ton. By that time Frick controlled four-fifths of the entire US coke production, and $3 on every ton went straight into his own pocket as profit. By the end of 1879 a hundred freight-cars of coke were being despatched every day to meet the demands of the Pittsburgh furnaces. On 19 December that year, Henry Frick celebrated his thirtieth birthday by popping into Uncle Martin's store and treating himself to a five-cent Havana cigar which he lit slowly and puffed with the greatest satisfaction. Earlier that day he had pored over his account books and concluded that he had now attained his first million. His personal fortune was now twice that of his grandfather when he died in 1870; Frick had realised his ambition. Like many other driven men who achieve the seemingly impossible goals they set themselves, Frick was not satisfied. Instead of sitting back and enjoying his wealth, he must redouble his efforts. He lived as frugally as ever, but worked even harder. More coal, more ovens, more freight-cars and barges to transport the coke to the mills – this was the restless pattern. By 1880 Frick had almost a thousand ovens and about three thousand acres of coalfields.

Judge Mellon continued to take an avuncular interest in the dour young tycoon and encouraged a friendship between him and Mellon's third son Andrew, who was five years younger than Frick. Though their friendship lasted half a century the two men never got on to first-name terms. In 1880 Frick and Mellon emulated Carnegie and went on a pleasure trip to Europe. A year later, on 15 December 1881, Frick married Adelaide Howard Childs of Pittsburgh, youngest daughter of wealthy and influential Asa P. Childs, and went off on a honeymoon through the major cities of the East Coast. Two holidays in as many years! Such behaviour was so utterly out of character that people began to wonder whether young Frick had lost his reason. But on the European trip Mellon was disconcerted when Frick brought along, as a travelling companion, a major rival in the coke business, a man who was regarded as a crashing bore into the bargain. But all was explained when they reached Venice and Frick told Mellon that he had persuaded the other fellow that the pursuit of pleasure was all that really mattered in life. Consequently, he had persuaded his rival to sell him his business; while Frick attended to the paperwork regarding the transfer of coalfields and cokeworks, the rival was planning to take an extended trip around the world.

Now, after a leisurely tour through Washington, Baltimore and Philadelphia, Frick was heading for New York; in his luggage he had a warm letter of congratulations from Andrew Carnegie and an invitation to call on him at the Windsor Hotel and dine with him and his mother. Carnegie was Frick's largest customer, and such an invitation was not to be sneezed at. A sixth sense told him that Carnegie was not anxious merely to toast the bridal couple, and he was right. For several years he and Tom Carnegie had done business, and it was Tom who had drawn his brother's attention to the energetic, efficient young Frick. Carnegie was anxious to secure vertical control of steelmaking, which entailed the management not only of the iron ore and the limestone but also the coal and the coke. Even before that momentous lunch at the Windsor, Carnegie had offered Frick $325,000 for an 11 per cent interest in his company, and this had been accepted. Frick was needing additional capital for further expansion; this and the promise of an assured market helped to clinch the deal. The final details of this deal were actually worked out on the very day that the Fricks dined with the Carnegies. The upshot was the formation, on 1 May 1882, of the H.C. Frick Coke Company with capitalisation of $2,000,000.

Subsequently this was increased by 50 per cent, the Carnegie brothers putting up the additional sum to become half-owners. Meanwhile, Carnegie had persuaded Frick's associates, the brothers E.M. and Walter Ferguson (who had purchased 60 per cent of the shares in the new company) to sell him a substantial slice of their stock. By the summer of 1883 Carnegie had become the largest single shareholder in the company. When Frick sought further expansion and wanted to raise the additional million dollars to do so, it was naturally to Carnegie that he turned. Carnegie only agreed with some reluctance, but when Frick importuned him the following November with the offer of stock that would give him 50 per cent of the company, provided he took over responsibility for all the debts Frick had incurred during his previous expansion, Carnegie leapt at the opportunity. Less than two years after that auspicious meal at the Windsor, therefore, Carnegie Brothers owned more than 50 per cent of Frick's company. Frick seems to have been quite happy with this arrangement; he was left with a free hand to run the company in his own dynamic way, and Carnegie was happy to let him, confident in

Frick's outstanding managerial skills. As Carnegie Brothers continued to expand their steel output, demand for coke rose commensurately. Whatever Carnegie demanded, Frick was more than able to supply. The symbiosis of Carnegie steel and Frick coke was unstoppable. In the first fourteen months of the reorganised company, Frick produced almost a million tons of coke, generating net profits of $400,000. In the ensuing three years the number of ovens rose from 1000 to 5000, and output rose sharply to over 6000 tons a day.[4]

Carnegie Brothers showed a net profit of $2,000,377.42 in 1881 and $2,128,422.91 in 1882.[5] The following year, however, coming at the end of a ten-year cycle, showed a sharp drop in business, with profits halved. Once more, the steel industry was going through a slump; but as others were offloading their stock at rock-bottom prices Carnegie was buying. Now his tight-fisted policy of keeping dividends low and reinvesting profits in the business or laying aside huge reserves for investment, paid off.

A couple of miles downstream from Braddock's Field was the great rival steel plant at Homestead on a bend in the Monongahela River. Some years previously seven Pittsburgh steel firms, fearing the rising power of the Carnegies, had joined forces as the Pittsburgh Bessemer Steel Company to create the most advanced steel plant in Pennsylvania. Had Homestead been run efficiently, it would have been a formidable opponent; but it lacked the leadership of a Bill Jones. From the outset, Homestead was bedevilled with labour troubles and tension among the various ethnic groups employed there. Where Bill Jones won the respect and love of his workforce, the men at Homestead had nothing but loathing and contempt for their general superintendent, William Clark. A steel boss in the old-fashioned dictatorial mould, he was determined to break the power of the Amalgamated Association of Iron and Steelworkers. This was an élite union which jealously guarded its rights and privileges and only admitted the most skilled workers, leaving the semi-skilled workers and labourers to fend for themselves. In its first six years, Homestead chalked up an unenviable record for strikes, lockouts, wildcat stoppages and even ugly, violent clashes between different sections of the workforce, between skilled and unskilled men, between German and Irish and other groups. The recession of 1883 was the *coup de grâce*, and the

Homestead partnership desperately sought a way out. At the right moment Carnegie Brothers offered to buy the plant, offering $350,000 – no more than what it had cost. This was to be paid in hard cash, or stock in a new company they proposed to form. Six of the seven Homestead partners took the money and ran. The seventh, W.H. Singer, mulled it over and told Andrew Carnegie that he would take stock. Within a few years Singer saw his modest $50,000 allocation of shares grow into many millions.

A new firm, Carnegie, Phipps & Company, was formed to operate the Homestead plant. Once more Carnegie's lucky star was radiant; the deal was no sooner concluded than the market recovered, railroads recommenced their expansion programmes, and demand for steel rails and girders soared. Within two years the outlay on Homestead had been handsomely repaid. Soon Julian Kennedy, formerly boss of the Lucy Furnace, was doing for Homestead what Bill Jones and Alexander Holley had done at ET. A stroke of Kennedy genius was the installation of machinery to produce beams and girders required for heavy construction work. Much of the first batch turned out at the new plant went into the erection of the Rookery in Chicago, America's first skyscraper, which was built in 1887. In 1884 the Carnegie partnership earned $1,103,180.28; in 1885 this crept up to $1,191,993.54; but in 1886, the first full year of operations at the newly reconstituted Homestead plant, profits soared to $2,925,350.08. More importantly, thanks to Andrew Carnegie, American steel production now exceeded the output of Britain for the first time, and thereafter it remained paramount.

What should have been Andrew Carnegie's most glorious year was marred by personal sorrow. In October he returned to Cresson Springs from New York, stricken by a high fever which turned out to be typhoid. Professor Fred S. Dennis was summoned from New York to treat him, and an attendant physician and a trained nurse were provided at once. For many days he hovered between life and death, but while he was seriously ill his brother took ill and died.

At the age of forty-three Tom Carnegie caught a cold which developed into pneumonia. Tom, the father of nine children, had developed a heavy drinking habit in recent years. To what extent this was stress-related is a matter of speculation. In character and temperament so very different from his ruthless elder brother, he was often put in an invidious position of having to mediate between Andrew and the other partners, and deal with a thousand and one problems on a daily basis, while Andrew was relaxing at Cresson Springs or New York or swanning off around the world on one of his prolonged trips.

With Andrew Carnegie still on the danger list, Tom's sudden death left his partners understandably jittery. Tom had a 17.5 per cent interest in Carnegie Brothers and a 16 per cent interest in Carnegie, Phipps & Company. These interests were the equal of the shares held by Henry Phipps and second only to Andrew's in extent. His death meant that a full and immediate settlement of his interests had to be absorbed. Had Andrew died, his 54.5 per cent interest in Carnegie Brothers and 52.5 per cent in Carnegie, Phipps would have been far more than the market could have absorbed, and his colossal empire would have been driven into bankruptcy. But unlike his brother, Andrew was virtually teetotal, and though he was undoubtedly carrying more weight than he should, his stamina and rugged constitution carried him through the typhoid fever.

Carnegie was past the crisis of typhoid fever but still recuperating in bed at Braemar Cottage when the second blow in a matter of weeks struck. Margaret had been in poor health for some time, but by the autumn of 1886 she was too frail to make the train journey back to New York for the winter. Then she, too, took to her bed and went into a steady decline. She was seriously ill when Tom died, and was never told of his death. Then, one cold November day, when snow lay deep on the ground, she passed away. 'My mother's and brother's serious condition had not been revealed to me, and when I was informed that both had left me forever it seemed only natural that I should follow them. We had never been separated; why should we be now? But it was decreed otherwise.'[6] For the first time in his life the stuffing was knocked out of him. The deaths of the two people closest to him within a matter of days, and his inability to attend their funerals, affected him deeply. His severe depression was matched by the weather, which was exceptionally cold with high winds and driving blizzards. Braemar Cottage was ill equipped for such severe weather, and it was imperative that the patient be moved to a warmer climate as soon as possible. Eventually he was fit enough to be dressed and driven to the nearest railway line where his old friend Bob Pitcairn had laid on a de luxe private railcar to take him south.

The partners had had a bad fright, and even before Carnegie himself was fully recovered, they took energetic measures to see that the situation should never arise again. Architect of the new 'Iron Clad' agreement, drawn up early in 1887, was Henry Phipps who based it on the articles of agreement for Kloman, Phipps & Miller. The essential feature of the Iron Clad was that it provided a painless method for the surviving partners to purchase the shares of a deceased partner. If a partner had 4 per cent of the business or less, the company had four months in which to purchase that interest. The higher the percentage, the longer the time allowed; in the case of Andrew Carnegie, the company had fifteen years in which to acquire his interest. The agreement also gave Carnegie and Phipps the means of ousting partners whose continued presence might be detrimental to the business. This move could be made if three-quarters of the other partners were in agreement, in which case the ejected partner would be compelled to sell his stock to the others at book value. This precaution was motivated by the bitter experience with William Shinn. This was the sort of agreement which Carnegie liked. As it also contained a clause requiring 'three fourths in value of said interests' to act together, as well as three fourths of the parties concerned, it effectively excluded any partner who had more than a quarter of the stock; and as Carnegie, with well over half, was the only partner in this category, he was exempt. Ironically, it was Phipps who had proposed this agreement, unduly concerned about the effect Carnegie's death would have had on the business. He was so anxious to get the Iron Clad drawn up that he neglected to note that it put his own position in jeopardy.

While he recuperated in Florida over the winter of 1886–87, Carnegie pondered on the meaning of life. With his parents and brother gone, he was all alone in the world. But his was too resilient a spirit to be kept down for long, and soon he began to think of the future. While not scheming over the reorganisation of his business empire in the light of his brother's death, he began to turn his thoughts towards a previously taboo subject. With Margaret barely cold in her grave, Carnegie, at the age of fifty-two, contemplated matrimony.

The lady he had in mind was Louise Whitfield, at twenty-eight barely half his age. She came from a respectable old Connecticut family and lived with her widowed mother at 35 West Forty-eighth Street. Carnegie first clapped eyes on Louise as she rode her pony in the park, and was immediately captivated by her beauty, sweetness and wholesome charm. But while Margaret was alive Carnegie believed that there was safety in numbers. Louise was only one of several young ladies with whom he rode and exchanged pleasantries. On his return to New York in the spring of 1887, however, he wasted no time in singling her out. According to his *Autobiography*, Carnegie originally felt that he had no chance of winning her hand, that Louise had plenty of admirers of her own age, that his age and wealth told against him: 'Her ideal was to be the helpmeet of a young, struggling man.' He implies that he courted her over quite a period of time, when Margaret was alive, but that Louise returned his letters and rejected his advances.

Her attitude changed when he fell desperately ill. She was touched when the first time he was fit enough to hold a pen to paper he had written to her from Cresson Springs. While recuperating at the home of Professor Dennis in New York, Carnegie had had a visit from Louise. Later, when he was well enough to go out of doors again, he invited her to dinner and escorted her to the theatre. Soon he was being entertained in Mrs Whitfield's drawing-room, listening to Louise as she played the piano. The courtship was brief, brisk and to the point. On 22 April that year, in the presence of a few close friends, Louise became Mrs Andrew Carnegie. Immediately before the ceremony Carnegie transferred to her sufficient securities to provide her with an independent income of $20,000 a year. As a wedding present, however, he gave her the imposing mansion at 5 West Fifty-first Street, formerly the property of Collis P. Huntington.

Despite the disparity in age, this turned out to be a happy marriage. Louise was sweet-natured, demure, docile and deferential, at least in public. She was elegant, a charming hostess, the jewel in his crown. Below the surface of docility, however, she exercised her subtle will on her all-powerful husband. The full extent of her influence over him has never been gauged, but marriage was definitely a watershed in his life. Perhaps she led by example, and her gentle qualities rubbed off on him; but from 1887 onwards he was definitely a more mellow person. The old combativeness, cockiness, arrogance and overweening confidence were toned down and in their place came a quieter, softer Carnegie. It might be argued that where Margaret Carnegie, who was cast in the same diamantine mould, had egged him on and wholeheartedly approved of his schemes and ploys, Louise made him pause and question his motives and tactics. To be sure, there would still be ample evidence that the old overbearing Carnegie was not dead, but in the thirty-two years of their marriage Louise had a decidedly softening effect on him.

The day after the wedding, the bridal couple took ship for Southampton and spent their honeymoon on the Isle of Wight. Uncle Lauder and one of Carnegie's cousins came down from Scotland to visit them, and shortly afterwards they headed north, taking the Perthshire estate of Kilgraston for the summer. Louise, who had been reared on the romantic novels of Walter Scott, was enchanted with Scotland. Her husband took a boyish delight in showing her Dunfermline, his birthplace and all the haunts of his youth. *En route*, they paused in Edinburgh long enough for Carnegie to receive the freedom of the city, the future prime minister, Lord Rosebery, delivering the eulogy. Louise was overwhelmed by the vast crowds who turned out in Edinburgh and Dunfermline to greet them. Until that time she had not appreciated just what a Scottish national hero she had married. At Kilgraston, they entertained old friends and new acquaintances, including Matthew Arnold, Senator Hale and his wife as well as James Blaine, Speaker of the House of Representatives, and his wife. Carnegie had poured vast sums of money into the Republican treasure-chest in support of Blaine's campaign for the presidency in 1884. But undoubtedly too close a connection with Carnegie, Cyrus Field, Jay Gould and other wealthy businessmen robbed Blaine of the prize which went to Grover Cleveland instead.

John Hay, who had been Lincoln's secretary during the Civil War, wrote to his friend Henry Adams from London soon after visiting the Carnegies: 'The house is thronged with visitors – sixteen when we came away – we merely stayed three days: the others were there for a fortnight . . . Carnegie likes it so well he is going to do it every summer and is looking at all the great estates in the County with a view of renting or purchasing.'[7]

In the summer of 1886 Carnegie had produced his third book, an economic survey of half a century of progress by the United States, which Scribner's published under the inspired title of *Triumphant Democracy*. This time Carnegie had hired a competent researcher, James Howard Bridge, to do the necessary spadework, but the text itself was in Carnegie's inimitably opinionated style. In rather simplistic terms he praised his adopted country to the skies and boasted of the superiority of its political system over the decadent monarchies of Europe. It was a recital of the facts in the letters to Cousin Dod thirty years earlier, writ large. The book was taken seriously and enjoyed a huge success, on both sides of the Atlantic. In particular it had been warmly received by William Ewart Gladstone, the grand old man of Liberal politics. As a result, Carnegie and Blaine, with their respective wives, were invited to dine at Lord Wolverton's townhouse in Piccadilly on the evening of Queen Victoria's Golden Jubilee (20 June 1887), amid a galaxy of aristocrats, socialites and captains of industry, including the octogenarian Gladstone, as alert and incisive as ever, despite advancing deafness. Later that night, as Blaine and Carnegie fought their way through vast throngs of revellers towards the Metropole Hotel, the latter heard a word or two spoken by a voice close to the building on his right.

I said to Mr Blaine: 'That is Mr Gladstone's voice.'

He said: 'It is impossible. We have just left him returning to his residence.'

'I don't care; I recognize voices better than faces, and I am sure that is Gladstone's.'

Finally I prevailed upon him to return a few steps. We got close to the side of the house and moved back. I came to a muffled figure and whispered: 'What does "Gravity" out of its bed at midnight?'

Mr Gladstone was discovered. I told him I recognized his voice whispering to his companion.

'And so,' I said, 'the real ruler comes out to see the illuminations prepared for the nominal ruler!'

He replied, 'Young man, I think it is time you were in bed.'

179

> We remained a few minutes with him, he being careful not to
> remove from his head and face the cloak that covered them. It was
> then past midnight and he was eighty, but, boylike, after he got Mrs
> Gladstone safely home he had determined to see the show.[8]

This encounter may have been innocent enough. On the other
hand, posterity knows what Carnegie did not: that Gladstone
indulged in nocturnal forays to chat up prostitutes.

Amidst the honeymooning and Jubilee revels Carnegie was
suddenly brought down to earth by a lengthy coded telegram from
Henry Phipps and John Walker, who was being groomed for the
difficult role of chairman in place of the late Tom Carnegie. Walker
was Phipps's brother-in-law and had been directly or indirectly
associated with Carnegie for fifteen years. In 1872 the older and less
profitable Lower Mills of the Union Iron Mills had been sold to a new
firm, Wilson, Walker & Company (in which Carnegie had a
substantial interest). Then, in 1881, Carnegie had disposed of the
Lucy Furnaces to this company. Five years later, when Carnegie,
Phipps & Company was formed, Carnegie took back the Lucy
Furnaces. John Wilson sold his interest to Carnegie while John
Walker, in agreeing to the merger, was made chairman of the new
company which included the Lucy Furnaces and the Homestead
mills. Phipps and Walker represented a majority interest on the
board of the Frick company and they were very worried because a
strike was paralysing the coke region. The workers were demanding
a 12.5 per cent pay increase but Frick and the other operators were
solid in refusing this claim. As a consequence the Carnegie blast
furnaces were banked up for lack of fuel and a complete shutdown
was imminent at both Homestead and ET. Carnegie's response was
brisk; he ordered Frick to concede the men's demand immediately.
Furious and humiliated, Frick promptly resigned as president and
general manager. In a letter addressed to Phipps and Walker, but
obviously aimed at Carnegie, Frick wrote:

> The loss to the Coke Company may be far more than made up, so far
> as you are concerned, by gains in your steel interests, but I object
> to so manifest a prostitution of the Coke Company's interests in
> order to promote your steel interests. Whilst a majority of the stock

180

entitles you to control, I deny that it confers the right to manage so
as to benefit your interests in other concerns at the loss and injury
of the Coke Company in which I am interested.'[9]

From Kilgraston, however, Carnegie fired off a series of flattering,
fawning epistles to Frick. To make matters worse, the other coke
operators denounced Frick for giving way and continued to hold out.
In the end their employees caved in and returned to work, so only the
Frick company was saddled with a higher wage scale.

Out of a job for the first time since boyhood, Frick decided to take
a trip to Europe. With his wife and two little children, Adelaide's
mother and sister in tow, he sailed for England. On checking-in at his
London hotel early in August he found a note from Carnegie,
extending the warmest invitation to the Frick family: 'It's superb –
Come and see what one gets in Scotland these summer days.' This
melted Frick's resolve to have nothing further to do with the tricky
Scot. The family went north and in due course the two men were
reconciled. In the spring of 1888 Frick accepted the unanimous
invitation from the board of the coke company and was re-elected
president. They both learned a valuable lesson from this episode.
Carnegie acquired a fresh appreciation of Frick's true worth and ever
afterwards was extremely careful to lavish unstinted praise on him.
Frick, on the other hand, now had no delusions about Carnegie:
pragmatism, not principle, was his guide at all times.

Frick's climb-down was made more palatable on two counts. In the
first place, the coke company continued to show a steady rise in
profits despite having to pay higher wages, and inevitably attracted
the cream of the workforce away from those firms which were
sticking to lower rates. In the second place, Frick's re-entry was
rewarded by swift advancement within the mainstream Carnegie
organisation. Within twelve months he had replaced Phipps as
chairman of Carnegie Brothers, accompanied by a hefty increase in
his interest, from 2 to 11 per cent, again without Frick having to pay
a cent in cash as it was apportioned from the profits. Congratulating
Frick on his elevation in January 1889, Carnegie penned an effusive
note: 'Take supreme care of that head of yours. It is wanted. Again,
expressing my thankfulness that I have found THE MAN. I am
always yours, A.C.'[10]

Frick proved his worth many times over. Within two years of his return to the fold he had gained control of two-thirds of the entire Connellsville coke region. When he was confronted with further labour problems, he was given an entirely free hand this time, and Carnegie wisely did not interfere or go behind his back. When the cokeworkers again went on strike, in the winter of 1889–90, Frick imported Hungarian and Polish strike-breakers and ruthlessly crushed the rebellion. For three months the Connellsville area was torn apart by riots, arson and even murder. Heavily armed mobs attacked the mines and coking plants, killing and wounding the black-legs and smashing the machinery. When deputy marshals tried to restrain them, the strikers openly defied them. If a particular village or community looked like giving way, marauding gangs descended on them in the dead of night and terrorised them. The situation was rapidly getting out of hand, and the region was sinking into open warfare, with pitched battles between the strikers and the forces of law and order. Foreseeing trouble, Carnegie had ordered the massive stockpiling of coke, so that he was prepared to back Frick to the bitter end.

And so the ugly dispute dragged on, until the strikers were arrested or driven out of the region. Matters were exacerbated by a sharp fall in demand for rails and girders; after a record profit of $3,441,887.29 in 1887, net profits shrank in 1888 to $1,941,555.54.

In fairness to Frick it should be noted that the late 1880s were a troubled time for American industry as the workers began flexing their muscles and demanding higher wages and shorter hours. In 1877 Captain Jones had been instrumental in getting Carnegie to agree to an eight-hour day for the men who worked at ET. By adopting a three-shift system, the blast furnaces were kept going right round the clock. In agreeing to this radical departure, Carnegie hoped that this example would soon be followed by rival firms, but they remained firmly committed to a two-shift system with men working twelve hours a day. By late 1887 Carnegie felt that he could no longer afford the eight-hour, three-shift system, and ordered Jones to come into line with other steelworks by 1 January 1888. In vain Jones protested against this move; when it was introduced at Carnegie's demand, the workers promptly came out on strike.

Carnegie was adamant that the works would remain closed till the men backed down, but after a delegation came all the way to New York to beard the lion in his den he did agree to come back to Pittsburgh and address the men and listen to their grievances. Three weeks later Carnegie, pint-sized but pugnacious, got up in front of a densely packed hall. In the wings stood Phipps and George Lauder, fearful that the meeting would erupt into violence. Carnegie, the master orator, began in a low-key manner, warming up his audience with wisecracks and soothing remarks, before asking for individual statements of grievance. There was an awkward pause, then one of the men slowly got to his feet and said, 'Mr Carnegie, take my job, for instance —'

Quick as a flash, Carnegie interjected: 'Mr Carnegie takes no man's job.'

The men were convulsed with laughter at this sally, stamped their feet and began chanting, 'Thou shalt not take thy neighbor's job!'

The atmosphere melted, and Carnegie, on his feet once more, rapidly outlined his proposals. The matter would be dealt with in a proper, democratic manner. They could take a vote on it. They could either have a continuance of the eight-hour day with reduced wages, or a return to the twelve-hour day with a profit-sharing sliding scale. Without pausing to give due consideration to these alternatives, the men shouted their approval, and in a secret ballot they voted heavily in favour of the latter. Too late they discovered that Carnegie had pulled a fast one. It was a case of 'heads I win, tails you lose'. Work resumed the very next day, and ever afterwards Carnegie could claim with hand on heart that the twelve-hour day had been secured by due democratic process.

Trouble next surfaced at the Homestead plant which had such a long history of poor labour relations. After his honeymoon, Carnegie got into the habit of spending the summer months each year in Scotland. In 1889 he departed, knowing full well that trouble was brewing over his attempts to extend the sliding-scale policy to Homestead. By now the workers had realised their mistake, and their counterparts at Homestead were determined not to fall into the same trap. Of the 3800 men in the Homestead workforce, about 800 were members of the Amalgamated Association of Iron and Steelworkers, paid on a flat tonnage basis. As output increased with improved machinery, naturally the wages of these élite workers rose. Any attempt to replace this system with the sliding scale was bound to be strenuously resisted.

The current contract was due to expire on 30 June, and six weeks previously the management announced that it would not be renewed. This was bad enough, but management's insistence that 'men desirous of employment will be required to sign an agreement' was taken by the union as a direct threat to its continued power. As a result, union members walked out on 30 June and the following day Homestead closed down entirely. From Scotland, Carnegie urged William Abbott, who had succeeded Phipps as chairman of Carnegie, Phipps in 1888, to stand firm. Abbott, however, advertised for strikebreakers early in July. Only a handful of immigrant and Negro labourers turned up, under the armed guard of the county sheriff and 125 deputies; but when they were confronted by almost 2000 angry, well-armed strikers, the sheriff, deputies and would-be blacklegs turned tail and ran for their lives. When the workers at ET threatened to come out in sympathy, Carnegie temporised, ordering Captain Jones to do his utmost to keep his men out of the Homestead dispute. Fortunately Abbott caved in. In return for full recognition of the union, the men agreed to a new sliding scale of pay that was to remain in force for three years. That oppressively hot July night the workers at Homestead rejoiced and sang the praises of the Little Boss who was perceived as having a hand in the conciliatory move. Had he not given a solemn assurance that he would not take his neighbour's job? To be sure, Carnegie had got his way over the sliding scale, but the union was now more firmly entrenched than ever. Thus was mapped out the collision course that was to have such terrifying results three years later.

The hero of this confrontation was a young man named Charles Schwab. Born at Williamsburg, Pennsylvania, the son of a German livery stable operator, he had been raised at Loretto, a remote settlement near Cresson Springs. He frequently set eyes on the great Carnegie when he rode out to Braemar Cottage with the mail each day. Aged seventeen, he left his father's livery stable and went to Braddock where he got a job as a clerk in a grocery store. One of the regular customers was Captain Jones, and one day young Charlie boldly asked if he might get a job at ET. Jones appraised the husky teenager and told him to report for work at seven the following morning. Thus Schwab started his career in the Carnegie empire as a stake-driver at a dollar a day. Promotion was meteoric; within six months he had been elevated to superintendent in charge of the construction of new blast furnaces. Schwab rose to the challenge and his success was crowned when he was asked to meet the Little Boss himself.

From then on he never looked back. Ambitious, eager, energetic and hardworking, he was exactly the kind of young man Carnegie sought out. Schwab had charm and a ready wit, qualities that Carnegie had himself in abundance. Before he was twenty, Schwab was Carnegie's protégé, and thereafter promotion was even swifter and more dramatic. His unfailing good humour was just what Carnegie needed as an antidote to Frick's dour taciturnity and Phipps's vapid timidity. At the age of twenty-five Schwab became general superintendent at Homestead, and he proved his mettle in his courageous handling of the 1889 strike, in contrast to the panicky behaviour of the chairman, Abbott. While Abbott was blamed for conceding too much, Schwab was praised for preventing violence.

The steel mills were just getting back to normal in the summer of 1889 when disaster struck again, from a totally unexpected quarter. On the night of 26 September one of the new blast furnaces at ET exploded with sudden and terrifying force. Bill Jones, who was standing near by, was thrown backwards by the blast, fracturing his skull on the side of an ore truck. He died two days later, without regaining consciousness. The greatest steelman in all America was dead, sincerely mourned by management and workers alike. Thousands lined the streets at his great public funeral and all the flags in Pittsburgh flew at half-mast.

Schwab was promoted to fill the vacancy. Comparisons are invidious, of course, but one cannot help speculating that had Jones lived the dreadful events that unfolded a few years later might have been averted. Schwab was a personable young man with a great deal of personal magnetism, but this was no substitute for the Jones charisma. Schwab's ready humour often saved the day when dealing with workers and union officials and, like Jones, he was not afraid of hard, physical labour and led from the front. Unlike Jones, though, he had taken a great deal of trouble to study chemistry and metallurgy and had acquired a sound knowledge of the technical intricacies of

185

steelmaking. But his ambition was more self-centred and less company-orientated than Jones's had been. At the same time he was more docile and tractable, and lacked the maverick element which had made Bill Jones his own man. Above all, Carnegie liked Schwab because he never wavered in executing the great man's orders. Jones could be as temperamental as a prima donna, with frequent threats of resignation; Schwab would have shrunk from such behaviour.

Schwab had one other thing in his favour – Henry Clay Frick. Frick heartily disliked Jones because of his independent spirit and because he was 'soft on labour'. Frick was quick to recognise Schwab's obedience to orders, and saw in Jones's death an opportunity to rationalise the business. He proposed to Andrew that Carnegie Brothers and Carnegie, Phipps should be amalgamated, that ET and Homestead should be run as a single concern. Furthermore, he argued cogently in favour of a larger capitalisation which would more truly represent the worth of the business, and at the same time give many of the promising young executives in the organisation initiative by way of a junior partnership and a chance to enjoy the fruits of their labour. This appealed to Carnegie, who had always preferred giving his 'young geniuses' a small partnership interest rather than a big salary. Frick backed his argument with the exceptionally satisfactory figures. In his first year as chairman of Carnegie Brothers, profits had almost doubled, from $1,941,555 to $3,540,000. Carnegie was finally convinced and gave the proposed merger the go-ahead. Under the terms of the new charter, due to take effect on 1 July 1892, Carnegie, Phipps & Company and Carnegie Brothers & Company were to sell their assets to the Carnegie Steel Company Limited. The combined capitalisation of the two companies at the time of the amalgamation was $10,000,000. Carnegie Steel was capitalised at $25,000,000, of which Andrew Carnegie would hold $13,833,333 or 55.33 per cent; Frick and Phipps would each hold $2,750,000 or 11 per cent, and the remaining nineteen partners would have 1 per cent each. This left 3.66 per cent which was to be held in trust by Francis Lovejoy, the company secretary, to be divided among deserving young men in the organisation whom Carnegie might later wish to admit to partnership. Schwab, still excluded from this magic circle, had his glittering eye on this reserve. He would not have long to wait.

EIGHT

Homestead

1892

Man's inhumanity to man
Makes countless thousands mourn!
Robert Burns, 'Man Was Made to Mourn'

KILGRASTON, OVERLOOKING THE RIVER TAY, WAS NOT WILD enough for Louise Carnegie who had a hankering after something more remote in the Highlands of Scotland. In Edinburgh, she had been captivated by the pipe band that attended the civic freedom ceremony in 1887, and begged her husband to have her own personal piper to play around the house at dawn and dinnertime. Casting around for a suitable piper, Carnegie was sent one by Cluny Macpherson, chief of the clan. At the end of the 1887 season the piper was one of a number of Scottish servants whom Carnegie took back to New York. The anonymous piper also influenced Carnegie in his choice of summer residence in 1888, for he rented Cluny Castle from the clan chief. Thereafter, each summer, the Carnegies fled from the heat and humidity of Pittsburgh and New York to their Highland retreat. Ever since he had been smitten with sunstroke in 1861, Carnegie had a marked aversion to hot weather, hence Braemar Cottage at Cresson Springs high up in the Alleghenies; but after Margaret died Carnegie closed it down and never went back there. All his mother's possessions were carefully packed away, but even her portraits were withdrawn from view. It was as if the memory of the one person he had loved wholeheartedly was too painful to bear.

Escaping to a cooler climate had other advantages for Andrew Carnegie; it enabled him to absent himself from Pittsburgh when trouble was brewing, and to remain out of the country when trouble actually erupted. Of course, he maintained close communications with his partners, thanks to the miracle of the transatlantic telegraph cable; but even if he were to respond to an urgent plea and head home by the first available boat, it would inevitably take him upwards of two weeks to get to the heart of the matter. Scotland was to provide Carnegie with a perfect alibi when violence erupted at the Homestead plant in the summer of 1892, the most disgraceful episode in the annals of American labour relations.

The man actually in command on the spot was, of course, Henry Clay Frick. From the moment that he took over as chairman of Carnegie Brothers at the age of thirty-nine, Frick demonstrated un-equivocally to Carnegie that he was just the man he had been seeking. One of his early successes was the takeover of the Duquesne Steel Company, formed by a consortium of Pittsburgh iron manufacturers who made it the most advanced steel plant in America. As Duquesne concentrated on the production of rails it posed a very real threat to the near-monopoly which Carnegie had previously enjoyed. With its state-of-the-art streamlined production methods, Duquesne could turn out rails more swiftly and cheaply than ET. Alarmed, Carnegie responded by blocking the company's admission to the current rail pool, and then sent letters to all the railroad companies warning them that Duquesne rails were bound to prove 'defective through lack of homogeneity'. Strangely enough, the direct rolling process pioneered at Duquesne was soon adopted at ET and other large steel mills.

Having failed to stop Duquesne, Carnegie next tried to buy them out. Early in 1889 Frick, at Carnegie's behest, offered $600,000 for the Duquesne plant, but the offer was rejected. The following year Frick raise his offer to a million in bonds of Carnegie Brothers. By that time Duquesne had been hard hit by a series of strikes as well as by Carnegie's obstructive tactics. In the end, William G. Park, Duquesne's main partner, reluctantly accompanied Frick to New York for a meeting at Carnegie's elegant mansion. A deal was finally hammered out in the library; as they went downstairs to the dining-room for lunch, Frick whispered to Carnegie that he thought the price could have been cut below the million mark.

'Never mind,' whispered Carnegie. 'We get the turkey. Let Park have the feathers.'

Late in 1890 Frick reorganised the Duquesne plant, installing as superintendent Thomas Morrison, another of Carnegie's young cousins who had emigrated to Pittsburgh and had worked his way up the corporate ladder, from a humble machinist at Homestead. Frick liked Morrison; the dour young Scot was every bit as taciturn as Frick himself. During 1891 the Duquesne plant was rationalised and linked to Braddock and Homestead by means of a private railway system. Duquesne was immensely profitable from the outset, actually paying for itself during the first year of operation. When the bonds fell due, it had netted over $6,000,000. Within a decade Duquesne would be turning out 750,000 tons of pig-iron and 600,000 tons of raw steel per annum using the new open-hearth process.

With Frick at the helm, it seemed as if the Carnegie enterprises were unstoppable. Every year production rose, and profits soared just as astronomically. Carnegie relied on Frick implicitly and felt free to indulge his passions for travel, writing, entertaining, public-speaking and socialising on a grand scale. In the earlier years he had been too busy making money to give much thought to politics, but as his businesses prospered he became more and more wedded to the high-tariff policies of the Republican party. It will be remembered that he had supported James Blaine's bid for the presidency in 1884. Four years later Blaine and his wife were the principal guests at Cluny Castle. Blaine and his diminutive supporter spent days fly-fishing on Loch Laggan and danced the night away in wild eightsome reels and Highland jigs. At the Republican convention in Chicago that autumn the band struck up 'My Heart's in the Highlands', a Burns song which was one of Carnegie's favourites, as Blaine made his grand entrance. Blaine, however, was reluctant to seek the nomination unless he had the support of John Sherman, the influential Senator from Ohio. Carnegie played a vital role as go-between in the subsequent wheeling and dealing with Senator Stephen B. Elkins of West Virginia. They were poised to support Blaine when he swithered, then decided to switch his allegiance to Benjamin Harrison who, in due course, was elected twenty-third President of the United States.

When Blaine stood down, Carnegie put all his weight behind the Harrison campaign, contributing heavily to the fighting fund and securing the appointment of Matthew Stanley Quay as campaign manager. Quay had succeeded Simon and Donald Cameron (father and son) as the political boss of Pennsylvania. Like the Camerons, he was a very close friend of Carnegie. His fellow-director of the Republican party machine was Bible-thumping Thomas Collier Platt of New York, who was also one of Carnegie's intimate cronies. Another of Carnegie's close buddies was Mark Hanna, Republican party agent in Cleveland, Ohio, and through him he advanced the career of a rather dull congressman named William McKinley whose brother Abner was a long-term resident of the Windsor Hotel and constant companion of the steel magnate. When Harrison entered the White House Blaine's loyalty was rewarded when he was appointed Secretary of State. In this manner Carnegie became a trusted confidant of the President and adviser of the administration. In 1891 he persuaded President Harrison to accompany him to Pittsburgh and formally inaugurate the Carnegie Library and Hall in Allegheny City. This was the first time that a President of the United States had ever visited Pittsburgh, and Harrison was frankly appalled by the place. 'Hell with the lid off' was his terse description of the steel city. The following morning he dutifully toured the Carnegie steel mills, an event that was covered by the world's press and was Carnegie's most spectacular publicity stunt.

The Carnegie Steel Company Limited formally came into being on 1 July 1892. No new capital was contributed, the capitalisation of $25,000,000 being raised simply by Carnegie declaring a 400 per cent stock dividend on the original $5,000,000 shares of Carnegie Brothers & Company. In this new organisation Carnegie held $13,833,333 of stock, Phipps and Frick held $2,750,000 each and George Lauder a cool million. William H. Singer, Henry M. Curry, Henry William Borntraeger and John G.A. Leishman each had $500,000. Otis H. Childs, Frick's brother-in-law, and John Vandevort, Carnegie's travelling companion, had $250,000 and $200,000 respectively. Francis Lovejoy had a personal interest of $166,666, twice that of the bevy of junior partners, but he also controlled the reserve of $918,055.

Only Carnegie, Phipps and Frick were credited with paid-up subscriptions. The others were 'debtor partners'; Carnegie had a firm grip on them because their interests, to be paid from bonuses and profits, could be rescinded any time at the whim of the majority stockholder. Harry Phipps took no active part in the company. The immigrant cobbler's son had now decided to return to England where he purchased a large country estate. This left Frick very much in sole command.

The 'debtor partners' were a colourful bunch of yuppies. John Leishman, a Scot, had been orphaned at a very early age and at ten he was already an office boy in an ironworks. Still in his teens, he had entered Carnegie's service as a salesman and soon made his mark in landing huge orders for steel rails. He would later abandon steel for the diplomatic service and became American ambassador to Switzerland and then Turkey. Abbott, who rose from a junior clerk at the Union Iron Mills to become chairman of Carnegie, Phipps, was a protégé of Harry Phipps. His chief claim to fame (apart from his dismal handling of the labour dispute of 1889) was to organise a highly skilled team of professional salesmen which included John C. Fleming and J. Ogden Hoffman who emerged in 1892 as junior partners. Abbott himself took early retirement at forty, preferring the pursuit of literature and congenial company, and thus missed his opportunity to become a multi-millionaire. Lovejoy had had a succession of low-paid jobs – laundry-man, oil-driller, telegraphist, newspaper reporter, stenographer and book-keeper – before joining Carnegie as an auditor. Catching the eye of the Little Boss, he enjoyed rapid promotion, becoming company secretary and treasurer in place of William Shinn, and winning his partnership at the age of thirty-seven.

Alexander Peacock, another young Scot, had been clerk in a dry-goods store when Carnegie's talent scouts had spotted him. Recruited by Abbott as a salesman, he excelled in this cut-throat medium. When he consistently beat the sales target, he was summoned to New York for an audience with Carnegie who asked him bluntly, 'Peacock, what would you give to be made a millionaire?' Without batting an eyelid, he replied, 'Two per cent discount for cash, sir.'

Henry B. Bope, on $27,777 the most junior of the partners, had until recently been a typist. William Blackburn (with an interest of $83,333) had been clerk in a village store. Apart from Otis Childs, the only junior partner who owed his position to his family connections was Phipps's son Lawrence, whose interest was likewise set at $83,333.

Day-to-day direction of Carnegie Steel was in the hands of Frick as chairman. Under him were Henry Curry (treasurer) and Francis Lovejoy (secretary). Frick, Curry and Lovejoy also ranked as managers, along with Lauder, Singer, Leishman and Lawrence Phipps. Between them, they had control of a multi-million-dollar enterprise with a workforce in excess of 30,000 men. It was the largest steel company in the world, with an output half that of the total steel production in Great Britain.

Even before Carnegie Steel formally came into being, trouble was brewing at the Homestead plant. The three-year contract with the Amalgamated Association of Iron and Steel Workers on wages and conditions of employment was due to expire on 1 July 1892. On 4 April that year, however, Carnegie sent Frick a notice which was to be published at Homestead. In this document the employees were informed:

> These works having been consolidated with the Edgar Thomson and Duquesne, and other mills, there has been forced upon this Firm the question Whether its Works are to be run 'Union' or 'Non-Union'. As the vast majority of our employees are non-union, the Firm has decided that the minority must give place to the majority. These works, therefore, will be necessarily Non-Union after the expiration of the present agreement.
>
> This does not imply that the men will make lower wages. On the contrary, most of the men at Edgar Thomson and Duquesne Works, both Non-Union, have made and are making higher wages than those at Homestead, which has hitherto been Union.
>
> The facilities and modes of working at Homestead Works differ so much from those of steel mills generally in Pittsburgh that a scale suitable for these is inapplicable to Homestead.
>
> A scale will be arranged which will compare favorably with that at the other works named; that is to say, the Firm intends that the men of Homestead shall make as much as the men at either Duquesne or Edgar Thomson. Owing to the great changes and improvements made in the Converting Works, Beam Mills, Open Hearth Furnaces etc., and the intended running of hot metal in the

latter, the products of the works will be greatly increased, so that at the rates per ton paid at Braddock and Duquesne, the monthly earnings of the men may be greater than hitherto. While the number of men required will, of course, be reduced, the extensions at Duquesne and Edgar Thomson as well as at Homestead will, it is hoped, enable the Firm to give profitable employment to such of its desirable employees as may temporarily be displaced. The Firm will in all cases give the preferences to such satisfactory employees.

This action is not taken in any spirit of hostility to labor organizations, but every man will see that the Firm cannot run Union and Non-Union. It must be either one or the other.[1]

Anticipating trouble when this bombshell was dropped, Carnegie sent a confidential memo to John Potter, the youthful superintendent at Homestead, urging him to '*roll a large lot of plates ahead*, which can be finished, should the works be stopped for a time'. This alluded to a major order from the United States Navy for armour plate, the only really urgent job then on hand. Satisfied that he had thought of everything, Carnegie and his wife departed for their annual sojourn in Scotland.

Frick merely filed the notice for the time being, but immediately began talks with the union and the various works committees concerning a reduction in the minimum wage scale and a reduction in the tonnage rate arising from the vastly improved output of the new machinery. On 30 May Frick told Potter to pass on to the works committees that 'these scales are in all respects the most liberal that can be offered', adding:

We do not care whether a man belongs to a union or not, nor do we wish to interfere. He may belong to as many unions or organizations as he chooses, but we think our employees at Homestead Steel Works would fare much better working under the system in vogue at Edgar Thomson and Duquesne.[2]

In fact, although Carnegie and Frick paid lip-service to the notion of good labour relations, neither of them had any liking for unions. 'For twenty-six years I had been actively in charge of the relations between ourselves and our men,' wrote Carnegie in his *Autobiography*, 'and it was the pride of my life to think how delightfully satisfactory these had been and were.'³ Both men were determined to break the power of the Amalgamated Association. With no more than 800 members among the 3800 men at Homestead, it struck Frick as unreasonable and undemocratic that the union should have such a stranglehold on wage rates and working practices, especially as they increased operating costs and reduced profits. Frick gave the union an ultimatum; 24 June was set as the deadline for acceptance or rejection of the company's offer. Meanwhile, from his Highland fastness, Carnegie kept in constant touch with Frick by cable. Telegrams sent over successive days to Frick bear this out. Thus, on 10 June, Carnegie wired:

> You have taken your stand and have nothing more to say . . . The chances are you will have to prepare for a struggle, in which case the notice should go up promptly on the morning of the 25th. Of course you will win, and win easier than you suppose, owing to the present condition of markets.

A week later he cabled, 'Perhaps if Homestead men understand that *non-acceptance means Non-Union forever*, they will accept.' On 28 June, four days after the deadline had expired, he telegraphed:

> Cables do not seem favorable to a settlement at Homestead. If these be correct, this is your chance to reorganise the whole affair, and someone over Potter should exact good reasons for employing every man. Far too many men required by Amalgamated rules.

In rejecting Frick's ultimatum the workforce fondly imagined that the company was bluffing. To be sure, they knew that Frick had resolutely broken the unions in the coke region, but they were convinced that the Little Boss would never engage in a head-on conflict with his beloved working men. They could quote Carnegie's prolific writings in *Forum* and other magazines and newspapers over recent years where he had expounded his gospel of labour. These articles gave the impression that Carnegie was in favour of unions. Had his readers closely analysed what he actually wrote, however, they would have seen that the quondam Chartist had moved a long way from the ideals held by his father and uncles. Carnegie approved of unionism, so long as it was company unionism. In other words, what he envisaged was the proper organisation of the workforce within each steel plant or factory, so that management knew exactly who they were dealing with. He had no time for national unions, representing a form of outside interference in the smooth running of his business. He would have been just as vehemently opposed to industrial cartels or investment syndicates for the same reason. Underlying much of Carnegie's voluminous writings on the subject was a spirit of paternalism which could be quite patronising at times, and found expression years later in some of the homely anecdotes in his *Autobiography*.[4]

More than two-thirds of the Homestead workforce were immigrants; a quarter of the total spoke no English. Only a quarter of the men belonged to the union. On these counts Frick was confident that the majority would give way and accept the new contract on 1 July, but just to be on the safe side he announced that he would close the works on that date and reopen them six days later with what new labour he could recruit. This roused the men; ominously they paraded outside the gates and burned effigies of Frick and Potter. When a junior executive was despatched to put out the flames and cut down the grotesque figures, the strikers turned the fire-hose on him.

Frick was taken aback by the solidity of the strike. On the fateful morning of 1 July the Homestead works were completely at a standstill. Meanwhile the Amalgamated lodges at Homestead appointed a forty-man strike committee headed by a fiery Irishman, Hugh O'Donnell, who issued a manifesto that reads more like a declaration of war:

> The committee has, after mature deliberation, decided to organize their forces on a truly military basis. The force of four thousand men has been divided into three divisions or watches; each of these divisions is to devote eight hours of the twenty-four to the task of watching the plant. The Commanders of these divisions are to have as assistants eight captains composed of one trusted man from each of the eight local lodges. These Captains will report to the Division Commanders, who in turn will receive the orders from the Advisory

Committee. During their hours of duty these Captains will have personal charge of the most important posts, i.e. the river front, the water gates and pumps, the railway stations, and the main gates of the plant. The girdle of pickets will file reports to the main headquarters every half hour, and so complete and detailed is the plan of campaign that in ten minutes' time the Committee can communicate with the men at any given point within a radius of five miles. In addition to all this, there will be held in reserve a force of 800 Slavs and Hungarians. The brigade of foreigners will be under the command of two Hungarians and two interpreters.[5]

O'Donnell was not the only man to be laying plans with military precision. On 25 June, the day after the deadline passed, Frick wrote to Robert A. Pinkerton, joint-principal in the famous detective agency which also specialised in industrial policing and protection. Previously he had sounded out Pinkerton about the possibility of getting armed men to guard the Homestead plant in the event of any strike taking a violent turn. Pinkerton had written to Frick on 22 June offering the services of his company. Now Frick responded in detail:

We will want 300 guards for service at our Homestead mills as a measure of precaution against interference with our plan to start operation of the works on July 6th, 1892.

The only trouble we anticipate is that an attempt will be made to prevent such of our men with whom we will by that time have made satisfactory arrangements from going to work, and possibly some demonstration of violence upon the part of those whose places have been filled, or most likely by an element which usually is attracted to such scenes for the purpose of stirring up trouble.

We are not desirous that the men you send shall be armed unless the occasion properly calls for such a measure later on for the protection of our employees or property. We shall wish these guards to be placed upon our property and there to remain unless called into other service by the civil authorities to meet an emergency that is not likely to arise.

These guards should be assembled at Ashtabula, Ohio, not later than the morning of July 5th, when they may be taken by train to

196

McKee's Rocks, or some other point upon the Ohio River below Pittsburgh, where they can be transferred to boats and landed within the inclosures of our premises at Homestead. We think absolute secrecy essential in the movement of these men so that no demonstration can be made while they are en route.

Specific arrangements for movement of trains and connection with boats will be made as soon as we hear from you as to the certainty of having the men at Ashtabula at the time indicated.

As soon as your men are upon the premises we will notify the Sheriff and ask that they be deputized either at once or immediately upon an outbreak of such a character as to render such a step desirable.[6]

No fewer than 3500 of the 3800 men at Homestead had downed tools and walked out. One of these was John McLuckie who was also mayor of the town of Homestead. McLuckie ensured that the town council and, indeed, the entire population of 10,000, was solidly behind the strike. O'Donnell's generalship was impeccable. In addition to the pickets that ringed the works, he had posted lookouts on the approach roads and bridges, and even had boats patrolling the Monongahela keeping a sharp watch for any untoward activity on the part of the management. The workers might have been locked out, but they, in turn, prevented anyone from approaching the works. When Frick sent a posse of deputy sheriffs to guard his property, the strikers had barred their progress, jostled and manhandled them, and even stripped one deputy of his badge. Then, for several days, there was an uneasy calm as the strikers watched and waited for Frick to make the next move. On 5 July the sheriff of Allegheny County made a second attempt to enter the plant. This time the manoeuvre was low-key, the sheriff being accompanied by only a handful of deputies. The strike committee responded by politely escorting the sheriff and his men round the perimeter. O'Donnell indicated his smartly dressed and well-disciplined pickets and asserted that they had been posted to protect the plant. Then he asked the startled sheriff to deputise his men as official law officers. Bewildered by this turn of events, the sheriff scuttled back to Pittsburgh to confer with Frick. It was at that point that Frick, having failed to get adequate protection from the proper forces of law and order, felt justified in pressing on with his plan to call in the Pinkertons. On the evening of 5 July he informed the sheriff of his intentions, and asked for a senior official to accompany the guards so that they could be deputised if the situation demanded. The sheriff accordingly detailed Colonel Joseph H. Gray, a deputy sheriff, to join the Pinkerton agents at Bellevue, but told him that he was there solely as an observer and that he must on no account deputise the Pinkertons.

During the first few days of July, however, O'Donnell and his committee made incessant attempts to contact the Little Boss. Enquiries at Cluny revealed that Mr and Mrs Carnegie were travelling in Europe and could not be contacted. In reality they had slipped away quietly to a remote hunting-lodge on the edge of Loch Rannoch, in one of the most isolated parts of the Highlands. The nearest railhead and telegraph office was thirty-five miles away. Here, Carnegie would not be disturbed. Frick, of course, had made arrangements to contact him should the occasion demand; but no one else was privy to his whereabouts.

The committee – indeed the Homestead workforce as a whole – continued naïvely to believe that the Little Boss was really on their side, if only they could get through to him and let him know what Frick was up to behind his back! Little did they realise that Carnegie had carefully planned out the strategy to smash the Amalgamated Association, and that Frick was only obeying his orders. Remembering the wisecracking little Scot and his familiar banter with them on his occasional forays on to the shop-floor, they could not imagine that he would do anything to harm them. So they watched and waited, and prayed fervently that the Little Boss would turn up at the eleventh hour and sort out the matter in his pawky fashion, joshing and joking with them as usual.

Then, about one o'clock in the morning of Wednesday, 6 July, the tugboat *Little Bill* was observed passing under the Smithfield Street Bridge in Pittsburgh, towing a couple of heavily-laden barges. Slowly the tug and its twin charges headed upstream through thick fog for the Homestead plant, some ten miles away. The hatches on the barges had been battened down and reinforced. Inside lay the three hundred special operatives despatched by Robert Pinkerton. They were equipped with food supplies, bedding and stores. Despite Frick's injunction that they should be unarmed, Robert Pinkerton

had taken the precaution of issuing side arms to his men. Some of
them, however, had equipped themselves with rifles and shotguns,
not to mention an ample supply of ammunition.

Frick planned to disembark his imported guards under cover of
darkness in the dead of night, when the strikers would all be abed
and the handful of pickets at their least vigilant. In this he had sadly
underestimated Hugh O'Donnell. Within minutes of the passage of
the barges under the Smithfield Street Bridge a warning was wired to
the strike committee's headquarters. When the barges passed the
first lock, three miles below Homestead, the first glimmer of dawn
was on the horizon but the Monongahela was still shrouded in
darkness. The tug continued on its way but as it approached the
Homestead works around 4 a.m. a siren suddenly rent the air.
Instantly a flotilla of small boats appeared out of the fog and
surrounded the tug and its barges. The men in the boats hurled
bricks and rocks at the intruders. Ominously, shots were also fired,
though no damage was done at that juncture.

The noise alerted the citizens of Homestead. Out of the houses
poured men, both strikers and supporters. Armed with rifles and
shotguns, crowbars, staves and fence-posts, they scurried along the
streets down to the riverside. Jeering and catcalling, this huge mob,
swelling by the minute, ran along the bank, keeping pace with the
slow-moving barges. By sheer weight of numbers they flattened the
fence surrounding the plant and by the time the tug reached the dock
by the pumping station over a thousand men were there to greet it.

The leading barge put out a landing-stage and Captain Heinde
made ready to lead his agents ashore. Their path was barred by an
impetuous youth who threw himself flat upon the gang-plank,
screaming, 'You will cross over my dead body!' From the crowd
behind him a shot rang out, and Heinde fell with a shattered hip.
Immediately the Pinkertons opened fire, killing two strikers and
wounding a third. This ragged volley opened the floodgates of hell.
The strikers went berserk. In the ensuing mêlée it was difficult for
O'Donnell's divisional commanders and their captains to control the
frenzied mob. Barrels of oil were tipped into the river and set alight,
with the aim of burning the barges and roasting the Pinkertons still
trapped in the holds. Mercifully the wind got up and blew the flames
away from the barges. Then a group loaded a flat-car with burning

199

rags and crates and sent it hurtling down the tracks towards the dock – only to see it leap the rails and turn over, ignominiously scattering fellow-strikers in its mad, erratic course down the slope. Mayor McLuckie had the bronze cannon, a Civil War relic, brought from its pedestal in front of the town hall and directed against the barges, but the novice artillerymen charged it with dynamite and the barrel exploded when it was ignited.

The Pinkertons were hopelessly outnumbered and every time one of them showed his face at a porthole or above the bulwark this prompted a withering fusillade. By mid-morning half a dozen agents had sustained gunshot wounds, and with great difficulty the casualties were bundled aboard the tug which took them upstream to safety. When *Little Bill* returned at midday it was enfiladed with accurate rifle fire and forced to withdraw. As the day wore on, the plight of the Pinkertons became more and more desperate. Several attempts had been made to destroy the barges with sticks of dynamite and home-made bombs. At one point a hatch was blown off, exposing the cowering agents inside, and immediately they were subjected to a hail of rifle fire. The blood lust of the mob was up, the situation made worse by a brawny striker who cried out, 'Our brothers have been shot down before our eyes by hired thugs! Men of Homestead, we must kill them! Not one must escape alive!' About four o'clock in the afternoon a white flag was tentatively pushed out of a porthole, only to be riddled with bullets. While the dynamiters continued to lob sticks at the barges, another attempt was made to pour oil on to the water and turn the Monongahela into a raging inferno.

At that point William Weihe, the burly president of the Amalgamated Association, arrived in a vain bid to calm the situation. Hundreds of strikers followed him into one of the mills where he tried to address them, but they shouted him down, with shrieks of 'Burn the boats!', 'Kill the Pinkertons!' and 'No quarter for the murderers!'.

Towards evening the Pinkertons, who had been cooped up in the blistering heat from a merciless sun as well as the fiery waters, raised a second white flag. This time O'Donnell himself came down to the embankment to parley with the panic-stricken agents. They besought his protection and a safe conduct out of town. O'Donnell assented and selected a troop of picked men to disarm the Pinkertons and escort them, two by two, to the Homestead rink. As the barges were evacuated it was found that only one agent had been killed, although eleven were wounded. As soon as the barges had been cleared, the mob stormed on to them, looting them of the bedding, foodstuffs, firearms, ammunition and personal belongings of the unfortunate Pinkertons. Then the barges themselves were stripped of every piece of equipment and finally they were set alight and cast adrift to sink in midstream.

While this orgy of destruction was taking place, the prisoners were marched through the yard and along the public road. O'Donnell's men were powerless to protect their charges from the fury of the Homestead mob. The womenfolk, in particular, behaved atrociously, attacking the 'Pinks' with stockings loaded with scrap iron. They were forced to run the terrifying gauntlet over a course of about a mile. By the time they had reached the safety provided by the sheriff and his deputies, the Pinkertons had taken a savage beating. Two were beaten to death, while a third was driven out of his mind and later committed suicide. Thirty others were maimed or severely injured and required intensive care in the Pittsburgh hospitals. None of the other men escaped without some brutal treatment, sustaining cuts and bruises from the beating, their uniforms torn to shreds. Naked and bloodied, covered in filth, these miserable wretches stumbled to safety. Ironically, a high proportion of the Pinkertons were men who had been taken on by the agency at very short notice, recruited from the ranks of the unemployed and given the blandishments of a bright blue uniform with shiny brass buttons and a dollar a day in their pockets. They had been intended for a purely passive role, that of guarding factory premises, a function which Pinkertons had been performing efficiently and honourably for four decades. Despite the length and ferocity of the battle, the casualties were surprisingly light – ten killed and fewer than seventy seriously wounded – but the incident was rapidly magnified to become the blackest day in American labour history. On numbers of casualties alone, this would be debatable; both before and after 1892 there were several ugly incidents which surpassed Homestead in the volume of blood shed. In terms of damage to property, only the two barges suffered destruction, and the Homestead plant itself was untouched.

Indeed, steel production resumed barely ten days later without a hitch. But Homestead, because of the peculiar nature of the circumstances, and the injudicious application of an illegal, armed force, came to symbolise the very worst of the war between capital and labour. It would ever afterwards besmirch the name of Pinkerton.

It took some time to restore law and order; and for several days the town of Homestead was subjected to a reign of terror. O'Donnell and his committee managed to reassert their authority, taking control of the telegraph office and the police station and rigorously censoring reports by newspapermen who flocked to the scene from every part of the country. Those whose despatches did not meet with approval were rudely bounced out of town. An emissary of Governor Robert E. Pattison, sent to observe conditions, was arrested three times and manhandled. Governor Pattison reacted by calling out the entire division of the Pennsylvania National Guard. Major-General Snowden and eight thousand guardsmen arrived on 12 July. It seemed as if there would be a second battle of Braddock's Field, but, heavily outnumbered by well-armed militia, the strikers caved in. Within a week certain departments at Homestead were back at work, mainly employing new men brought from outside. Frick had notices posted at the gates letting the strikers know that:

> Individual applications for employment at the Homestead Steel Works will be received by the General Superintendent either in person or by letter until 6 p.m. Thursday, July 21, 1892. It is our desire to retain in our service all of our old employees whose past records are satisfactory and who did not take part in the attempts which have been made to interfere with our right to manage our business. Such of our old employees as do not apply by the time above named will be considered as having no desire to re-enter our employment, and the positions which they held will be given to other men.[7]

Only a handful of the original workforce responded to this announcement, and the plant was reopened with about seven hundred imported strike-breakers, who were boycotted by the Homestead community. Towards the end of the year, as harsh winter loomed, the strikers wavered, and gradually they drifted back to work, assuming of course that they still had jobs to go to. Throughout the summer of 1892, though, the atmosphere remained tense. In the immediate aftermath of the battle, Frick was seen as the single figure of hate, the target of countless articles and editorials. Through this hurricane of criticism, Frick himself remained unperturbed, stating flatly: 'We propose to manage our own business as we think proper and right.'

While Frick was bearing the crescendo of hostility in the world's press, the question was frequently posed: 'Where does Carnegie stand?' The Little Boss was incommunicado; apparently no one knew where he was. On the whole, the world's press was at first inclined to give him the benefit of the doubt. Readers were constantly reminded that Carnegie had enunciated the eleventh commandment: 'Thou shalt not take thy neighbour's job', and had written: 'Workmen resent the employment of new men. Who can blame them?' Unbeknown to the public, however, there had been a frenzied exchange of telegrams, even as the battle raged. On first hearing of the bloody fracas, Carnegie's instinct had been to return to America immediately. This set a panic in the breasts of Phipps and Lauder, convinced that Carnegie would repudiate Frick and leave the latter with no alternative but to resign forthwith. Both men were actually in England at the time and it was they who wrote frantically to Carnegie telling him to stay put and lie low for the time being. Given this unpalatable choice, Carnegie had cabled Frick the day after the Homestead affray:

> Cable received. All anxiety gone since you stand firm. Never employ one of these rioters. Let grass grow over works. Must not fail now. You will win easily next trial only stand firm law and order wish I could support you in any form.[8]

To Lauder he wrote at greater length, critical of Frick in general for having aggravated the lockout by trying to bring in strike-breakers. Moreover, he was furious with Frick's bungling of the whole affair, writing trenchantly to cousin Dod:

> Matters at home *bad* – such a fiasco trying to send guards by Boat and then leaving space between River & fences for the men to get

opposite landing and fire. Still we must keep quiet & do all we can to support Frick & those at the Seat of War. I have been besieged by interviewing Cables from N York but have not said a word. Silence is best. We shall win, of course, but may have to shut down for months.'

A few days later a correspondent of the *New York World* managed to track the great man to his lair on wild Rannoch Moor, and in due course reported:

> Asked if he had anything to say concerning the trouble at his mills, Mr Carnegie replied:
>
> 'I have nothing whatever to say. I have given up all active control of the business and I do not care to interfere in any way with the present management's conduct of this affair.'
>
> 'But do you not still exercise a supervision of the affairs of the company?'
>
> 'I have nothing whatever to say on that point, the business management is in the hands of those who are fully competent to deal with every question that may arise.'
>
> 'Have you heard from Homestead since the riot occurred?'
>
> 'I have received several cables and among them several asking my interference with the parties in control.'
>
> 'But you must have some opinion in the matter that you are willing to express.'
>
> 'No, sir. I am not willing to express any opinion. The men have chosen their course and I am powerless to change it. The handling of the case on the part of the company has my full approval and sanction. Further than this I have no disposition to say anything.'[10]

This less-than-straightforward attitude swung public opinion behind the strikers, though Frick noted the report with approval. He informed the press that more than two hundred men had gone back to work. When asked whether it was true that there had been threats on his life, he dismissed the notion contemptuously. A reporter from the *New York Times* noted that there had been numerous statements in the press that Mr Frick was under constant guard by detectives, but discounted this by saying: 'There is no sign of a guard in his office.

He can be seen at his desk from the public hall of the building, and anybody can reach the hall by going up in the elevator.'[11]

On Saturday afternoon, 23 July, Frick was seated at his desk as usual, chatting with John Leishman, when a pale, nervous young man named Alexander Berkman, recently migrated from Lithuania, burst in and shot Frick twice with a small pistol at close range. The first bullet pierced Frick's left ear-lobe, entered his neck and penetrated to the middle of his back. The second lodged in the right side of his neck. Before Berkman could discharge a third shot, Leishman lashed out and sent the bullet wildly through the ceiling. As Berkman and Leishman wrestled on the floor, Frick grabbed his assailant by the waist. Berkman succeeded in disentangling himself and drew a sharpened file from his pocket, stabbing Frick three times, in the hip and legs. By now the commotion had roused the staff in the outer office and they rushed in to try and overpower the frenzied assassin. Finally a deputy sheriff appeared with his revolver drawn. He took aim and was about to shoot Berkman, when Frick himself ordered him to put up his weapon: 'Leave him to the law,' he said. 'But raise his head and let me see his face.' Then he realised that Berkman was chewing furiously. The deputy forced open his jaws to disgorge a capsule containing fulminate of mercury, enough explosive to have blown the room to smithereens. As this dawned on Leishman, the Scotsman collapsed in a dead faint.

Frick sat impassively in his chair while a surgeon worked feverishly and without anaesthetic to remove the bullets from his back and neck. Though covered in his own blood, Frick was impatient to return to work. As soon as his wounds had been stitched and bandaged he was back at his desk, almost as if nothing had happened. His first act was to wire his mother: 'Was shot twice but not dangerously.' In a similar cable to Carnegie, he added: 'There is no necessity for you to come home. I am still in shape to fight the battle out.' Then, while his dumbfounded doctor and office staff looked on, he coolly resumed work on the papers on his desk, checking the complex details of a loan he was negotiating, wrote several letters and finally prepared a statement for the press: 'This incident will not change the attitude of the Carnegie Steel Company toward the Amalgamated Association. I do not think I shall die, but whether I do or not, the Company will pursue the same policy and it will win.'

Then, and only then, would he consent to be taken home by ambulance. At home, he halted the stretcher carrying him past his wife's bedroom and called out, 'Don't worry, Ada, I'm all right. I may come in later to say goodnight. How is the baby?'

His third child, Henry Clay Frick Junior, had been born on the day of the Homestead battle. The baby died on 3 August.

The news of the attempted assassination convulsed America. Berkman was a Nihilist who had fled from the attention of the Tsarist police. He had no connection whatsoever with the Amalgamated Association or the Homestead strikers, but the gory details of the shooting and stabbing were all over the Monday newspapers and inevitably swung public opinion back in sympathy for Frick, especially when it was learned that he had just lost his only son. Two days after the baby's funeral, Frick was back at his desk as usual by eight o'clock. Even his bitterest critics had to admire his courage and fortitude. This sympathy was shortlived, for the very next day the same papers carried the horrific story of the young National Guardsman, Private Iams who, on hearing of the attempt, had cried out 'Hooray for the anarchist'. For this intemperate outburst he was immediately sentenced by General Snowden to be strung up by his thumbs till he lost consciousness. In truth, he was only suspended for thirty minutes; but by the time the story reached the other side of the Atlantic the British and Continental papers were claiming that Iams had been crucified. This, the ultimate atrocity, with its biblical undertones, shocked the world. More than anything else, Iams's 'martyrdom' turned world opinion against Frick, and soon also against Carnegie.

Berkman was in due course convicted of attempted murder and sentenced to twenty-one years in the state penitentiary. He served less than thirteen years before being paroled. Later he married Emma Goldman, a noted feminist anarchist, and the couple were deported from the United States as undesirable aliens on 21 December 1919. By a strange coincidence, Frick, then aged sixty, had died nineteen days earlier. Asked for a comment on this as he was being hustled aboard ship, Berkman, unrepentant to the last, observed, 'Frick left the country before I did.'

Within a day of the Braddock's Field battle Hugh O'Donnell had been seized by deputies and charged with the murder of the

Pinkerton agents. Somehow he managed to escape from custody and fled to New York where he made a beeline for the Republican party headquarters, shrewdly reasoning that his version of what had happened might be useful as a bargaining factor. Whitelaw Reid, editor and proprietor of the *New York Tribune*, who had only recently received the vice-presidential nomination at the Republican National Convention, was uneasy at the long-term implications of the Homestead troubles. The Democrats were actively wooing the labour vote and making loud noises about bloated capitalists grinding the faces of the decent working men into the mud and of Big Business flouting the law. Reid got O'Donnell to write a letter as if it were from Homestead, and then wired it to Carnegie along with his own endorsement. Sitting in Reid's office, O'Donnell wrote a carefully worded plea to the Little Boss, cleverly turning Carnegie's own words back on himself. O'Donnell was conciliatory and diplomatic, persuasive and articulate. The men would not oppose the principle of a wage scale or working hours, so long as Carnegie would recognise the union. That was all that they asked. The men deplored 'the recent sad occurrence as much as any other class of people in the whole country', and he implored Reid 'to do what you can in every honorable way to bring about an amicable settlement'.

On Reid's advice O'Donnell went back to Pittsburgh and gave himself up to the sheriff. Meanwhile Reid (who had just permitted the Typographers' Union to establish a branch in his works) tried to elicit Carnegie's whereabouts in order to send the telegram; but Frick refused to divulge this. In the end, Reid sent the cable care of the American Consul General in London, adding his personal plea to prevent a prolongation of 'this distressing and bloody strife which may spread so widely'. It was not until 28 July that Carnegie received these messages, however. His immediate reaction was to accept O'Donnell's proposal. By now Carnegie was getting a great deal of unfavourable comment in the British press and this piqued him immensely, so he wired Frick urging him to negotiate with the union. Then he had second thoughts, recalling no doubt that it was with the intention of breaking the power of the union that the dispute had been engineered in the first place.[12] The following day Frick received a second cable:

> After due consideration we have concluded Tribune too old. Probably the proposition is not worthy of consideration. Useful showing distress of Amalgamated Association. Use your own discretion about terms and starting. George Lauder, Henry Phipps, Jr., Andrew Carnegie solid. H.C. Frick forever![13]

As a result, Frick dug in his heels and refused to negotiate with the union. Gradually this hardnosed policy paid off as the strikers were forced by hardship to beg for their jobs on any terms they could get. As the limelight moved from Frick, it settled harshly on the man whose practices were so much at variance with his public statements. Even his old Civil War colleague, General Ben 'the Beast' Butler vociferously demanded Carnegie's extradition from Britain on a charge of murder. General Grosvenor of Ohio denounced him as 'the arch-sneak of this age'. He was burned in effigy in many parts of the United States and numerous social and political clubs, community organisations and even church groups passed resolutions condemning the arch-capitalist. Frick's attitude towards the unions was well known, and thus he escaped opprobrium because he had stuck to his principles. But Carnegie was perceived as a turncoat. On 12 July 1892, *The Times* of London commented magisterially:

> Mr Carnegie's position is singular. The avowed champion of trades-unions now finds himself in almost ruinous conflict with the representatives of his own views. He has probably by this time seen cause to modify his praise of unionism and the sweet reasonableness of its leaders. Or, are we to assume that this doctrine is true in Glasgow but not in the United States, or that it ceases to be applicable the moment Mr Carnegie's interests are touched?

The same newspaper also pointedly remarked that next time the Americans agitated for Home Rule in Ireland they would do well to remember Pittsburgh and put their own house in order: 'Every country, however fortunate, will always have its hands full if it attends to its own affairs.' The *Edinburgh Dispatch* smugly described Carnegie's position as 'certainly a most unenviable one', reflecting that even the bitterest labour dispute in Britain never descended to the horrific violence that was so common in America, the land of so-called 'Triumphant Democracy'. The unkindest cut of all came from the *Dunfermline Journal*, which taunted the town's most famous son by saying that 'even in the boasted land of freedom the sons of toil are still a considerable distance from an industrial millennium'. The *Sheffield Daily Telegraph* poured ridicule on Carnegie's books by suggesting that the next one should be entitled *The Tyrannies of Democracy*, and derided the 'millionaire man of the people, the great protector of tariffs and Pinkertons'.

The constrictions of the Liberal press were bad enough, but Carnegie had to put up with the scorn and ridicule of the Tory newspapers, which took their sweet revenge on a man who had so often irritated them in the past with his unsolicited advice. *St James's Gazette* neatly summed it up when it observed: 'Mr Andrew Carnegie has preached to us upon Triumphant Democracy, he has lectured us upon the rights and duties of wealth . . . It is indeed a wholesome piece of satire.' The *Financial Observer* sneered at 'this Scotch-Yankee plutocrat meandering through Scotland in a four-in-hand opening public libraries and receiving the freedom of cities while the wretched workmen who sweat themselves in order to supply him with the ways and means for his self-glorification are starving in Pittsburgh'.

In the United States the press was even more forthright and remorseless. The harshest criticism came in an editorial in the *St Louis Post-Dispatch*:

> Count no man happy until he is dead. Three months ago Andrew Carnegie was a man to be envied. Today he is an object of mingled pity and contempt. In the estimation of nine-tenths of the thinking people on both sides of the ocean he has not only given the lie to all his antecedents, but confessed himself a moral coward. One would naturally suppose that if he had a grain of consistency, not to say decency, in his composition, he would favor rather than oppose the organization of trades-unions among his own working people at Homestead. One would naturally suppose that if he had a grain of manhood, not to say courage, in his composition, he would at least have been willing to face the consequences of his inconsistency. But what does Carnegie do? Runs off to Scotland out of harm's way to await the issue of the battle he was too pusillanimous to share. A

single word from him might have saved the bloodshed – but the word was never spoken. Nor has he, from that bloody day until this, said anything except that he had 'implicit confidence in the managers of his mills'. The correspondent who finally obtained this valuable information expresses the opinion that 'Mr Carnegie has no intention of returning to America at present'. He might have added that America can well spare Mr Carnegie. Ten thousand 'Carnegie Public Libraries' would not compensate the country for the direct and indirect evils resulting from the Homestead lockout. Say what you will of Frick, he is a brave man. Say what you will of Carnegie, he is a coward. And gods and men hate cowards.[14]

Not so long before, Carnegie had been cheered by the Glasgow Trades Council. Now they passed a resolution declaring him to be 'a new Judas Iscariot', but thanked him with ironic politeness for drawing their attention to the plight of labour. The Labour Representation League of Great Britain urged all workers to refuse any future gifts from Carnegie. George Bateman, formerly a staunch ally of Carnegie in the Liberal party, now moved that he be expelled from membership. Keir Hardie, who had received £100 from Carnegie as a contribution to his campaign to win a seat in the recent Parliamentary elections, sent the money to the Homestead strike committee. While a monster petition circulated in Pittsburgh urging the local art association to reject Carnegie's offer of a public library and art gallery, the ultra-conservative Chamber of Commerce in Cleveland, Ohio, blackballed him from honorary membership. Carnegie was thus reviled in every quarter, from the extreme right to the far left. Never before had people of every political persuasion and outlook been so united in their condemnation. Carnegie was dismissed as a leper, a pariah. Those who clamoured for his extradition and trial on capital charges were matched by those who clamoured for his exclusion from re-entering the United States. It was small consolation that Carnegie should receive soothing reassurances from such eminent figures as Gladstone, Rosebery and Morley. He clutched at these platitudinous straws. To Gladstone's message of sympathy, written in September 1892, he responded in a characteristically pugnacious vein that he had written a book dealing with the burning questions of wealth, labour, short hours, trade unions and so forth: 'It is intended for my fellow workmen and I think will do good both to Capital & Labor.'[15]

The bitter memory of Homestead bedevilled American labour relations for many years; even today, more than a century after the event, the very name of Homestead is enough to remind people of the bloody struggle. It would remain at the back of Carnegie's mind for the rest of his life; although by the time he came to write his *Autobiography* it was glossed over as 'the one really serious quarrel with our workmen in our whole history'.[16] The ensuing pages of self-justification, distortion of the facts and downright untruths show how the wretched affair had become blurred in Carnegie's highly selective memory. He even convinced himself that the union officials at Homestead had sent him a telegram that read: 'Kind master, tell us what you wish us to do and we will do it for you.' Rather embarrassingly, however, he could find no record of this cable among his meticulously filed papers, and even sent Alexander Peacock off on a wild-goose chase for weeks on end trying to track it down. Peacock, of course, drew a blank; but Carnegie printed the story just the same.[17] That Carnegie could imagine for one moment that his workmen regarded him as their 'kind master' tells us a great deal about his attitudes. Some years later a European businessman visited the Homestead plant and reported that what was being trumpeted as 'Triumphant Democracy' was nothing more than 'Feudalism Restored'.

Characteristically, Carnegie filled the ensuing pages of his *Autobiography* with anecdotes dressed up to show how much sympathy and support he had received at this trying time, even from the erstwhile strikers themselves. Typical of this was the long rambling tale about John McLuckie. In his capacity as mayor of Homestead, McLuckie had ordered the arrest of the Pinkerton agents. After the battle he was indicted for riot, affray, murder and treason, and fled from Pennsylvania until the trouble blew over. The poor man lost everything, his house, his wife and his livelihood, for he was blacklisted and could not get work in any steel mill. Eventually he went to Mexico where he worked as a mine labourer and was virtually destitute when he was discovered at La Noria Verde by John C. Van Dyke of Rutgers College in 1900. Van Dyke immediately wrote to Carnegie, telling him what had befallen

McLuckie. Carnegie replied by return telling Van Dyke to 'give McLuckie all the money he wants, but don't mention my name'. Even so, McLuckie was too proud to take a handout from a fellow-American, but Van Dyke succeeded in getting him a job with the Sonora Railway, and when next Van Dyke was in Mexico he found McLuckie as superintendent of the railway workshops. He had married a Mexican girl and was prospering at last. Van Dyke then told him that the money which had been offered had been Carnegie's. McLuckie was fairly stunned, and all he could say was: 'Well, that was damned white of Andy, wasn't it?' Carnegie was extremely moved on hearing this story, and reproduced it in his *Autobiography* at great length. He would rather have McLuckie's verdict 'as a passport to Paradise than all the theological dogmas invented by man'.

Meanwhile in 1892, as Frick remained obdurate about ending the lockout, the Republican party bosses began to worry about the forthcoming election. Carnegie had heavily backed Benjamin Harrison for the presidency in 1888 and had been rewarded by protectionist legislation that had helped boost his profits. Now it was time to repay the favour. John E. Milholland, acting on behalf of the President and the Republican National Committee, went to Pittsburgh on 30 July to urge Frick to come to terms with the Amalgamated Association. With extraordinary vehemence, Frick declared: 'I am going to fight if it takes all summer and all winter and all next summer and all next winter. Yes, even if it takes my life. I will never recognize the union, never, never!' He was never known to have said so many words all at one time before.

The Republican leaders still hoped that Carnegie himself would intervene, or at least make a very generous donation to the campaign fund. When Stephen B. Elkins, then Secretary of War, told Frick a few weeks later that Carnegie had promised $50,000, Frick gave him a cheque for half that sum. Carnegie would later belatedly cable Frick saying that no more than $10,000 should be contributed. He realised that the Republicans had no hope of re-election, thanks to the festering sore of Homestead which had now become a national issue. Inevitably the Democrats made full use of the affair, lampooning Carnegie and Frick in editorials and savage cartoons, even in posters and billboards. When Grover Cleveland was elected by a landslide victory that November, Carnegie cabled Frick philosophically: 'Well we have nothing to fear and perhaps it is best. People will now think Protected Manfrs. will be attended to and quit agitating. Cleveland is a pretty good fellow. Off for Venice tomorrow.' While thousands of haggard men and their starving families faced a bleak future, and others were hounded from state to state or fled the country, the Carnegies junketed in Italy. They were basking in the late-autumn sunshine in Florence when Frick sent a telegram on 21 November saying that the strike had been officially declared at an end.

The five-month struggle had cost the company $2,000,000, the workmen $1,200,000 and the state of Pennsylvania $1,600,000. Incredibly, despite the strike, Frick informed Carnegie that net profits for 1892 would fall only $300,000 short of the $4,300,000 earned the previous year. Carnegie's telegraphic response was: 'Life worth living again! First happy morning since July – surprising how pretty Italia – congratulate all round – improve works – go ahead – clear track – tariff not in it – shake.' And from Rome a few days later, he wrote:

> I am well and able to take an interest in the wonders we see. Shall see you all early after the New Year. Think I'm about ten years older than when with you last. Europe has rung with Homestead, Homestead, until we are all sick of the name, but it is all over now – So once again happy New Year to all. I wish someone would write me about your good self. I cannot believe you can be well.
>
> Ever your pard, A.C.[18]

Those men who did manage to get their jobs back found, to their cost, that their wages were slashed. Carnegie had boasted that, with the new machinery, they would easily clear $9 a day. Instead, the rates for rollers, shearmen, tablemen and heaters were cut from an average of 9.6c to 4.4c a ton. The minimum for the sliding scale was abolished when the strike ended, and the entire sliding scale principle was abandoned in 1894. As the century drew to a close the price of steel rose by 40 per cent, but wages at the Carnegie steel plants rose by only 10 per cent. The men continued to slave a twelve-hour day, seven days a week. Meanwhile, Carnegie founded countless libraries and sometimes wondered why so few adults used these marvellous facilities.

Carnegie did not venture back to the United States until the spring of 1893, by which time he had been out of the country for almost a year. Appalled at the universal resentment and the way in which his name was reviled, he continually reiterated: 'I am not an officer of the company but only a shareholder. Four years ago I retired from active business. I am selling portions of my interests to such young men in our service as my partners find possessed of exceptional ability.' Of course, nobody believed him. Eventually he faced up to the spectre of industrial unrest and went back to Pittsburgh. Later he wrote to John Morley: 'I went to Homestead & shook hands with the old men, tears in their eyes & mine. Oh, that Homestead blunder – but it's fading as all events do & we are at work selling steel one pound for a half penny.' [19] And that said it all.

Of course there was a series of enquiries by the House and Senate into the Homestead affair, but though they were generally sympathetic to labour no firm conclusions were drawn. The Pinkertons were made the scapegoats. State after state passed laws forbidding the use of such mercenaries; but the employment of outside guards obscured the real issue. Unionism in the steel industry was effectively destroyed by the dispute, and the Amalgamated Association lost its last representation in Jones & Laughlin and Illinois Steel without any show of resistance. There would be no unions in the American steel plants again till 1937, the era of Franklin D. Roosevelt.

A bad atmosphere remained at Homestead for many years after the events of 1892. Successive writers and commentators who visited the town and its steelworks were appalled by the demoralised, cheerless spirit of a cowed, sullen, resentful workforce. But back in New York Carnegie was well satisfied when he studied the balance sheet. Homestead was busier than ever, and it had a brilliant, dynamic, vibrant young manager, Charles Michael Schwab.

NINE

The Greatest Business in the World

1893–1900

All you who follow wealth and power with unremitting ardour, O
The more in this you look for bliss, you leave your view the farther, O
Robert Burns, 'My Father Was a Farmer'

EVEN BEFORE HE LEFT SCOTLAND EARLY IN THE SPRING OF 1893, Carnegie had decided on sweeping changes at the troubled plant. To this end, he cabled Pittsburgh urging that Charles Schwab be sent back to Homestead. He had only recently been promoted to the Edgar Thomson works. 'Had he remained at the Homestead Works,' wrote Carnegie, 'in all probability no serious trouble would have arisen. Charlie liked his workmen and they liked him.'[1]

A decade earlier, Bill Jones muttered a string of obscenities when he received a communication from the Pennsylvania Railroad stating that the rails should be of a specific composition. Such terms as carbon and manganese were meaningless to him. 'Charlie,' he said in disgust to his youthful assistant, 'this damned chemistry is going to ruin the steel business yet.'

Charlie calmed him down, quietly assuring him that he would make sure that the rails were of the correct chemical composition. He had been studying metallurgy and chemistry in his spare time, and was well ahead of the game. At that time Schwab rented a room in a boarding-house, but was allowed a shack in the back yard where he had rigged up a primitive laboratory. Here he spent all of his spare time, after a busy day at the plant or giving piano and violin lessons to augment his meagre wages. Charlie's aptitude for music had been recognised at a very early age by Father Bohn, chaplain of the

Franciscan College in Loretto, and a one-time pupil of Franz Liszt. A talented pianist, Charlie also played the organ in the Loretto church, sang in the choir and helped serve Mass. He was a sweet, gentle child; perhaps too soft for his own good. His own younger brother had been quick to sense this, and bullied him mercilessly. After one severe beating, when Charlie had run off in tears to his parents, they had advised him to stand up to his little brother in future. The next time Joe chased Charlie, the latter rounded on his persecutor and timorously slapped his brother lightly on the cheek. Then, before Joe could strike back, Charlie threw his arms around him, burst into tears and cried, 'There now, Joe. I've licked you and we won't ever fight again.'

And, surprisingly enough, this tactic worked. In later life Charlie Schwab would win many a victory by similar means.

At seventeen, and in his second year at the Franciscan College, Charlie fell madly in love with an older woman. She had ambitions to go on the stage, and encouraged Charlie, who sang so sweetly and played the piano so sensitively; but old Frau Schwab soon put an end to that nonsense. The would-be actress departed the scene and Charlie went to work in A.J. Spiegelmire's general store over in Braddock. For a few months Charlie drudged morning, noon and night in the store; but there had to be more to life than bagging sugar and cutting lengths of gingham. The story of his approach to Bill Jones for a job has already been told. Working as a stake-driver for a dollar a day was not even the lowest rung on the ladder, but it was a start. Charlie took to steel like a duck to water. Not content merely with the tasks assigned to him, he explored the ET works from top to bottom, asked myriad questions, borrowed textbooks and studied far into the night. Such enthusiasm and energy were bound to pay off.

Within six months Captain Jones had taken him off the stake-driving gang and appointed him assistant engineer. At twenty he was made chief engineer and assistant superintendent. Jones was his guru, his mentor, his role model and his idol. From his books and experiments he could learn all there was to know about the physical and chemical properties of steel, but from Bill Jones he learned all there was to know about men and how to get the best out of them. Charlie had one other quality which Jones later exploited to the full – the younger man got along very well with Carnegie. Jones was often more than mildly irritated by the way the Little Boss came buzzing round the works like a busy little bee. One day he introduced Schwab to Carnegie with the blunt statement: 'Andy, here's a lad who knows more about the mill than I do.' Henceforward, whenever ticklish problems arose or confidential reports had to be delivered to headquarters, Jones detailed Charlie to deal with them. Charlie, in turn, was not slow in making the most of these opportunities.

Carnegie took to Charlie from the outset, seeing something of himself at that age in the sturdy boy with blond hair, small sparkling eyes, full, tanned cheeks, a voice of bell-like purity and a dimpled smile that lit up his broad face. His personality crackled and vibrated. He exuded self-confidence. His energy was superhuman. His mind was chain lightning, coupled with an encyclopaedic memory-bank in which were stored the minutest details of the ET works. There was also that element of tractability which Carnegie sought in his 'young geniuses', that quality which meant that he could mould them to his will and way of thinking. Being groomed for senior executive rank by Andrew Carnegie was a daunting prospect; many were called but few, in the long run, were chosen. Charlie Schwab, however, passed with flying colours. In addition to his many abilities, Charlie had a gift for flattery and a fine line in deceptive humbug which could match Carnegie's any day. He was not slow in perceiving that the Little Boss was an exceptionally vain individual; well, then, he would feed that vanity. Smiling Charlie, as he was popularly known, soon became unofficial court jester. Years of fawning paid off when, in 1887, he was appointed superintendent at Homestead on Jones's recommendation. Charlie's major contribution to the mills was the system of continuous production, from raw material to finished steel, which saved the company millions of dollars.

Jones's untimely death brought Schwab back to Braddock as general manager; three years later, after the labour uprising, he returned to Homestead. This was the greatest challenge of his young life. The plant was seething with unrest and a firm hand was needed, as well as all the skills of man-management that Charlie could muster. For three days he worked round the clock without sleep and scarce a moment to bolt his food. For two weeks he never left the plant or changed his clothes. His daemonic energy galvanised the men. His warmth, emotionally charged sincerity and eagerness, coupled with his artful application of the Jones psychology, gradually restored calm. Acts of sabotage ceased and the men eventually settled back into a routine. Homestead would never be a happy place in which to work: that was the bitter legacy of July 1892. But under Charlie Schwab the plant slowly recovered and within a year was even more profitable than before.

Thereafter Charlie's advancement was meteoric. Carnegie first made him general superintendent at both Braddock and Homestead, then showered him with bonuses and gave him a stock interest of 0.33 per cent. Charlie responded to this lavish treatment, bombarding Carnegie and Frick with ideas and suggestions. His incredible mastery of the finest detail of steelmaking, coupled with organisational genius, resulted in countless labour-saving devices and ways of streamlining production. He squeezed every ounce of efficiency out of the twin plants, cutting costs, maximising profits, even, let it be said, ensuring that the workmen got their fair share of the resulting benefits. In time, the men adored him, and Carnegie was unstinting in his praise. At the same time, Charlie was not slow in advocating massive capital outlay if it meant a considerable saving in the long-run. This was merely following the Jones principle, which had put Braddock so far ahead of its competitors, but sometimes Carnegie suspected that his impetuous young general superintendent was inclined to extravagance. On one occasion, when Schwab cabled Carnegie at Cluny Castle for permission to erect a new rolling-mill, saying, 'It will be a success. I will guarantee it,' Carnegie had drily cabled back, 'But who will guarantee the guarantor?'

On another occasion Carnegie, alarmed at the costs Schwab was incurring at Braddock, summoned him to New York. 'I am told that you are personally extravagant,' Carnegie upbraided him. 'Here you are, a poor country boy and yet you spend every cent you make.'

Charlie hotly denied the charge, and deftly turned the argument with a string of amusing anecdotes. Hours passed. Roar after roar of laughter came from Carnegie's library. Finally, George Irvine, the butler, came in quietly and said to Schwab: 'Pardon me, sir, but that cabman from the Holland House says he'd like to be paid or dismissed. He's been waiting for you since nine o'clock.'

Crestfallen, Schwab looked at Carnegie. The latter was convulsed with laughter. Anyone else would have got a severe dressing-down.[2]

On the surface things were now back to normal at Homestead when, in September 1893, James H. Smith, a Pittsburgh lawyer, called on Hilary A. Herbert, Secretary of the Navy in the new Democrat administration. Smith said that he was acting for four employees of the Homestead mills who claimed to have proof that the Carnegie Steel Company was defrauding the government. The plant had a highly lucrative contract to supply armour plate for the Navy's new Dreadnought battleships, and the men claimed that costs were being cut by the substitution of inferior materials. The men were prepared to produce this damning evidence in exchange for a percentage of the penalties collected, should the company be prosecuted. Herbert interviewed the men and was convinced that there was a *prima facie* case. After conferring with the Attorney-General, he signed an agreement to pay the informants 25 per cent of such sums as might be recovered. The charges against the company were summarised by Herbert in a report to Congress:

> These men had been gathering information for a long time and this they submitted to the department in great detail. The allegations were that the company's employees had failed to temper armor evenly and properly, had plugged and concealed blow-holes, which would probably have caused a rejection of plates by the government inspectors, and had re-treated, without the knowledge of the inspectors, plates which had been selected for ballistic test, so as to make these plates better and tougher than the group of plates represented by them.
>
> The department had naval officers employed at these works as government inspectors. It was the duty of these officers to inspect all the plates as manufactured, to select from each group when completed one plate as a representative for ballistic tests, the physical qualities of which plate were to fulfil certain requirements before it could be sent to the proving grounds. These tests were made by taking pieces from different parts of the plate, turning them down into cylinders and breaking them in machines at the works, so as to exhibit their elasticity, tensile strength and elongation. The results of these tests at the works were carefully noted, and in each case forwarded to the department. The ballistic plate so selected was forwarded to Indian Head, where two shots of

a calibre and velocity proportioned to the thickness of the plate were fired at it. If the plate withstood the prescribed test the group of plates represented by it was thereupon accepted.

The informants stated that some of these plates, after they were selected by the inspector at the works, had been secretly and without the knowledge of the government inspector, re-treated at night – that is, reannealed and retempered, so as to make them better and tougher than the group of plates of which they were supposed to be the least resisting. It was the duty of the Carnegie Steel Company also to submit to the inspectors at the works, to be forwarded to the department, statements showing the length of time each plate had been subjected to the heating and annealing processes.

It was the custom of the heaters at the Carnegie works to hand in statements showing this upon little slips of paper marked in pencil. These statements were subsequently copied and sent to the inspectors to be forwarded.

The informants stated that under the direction of Super-intendents Schwab, Corey and Cline, the statement furnished to the government inspectors were in many cases false, and they submitted many original memoranda handed in by the heaters, which showed on their face in pencil marks that they had been altered. It was from these altered and false statements, the informants said, that the statements were made up that were sent to the inspector. These original memoranda were supposed to have been destroyed, but they have been preserved and sent to the department.'

The press, still mindful of the labour troubles at Homestead, had a field day when these charges were eventually made public several months later. One cartoon in the *New York Herald* showed a kilted Carnegie cowering behind a steel plate, while a naval officer aimed a cannon labelled 'Investigation' at him. The trembling Carnegie was made to cry, 'Hold on! Don't shoot. I made this plate.'

Captain William Thomas Sampson, chief of the Bureau of Ordnance, and his experts were assigned to investigate the charges. The charge concerning blow-holes, though it subsequently received the widest publicity in the press, was easily disposed of as unimportant and irrelevant. Plugging such holes was standard practice to produce a smooth surface; besides, these bubbles had no bearing on the strength of the steel. But the charge of deliberately treating the plates selected for testing was serious enough. The company was found guilty of fraudulent practice, even though the specially treated plate was found, on examination, to be below the standard of every plate which the investigators chose at random. Sampson recommended that penalties be assessed at 15 per cent on the amount of armour delivered, together with all premiums paid by the government. This yielded damages totalling $288,000. Frick was then summoned to Washington. For moral support he brought along his aide, Millard Hunsicker, a flamboyant dandy who was leader of the sales team. Secretary Herbert confronted them with the unpalatable conclusions of Sampson's enquiry and demanded satisfaction for the damages resulting from these 'irregularities'. Frick and Hunsicker promised to investigate the charges and return a few days later with Schwab's answers. On the subsequent interview with Herbert, Frick and Hunsicker were accompanied by Carnegie himself, together with Philander C. Knox, the company's senior counsel. Their statements were turned over to Sampson who finalised his report to the Navy Board on 16 December 1893.

In this Sampson laid the blame for fraud fairly and squarely at Schwab's door, concluding with the damning statement:

> Finally, there is nothing in Mr Schwab's statements which would modify the bureau's opinion that fraud was practised against the government at the works of the Carnegie Steel Company, with the knowledge and under the direction of the superintendent and other leading men.

Four days later Carnegie marched up to the front door of the White House and had a long interview with President Grover Cleveland. At the outset of the meeting Carnegie went on the attack, handing the President a handwritten, confidential letter in which he angrily protested against having 'been accused, tried, found guilty & sentenced without ever having been heard' and ending on a highly petulant note:

> I feel like Hotspur after he had won the battle . . . Spent millions, subordinated every other Branch of our business to the Govt's needs, succeeds — & then upon the testimony of spies we are charged with irregularities & our men with fraud — I cannot stand this — even at the risk of offending the Secretary [Herbert], good honest man, but overzealous in this affair.[4]

It is not known what was said or discussed in light of this extraordinary epistle, but apparently there was a bit of wheeling and dealing; for on 8 January 1894 Carnegie surprised and angered his protectionist cronies in big business by his *volte face* on high tariffs on imports. Now, he was pleading with fellow Republicans and manufacturers in general to support Cleveland's pet project on tariff reform, the Wilson–Gorman bill. This was almost three months before the slightest hint of the armour fraud leaked out to the general public.

Two days after Carnegie's sudden conversion to tariff reform, Grover Cleveland himself wrote at length to Hilary Herbert. While he conceded that Carnegie Steel had been guilty of producing armour plate of an inferior quality, and that this constituted a default entitling the government to damages, he continued:

> It is, however, an exceedingly difficult matter to extract from the fact developed a satisfactory basis for the assessment of such damages, and, inasmuch as my decision of the matter is final, I am naturally anxious to do justice to the company and to avoid presumptions against it not fully warranted.
>
> The award of the board, although exhibiting an honest desire to meet the case fairly, does not satisfy my inclination to give the company all reasonable benefit of the indefiniteness of the proofs obtained.[5]

Furthermore, went on the President, he had signed testimony from Schwab and others that the irregularities, which began on 3 November 1892, had been eliminated on 16 September 1893. Consequently, he thought it fair to deduct 10 per cent from the price of all armour manufactured between these dates. In point of fact, 3 November 1892 was the date on which the informants discovered that irregularities were taking place, and had presumably been going on for an unspecified time prior to that, probably right back to 1889, but Cleveland calmly ignored this. The value of the 2,647,937 tons of armour produced between November 1892 and September 1893 was estimated at $1,404,894.41, 10 per cent of which was $140,484.94 (less than half the sum suggested by Samson), 'and this amount in my opinion should be forfeited by the company to the government'.

Cleveland's mild rebuke to Carnegie Steel and his bland disposal of the scandal enraged Sampson and his brother officers. It was they who made sure that word of the disgraceful affair leaked out to the newspapers in March. The world's press tarred Carnegie and Cleveland with the same brush, and in due course the luckless President was compelled to yield to a congressional committee of enquiry. In August, the committee delivered a damning report which lambasted the company and deplored the lack of legal machinery for dealing with crimes of such magnitude. The *New York Tribune* pilloried Frick and Carnegie as 'sordid and ignoble' in a devastating editorial which continued:

> In palming off those defective and inadequate armor plates upon the government they were imperilling the lives of thousands of our seamen and jeopardizing the nation's honor and welfare, but they were making money. It is an appalling conclusion. One shrinks from believing a thing so monstrous. And yet there is the record in all its hideous simplicity and clearness. It is a record rich in instances of craft and avarice, but utterly destitute in fruits of candor and good faith . . . The expenditure of money in ostentatious charity and beneficence will not excuse the shameful means by which that money was acquired. The relinquishment of a moiety of plunder does not condone the theft. Messrs. Carnegie and Frick will go down in history covered with the odium of the Cummings report.[6]

Adding injury to insult, Carnegie Steel was forced to pay out $35,121.23 to the four informants as required by law. This made them the highest paid workmen anywhere in the United States that year, although their bonus was also their severance pay.

Despite the notoriety of the case, and the much-publicised penalties, Carnegie Steel managed to cling on to their government contracts. In point of fact, rigorous testing of armour plates selected by government inspectors at random in the aftermath of the original enquiry could not fault them in any respect. When Frick sent Carnegie a report on one of these tests, the little man could not contain himself. Immediately he fired off a cable to President Cleveland complaining that $15,000 of the taxpayers' money was being wasted on a needless test: 'This is inspection run mad, caused by the hasty, overzeal of an inexperienced Secretary who charges fraud upon people (Mr Schwab & others) quite as incapable of attempting to defraud the Government as the Hon. Sec'y himself.'[7]

By the time the Cummings report had been delivered to Congress, however, Carnegie was safely back in his beloved Highland glen, fly-fishing on Loch Laggan as if nothing had happened. It was no more than a temporary hiccup. Charlie Schwab likewise weathered the storm, and continued as general superintendent of all the Carnegie steel mills. Despite penalties and opprobrium, the company turned in a profit in excess of $4,000,000 in 1894, even though the country was going through the next depression in the ten-yearly cycle. Business recovered within a year, and profits rose sharply in 1895 and in each successive year. By 1899 they had risen to a staggering $21,000,000.

There is no record that Andrew Carnegie and Cecil Rhodes ever met, though they had a great deal in common. They both made vast fortunes but sold out their principles (in Rhodes's case, the champion of the black African would sow the seeds of Apartheid). Both men developed a peculiar form of megalomania, fuelled by their limitless wealth and infinite power. In a positive, harmless way this led to good works: with Carnegie it was libraries, with Rhodes it was scholarships. But both men had ambitions to fulfil some greater destiny, if not to play God then certainly to leave an indelible mark upon the world. Rhodes dreamed of a British Africa from Cape to Cairo. Carnegie dreamed of his adopted country taking over the whole of the American continent. Both had an almost Messianic view of the Anglo-Saxon race as masters of the world. In Carnegie's case, the English-speaking peoples would some day come together in one vast republic from Canada and the United States to Australia and

New Zealand. Britain and Ireland would, naturally, be an integral part of this super-state which would one day rule the world. Just how this global government was to be achieved was never fully worked out, though Carnegie, mindful of his pacifist upbringing, saw the Anglo-Saxon alliance as an instrument of world peace, not world conquest.

To Carnegie, who spent half his year in Scotland and the other half in America, his native and adopted countries were all one to him, and he turned a blind eye to the fact that they were very different places, with very different outlooks and interests. He had forgotten how these interests had been diametrically opposed during the Civil War; now he was rudely confronted with a clash of interests which brought Britain and the United States to the brink of war. The bone of contention was in South America, where Venezuela and British Guiana wrangled over their common frontier in the gold-rich Orinoco valley. Cleveland offered to arbitrate in the dispute but Britain, acutely aware of America's pro-Venezuelan stance, declined. The refusal to accept arbitration was therefore regarded as a belligerent act: if Britain refused to disgorge territory that rightfully belonged to Venezuela, what was to stop her seizing the whole of that country? The answer was the Monroe Doctrine, named after President James Monroe who, three-quarters of a century earlier, had declared that any act of aggression by a European power against any part of the American continent would be regarded by the United States as an act of aggression against that country. In the end, however, Britain backed down, and Carnegie was not forced to choose between the two countries he loved so passionately. The matter was put to arbitration and honour was satisfied on all sides, not least on Carnegie's. His attitude to the affair was summed up in an article with the provocative title 'Does America Hate England?', published in the *Contemporary Review* in the autumn of 1897. Carnegie concluded magnanimously that the answer was 'no', even though 'there was still the old sore, called Canada, and those new smarting irritants called imperial preferential tariffs'. These were nothing more than surface bruises which concealed 'the genuine respect, admiration and affection for the old home. The pride of race is always there at the bottom.' Thus Anglo-American relations were tied up in this sentimental, simplistic fashion.

Queen Victoria celebrated her Diamond Jubilee on 22 June 1897 and Carnegie, just as he had done at her Golden Jubilee, was one of the countless thousands who witnessed the pomp and pageantry in the streets of London. The old Radical Chartist and rabid republican was moved by the splendour of the occasion and emotionally described the event in the *North American Review*, pulling out every stop in his fulsome praise of the little old widow of Windsor:

> . . . prudence, patience and rare judgment have made of this good, able, energetic, managing, and very wise woman a saint, whom her subjects are as little capable and as little disposed to estimate critically as the American schoolboy can imagine or is disposed to imagine, Washington as possessed of human frailties. Washington, Tell, Wallace, Bruce, Lincoln, Queen Victoria or Margaret are the stuff of which heroes or saints are made . . . When a nation ceases to create ideals its glorious days are past. Fortunately for the world, both the republic and the monarchy have the future before them.[8]

This reconciliation of two opposing political philosophies would have been unthinkable when Carnegie was an angry young man; but now, at sixty-one, he was in mellow mood, at peace with the world. The previous year Cleveland and the Democrats had been ousted, and conservative Republicanism, epitomised by the stout, pompous figure of William McKinley, had been restored to power. Carnegie's sense of well-being was intensified by the fact that, after ten years of marriage, he had become a father. At the age of thirty-eight, Louise had given birth to a daughter. The baby, born on 30 March 1897, was christened Margaret after Carnegie's sainted mother. When he heard that the tenants of the Cluny estate had lit bonfires on nine hilltops in celebration, he was suitably touched; but paradoxically the birth was the cause of Carnegie severing his long connection with Cluny Castle. On several occasions he had tried to persuade Cluny Macpherson to sell the castle, but Macpherson, impoverished though he might be, refused to part with his patrimony. The birth of little Margaret now impelled Carnegie to seek out a Scottish home that he could truly call his own. According to his *Autobiography*, it was Louise who took the initiative, saying, shortly after the baby's birth: 'We must get a summer home since this little one has been given us. We cannot rent one and be obliged to go in and out at a certain date. It should be our home . . . I make only one condition. It must be in the Highlands of Scotland."[9]

That summer would be their last at Cluny Castle. With characteristic energy Carnegie now cast around for a place of his own and notified all his friends and estate agents in Scotland. In the end it was Hew Morrison, head of the Carnegie Library in Edinburgh, a distant cousin and unofficially Carnegie's man of affairs in Scotland, who found the ideal spot. Skibo in Sutherland, nestling in the slopes on the northern side of the Dornoch Firth, had once been the temporal estate of the Bishops of Caithness. The medieval castle was no more than a picturesque ruin, but it afforded a panoramic view over the firth to the North Sea beyond, and due south across the windswept moors of Easter Ross. It was magnificent, and Carnegie immediately fell in love with the place. The south-facing Skibo enjoyed a surprisingly mild climate for a situation so far north. Carnegie bought the estate from George Dempster for £85,000 and immediately made plans for a baronial mansion on the grand scale. In due course a splendid castle would rise from the ruins of the old, and from its battlements would fly a banner with a strange device. On one side it showed the Union Jack, but on the other was the Stars and Stripes. The two flags had been sewn back to back.

Back in Pittsburgh Frick was still in overall command. In the space of only five years he would transform Carnegie Steel into the largest company in the world. When he encountered problems with the several railroad companies that served the scattered plants and demanded increased haulage rates, Frick solved the problem by building his own private railway connecting the mills and mines, and then demanding – and getting – a rebate of 25c a ton from the giant Pennsylvania Railroad. With the Carnegie contract worth 16,000,000 tons of freight a year, the mighty Pennsylvania was in no position to argue.

Frick's coke plant grew enormously in the same period, rising from 5000 coke ovens to over 12,000. He also acquired vast deposits of high-grade Bessemer ore, acting in concert with Henry W. Oliver – the Harry Oliver who had once sat on the telegraph messengers' bench with skinny little Andy Carnegie. In the intervening years Oliver had established a mining company at Mesabi in Minnesota. Squeezed by the panic of 1893, however, he needed an urgent cash injection to carry on, and offered Carnegie Steel a half interest in exchange for $500,000 for further development. Interestingly, Carnegie opposed this deal, writing to Frick from Rannoch Lodge:

> Oliver's ore bargain is just like him – nothing in it. If there is any department of business which offers no inducement, it is ore. It never has been very profitable, and the Mesabi is not the last great deposit that Lake Superior is to reveal.[10]

Frick pointed out that they were going to get a half interest in Oliver's company by making a loan, not an investment. With the support of the other partners, Frick pushed through this deal soon after the Homestead strike was settled. Carnegie, who knew Oliver's mercurial temperament only too well, remained unhappy with this deal, and throughout 1893 and 1894 continually bombarded Frick with letters and memoranda which articulated his grumbles. Gloomily he prophesied that no good would come of the deal. Only when he discovered that his arch-rival in plutocracy, John D. Rockefeller, had been investing heavily in the ore region of Minnesota, did Carnegie begin to sit up and take notice. Perhaps Rockefeller intended to do for iron what he had done for oil – create a giant trust in one of America's basic industries. In confidential correspondence Carnegie habitually referred to his *bête noire* as 'Reckafellow', and in one letter rubbished his business acumen:

> I don't think Standard people will succeed in making ore a monopoly like oil, they have failed in every new venture and Rockefeller's reputation now is one of the poorest investors in the world. His railroads are almost worthless.[11]

The rest of the business community sat back and watched with bated breath as the two titans of industry squared up to each other. While Carnegie had continual misgivings about the ore venture, Frick and Oliver began manoeuvring with Rockefeller. In 1896 they arranged to lease the Rockefeller mines on a royalty basis of 25c a ton, well below the market price, in exchange for an agreement to ship 1,200,000 tons a year over Rockefeller rail and steamer routes to the ports on Lake Erie at $1.45 a ton. Frick estimated that this deal alone would save at least $500,000 a year. Oliver went to New York to discuss the proposal with Carnegie who, understandably, was less than happy at the idea. Later Carnegie wrote grudgingly to Frick:

> Oliver called today. He has got matters really in good shape – so HE SAYS. Hope he will have final papers to submit when you come. He may be too sanguine about closing on basis reported.

Shrewdly judging that Oliver was undercapitalised, Carnegie demanded of his old chum a five-sixths interest in the Oliver Mining Company. Oliver had no option but to give way. It would turn out one of the best bargains Carnegie had ever made. Keen competition forced down the freight rates on Lake Erie and triggered a panic among the stockholders of rival mining companies. Oliver and Frick seized the opportunity to gain options on the stock of the three main mining concerns. Oliver proved his worth by tramping energetically round the Minnesota mining interests, and sewed up four hundred options. Fearing resistance from the Little Boss, Frick crossed the Atlantic and trekked all the way to Cluny Castle that eventful summer of 1897 to lay all the facts and figures before Carnegie. Frick was chagrined when Carnegie swept the papers aside and rejected the deal, chiding Frick for his unwonted enthusiasm. Frick listened impassively, his inscrutable features concealing his anger, and swept out without a word. Back in America, he told Oliver what had happened. Oliver immediately wired Carnegie at Laggan Lodge imploring him to reconsider. There would never be another opportunity to secure options at such advantageous terms. And, he concluded: 'I will guarantee, counting the surplus they have in their treasury, to return in profits every dollar we invest in two years. Do not allow my hard summer's work to go for naught.' Where Frick's cold logic had left Carnegie unmoved, this *cri de coeur* from Oliver did the trick. Without offering any explanation, Carnegie reversed his decision, and cabled the go-ahead within hours of the deadline for accepting the options. As Oliver had predicted, within two years the Carnegie–Oliver alliance owned two-thirds of the finest grade

Bessemer ore deposit on earth. Without batting an eyelid, or remembering his recent confrontation, Carnegie wrote to Frick on 9 October 1897: 'I am happy that we are now secure in our ore supply; it was the only element needed to give us an impregnable position.'

To facilitate the transportation from mines to furnaces, Carnegie now purchased a derelict railway called the Pittsburgh, Shenango & Lake Erie Railroad. Soon the two hundred miles of track had been relaid and the rolling-stock modernised. In just over twelve months this outfit was relaunched as the Pittsburgh, Bessemer & Lake Erie Railroad, and shortly thereafter enormous trains of thirty-five freight trucks were making the daily haul from the mines to the blast furnaces. An exclusive communications link a thousand miles in length was completed by the purchase for the Oliver Mining Company of six large ore-carrying steamers.

Now Carnegie controlled every aspect of steel, from the raw materials to the finished product, as well as the transportation of ores and the movement of the marketable commodity. Carnegie now had in his pocket the means of production and distribution, and every cent of profit from the ore in the ground to the finished rail or girder stayed within the company of which he was by far the largest shareholder. This great feudal empire within a republic depended on the will of one man, more autocratic than the Tsar of All the Russias. As his wealth and power increased, Carnegie became more arrogant, more jealous to the point of paranoia. Fearing that Frick was getting above himself, for example, Carnegie began advancing his 'bright young geniuses' at Frick's expense. The die was cast when, towards the end of 1897, he made Charlie Schwab president of the company so that he could 'share some of Mr Frick's burdens'. Over the preceding four years Smiling Charlie was permitted to increase his interest from 0.33 per cent to 6 per cent. At the same time Frick, of his own volition, had reduced his interest from 11 to 6 per cent, bluntly telling the Little Boss that he had no desire to be in his debt. Frick continued to dominate the Frick Coke Company but increasingly he was becoming drawn into the orbit of that rising star in politics and high finance, Andrew W. Mellon.

Gradually, almost imperceptibly, a rift developed between Carnegie and Frick. Only icy self-interest had frozen over a decade of fundamental differences in temperament. As Frick began to cut a figure for himself in the financial, social and cultural world, Carnegie was increasingly irritated at his partner's growing prestige. Frick, on the other hand, chafed against the little man's delusions of empire. Sooner or later, the trouble between them was going to erupt.

Although memoranda, telegrams and letters came from New York or Scotland at frequent intervals, Pittsburgh saw nothing of the Little Boss for almost a year. For much of that period Carnegie was distracted by matters far above and beyond the narrow world of steelmaking. At first he was horrified when his beloved United States embarked on war with Spain over Cuba, but he soon swallowed his pacifist scruples and even bombarded General Nelson Miles, commander of the American expeditionary force, with tactical advice. In his own autobiography Miles acknowledged the sound advice he had received from Carnegie and which he had laid before President McKinley. As a result of Carnegie urging that Puerto Rico should be attacked and taken on account of its strategic value, McKinley authorised the invasion of that island.[12] To Carnegie, the Spanish-American War was fought that Cuba might be free from domination by a decadent European power. He was less than happy when America seized not only Cuba and Puerto Rico but the Philippine Islands, half a world away in the western Pacific. In the same year the United States annexed Hawaii, whose ancient tribal kingdom had been overthrown by a combination of American missionaries and business interests some five years previously. Now, it seemed, the United States was bent on pursuing an imperial policy, just like Britain and France. Interestingly, Frick was far more vehemently opposed to America's foreign adventures than Carnegie, reasoning that war was bad for business. Fortunately, Frick was soon proved wrong – and business, stimulated by the war and colonial expansion, boomed as never before.

Carnegie's swallowed scruples became easier to digest when President McKinley let it be known that he had no intention of holding on to Cuba. The war had been fought to make the island free and, indeed, in 1902 the American military administration handed over the nominal reins of power to the Cuban government. The war in the Caribbean and the Pacific, however, was soon followed by the outbreak of war in South Africa, as the imperial might of Britain and her colonies took on Paul Kruger and the Boers. The British had been taken by surprise and suffered a series of humiliating defeats; but after these initial reverses the resources of the British Empire swung into motion, and in the year that Cuba won her freedom the Boers finally surrendered. The South African War was at its height when trouble broke out in another quarter, which would witness the strange sight of British and American troops fighting on the same side for the first time since the reign of King George III. Rebellion in China swiftly sucked in the forces of a dozen nations including Germany, Russia and Japan. Appalled at the way the world was going, Carnegie began giving much more serious thought to his aim of securing world peace. It was Tsar Nicholas II, apprehensive at the arms race between Britain and Germany which had been developing over the previous four years, who proposed a Peace Conference at The Hague in 1899. From the very moment that this summit was proposed, Carnegie had been a vociferous enthusiast for some permanent international body that would prevent future wars by forcing the contending powers to submit to arbitration. In the spirit of putting his money where his mouth was, Carnegie was urged by the Russian diplomat of Dutch origins, Frederic de Martens, that he could confer no greater benefit on mankind than by erecting a great Peace Palace at The Hague. 'This will render the man who makes the gift a benefactor to every nation and all mankind – acknowledged as such through all time'.[13]

When this notion had first been tentatively floated by Frederick Holls, secretary of the American delegation to the Peace Conference, in November 1899, Carnegie was 'pleasant but not responsive', but over the ensuing months the idea grew in his mind.

In the intervening weeks business matters moved at a cracking pace. In November Carnegie attended a board meeting of Carnegie Steel in Pittsburgh. It was his first visit to his fiefdom in over a year, but he was newly returned from his splendid new demesne on the Dornoch Firth and was in an unusually affable and expansive mood. He had spent the summer supervising the finishing touches to his great castle, landscaping the grounds, even creating a huge waterfall for Lou's delectation, and cruising the calm waters of the firth in his spanking new steam yacht *Sea Breeze*. The tenants of the Skibo estate were, for the most part, poor crofters barely eking out a subsistence on the sour Sutherland moors. They had been accustomed to generations of rackrenting and absentee landlords who took far more than they gave back. The 'wee lairdie' from America was a totally new experience, providing much-needed work for all on his building and landscaping projects and injecting capital back into a generally impoverished region. At long last things were beginning to look up, and it was with genuine warmth for their new master that the tenantry dutifully doffed their bonnets and tugged their forelocks. They marvelled at his waterfall and his fishponds, just as they marvelled at the magnificent organ installed in the castle and the Hungarian virtuoso hired to play it for the entertainment of the house guests.

As he boarded the luxury liner *Oceanic* for the voyage back to New York that autumn, Carnegie had granted an interview to a group of British journalists, and told them solemnly of his Golden Rule of Business:

> Gentlemen, my partners are not only partners but a band of devoted friends who never had a difference. I have never had to exercise my power and of this I am very proud. Nothing is done without a unanimous vote and I am not even a manager or director. The way my young partners differed from me and beat me many a time was delightful to behold. I never enjoyed anything more than to get a sound thrashing at the hands of these young geniuses. No man will make a great business who wants to do it all himself, or to get all the credit for doing it. That spirit is fatal and sure proof of a small mind.[14]

He made no mention of a matter that was worrying and annoying him: Frick was making trouble over the price Carnegie Steel was having to pay for coke from the Frick Coke Company. Frick had promised to sell coke at $1.35 a ton, but balked at signing a formal contract because Carnegie had informed him verbally that he would expect coke cheaper than that if the market dropped. So they had parted company on bad terms, and now Carnegie feared that coke might rise as high as $3.50 a ton, and he was cursing that he had not pinned Frick to a written contract at $1.35. How could he have known that coke was going to rise in price? Knowing what a stickler Frick was for his rights, Carnegie feared trouble when he disembarked. As the *Oceanic* sped westwards, he had ample time to muse over his predicament. Niggling all the time was the feeling that Frick was getting far too big for his boots. Recently he had been making statements to the press as if he owned Carnegie Steel. Even worse, the public was beginning to believe that he did.

By the time he got to New York, Carnegie was determined on a showdown with Frick. The opportunity came when the board meeting took place on 17 November. During the meeting itself Carnegie sat quietly on the sidelines, watching the chairman run through the agenda with the precision of a parade-ground martinet. Even when it was proposed, and unanimously agreed, that the company purchase a large tract of land on the Monongahela at $3500 an acre from the owner, Henry Clay Frick, Carnegie assented without a murmur. At the conclusion of the meeting he chatted affably with Frick, Schwab and the rest of 'his boys'; but that afternoon he dropped in on John Walker and other old associates. To several of them he made the quip that Frick seemed to be making 'a pretty good thing' out of the land deal. To Walker he cracked, 'Frick always manages to look out for Number One first, doesn't he?' Then he contrasted this with Frick's refusal to sell coke to the company at $1.35. 'Pretty snide, I call it.'

'Well,' replied Walker bluntly, 'it would be a gift at that price.'

Walker was a close friend of Frick and had a large interest in the coke company. Not surprisingly, he had voted with Frick to ignore the unsigned coke contract. As Carnegie had intended, of course, Walker lost no time in relaying the jibes of the Little Boss. Exactly what he had hoped to gain by this manoeuvre is hard to determine, but it soon became apparent that he had misjudged Frick's combativeness. At the next board meeting (Carnegie being absent), on 20 November, Frick immediately went on the offensive. It was duly minuted that he threw down the gauntlet in no uncertain terms, reading out a carefully prepared statement:

> Mr Carnegie stated, I am told, while here that he had purchased that land from me above Peter's Creek; that he had agreed to pay market price, although he had his doubts as to whether I had any

right, while Chairman of the Board of Managers of the Carnegie Steel Company, to make such a purchase. He knows how I became interested in that land, because I told him so in your presence, the other day. Why was he not manly enough to say to my face what he had said behind my back? He knew he had no right to say what he did. Now before the Steel Company becomes the owner of that land, he must apologize for that statement.

I learn that Mr Carnegie while here, stated that I showed cowardice in not bringing up the question of the price of coke as between Steel and Coke Companies. It was not my business to bring that question up. He is in possession of the Minutes of the Board of Directors of the Frick Coke Company, giving their views of the attempt, on his part, to force them to take practically cost for their coke.

It is the business of the Presidents of the two Companies to make contracts of all kinds. Mr Carnegie has no authority to make a contract that would bind this Company. Neither have I any authority to make any contract that would bind the Frick Coke Company, and, at any rate why should he, whose interest is larger in Steel than it is in Coke, insist on fixing a price which the Steel Company should pay for their coke?

The Frick Coke Company has always been used as a convenience. The records will show that its credit has always been largely used for the Steel Company, and is today, to the extent of at least $6,000,000. The value of our coke properties, for over a year, has been, at every opportunity, depreciated by Mr Carnegie and Mr Lauder, and I submit that it is not unreasonable that I have considerable feeling on this subject.

He also threatened, I am told, while here, that, if a low price did not prevail, or something was not done, he would buy twenty thousand acres of Washington Run coal and build coke ovens. That is to say, he threatened, if the minority stockholders would not give their share of the coke to the Steel Company at about cost, he would attempt to ruin them . . .

Harmony is so essential for the success of any organization that I have stood a great many insults from Mr Carnegie in the past, but I will submit to no further insults in the future.

There are many other matters I might refer to, but I have no desire to quarrel with him, or to raise trouble in the organization, but, in justice to myself, I could not at this time, say less than I have.[15]

This statement, probably the longest utterance the normally monosyllabic Frick ever made, was greeted with stunned silence. For several days Charlie Schwab and the other partners tried to talk Frick into toning down, if not fully withdrawing, his accusatory statement before a copy was sent to the Little Boss, but Frick was adamant. 'I have stood enough,' he said. 'Mr Carnegie can do as he pleases. I am willing to resign at any time.' Eventually, however, he agreed to let Schwab and Henry Phipps go in person to New York to mediate. Meanwhile, a copy of this minute was despatched to Carnegie. The silence from New York was deafening. Carnegie made no direct reply and, of course, did not tender the apology that Frick demanded. When Schwab and Phipps reached New York they found Carnegie in a towering rage. He ranted and raved at the luckless emissaries; in particular he virtually accused Schwab of betraying him, and reminded the younger man that he had 'made' him. As he stood there in Carnegie's library, Schwab could not help comparing this unfair treatment with the way Frick had stood by him loyally during the armour-plate scandal, and had, on more than one occasion, saved him from humiliation at the hands of the mercurial little bully now before him. Charlie stood his ground, and let Carnegie go berserk. Eventually the Little Boss ran out of steam, and Schwab tried to placate him, summoning up all the fawning sycophancy he could muster. But even his soothing flattery failed to move the implacable tycoon. Schwab's eye never flickered as he gazed impassively over the silvery head at the marble open book carved above the mantelpiece with its solemn words: 'He that cannot reason is a fool. He that will not a bigot. He that dare not a slave', while Carnegie slavered, 'Frick must resign! If he doesn't get out voluntarily, I'll kick him out!'

In despair Charlie returned to Pittsburgh. The following day, Sunday, 3 December, he wrestled with his conscience. His better nature urged him to side with Frick against the little tyrant; but he was hardheaded enough to know that the wrong move at this delicate juncture would be the end of his career. At thirty-eight, the president of Carnegie Steel had far too much to lose: wealth, power, position, social standing, prestige. That evening he wrote a long letter to Frick which was despatched immediately by special messenger. In it, he warned Frick that Carnegie was on his way to Pittsburgh and would be there in the morning. He dismally reviewed the situation and came to the conclusion that the partners would close ranks behind the majority stockholder. 'Under these circumstances there is nothing left for us to do than to obey, although the situation the Board is thus placed in is most embarrassing.' Finally Charlie appealed to Frick 'to sacrifice considerably if necessary to avert this crisis'. And he ended on a poignant note that showed the turmoil of his soul:

> Personally my position is most embarrassing as you well know. My long association with you and your kindly and generous treatment of me makes it very hard to act as I shall be obliged to do. But I cannot possibly see any good to you or anyone else by doing otherwise. It would probably ruin me and not help you. Of this as above stated I am well advised by one most friendly to you. I beg of you for myself and for all the Junior Partners, to avoid putting me in this awkward position, if possible and consistent.[16]

Carnegie arrived on 4 December and immediately called a special board meeting at which he forced the managers to sign a demand for Frick's resignation. Frick replied the following day in a one-sentence letter: 'Gentlemen, I beg to present my resignation as a member of your Board.' Carnegie, however, was not content to leave matters at that. On 8 January 1900 he barged into Frick's office unannounced and came straight to the point. Ignoring the personal issues between them as if nothing had happened, he proposed a two-year coke contract at $1.35. Frick, who had only 23 per cent of the company that bore his name, was powerless to object, but tried to parley, offering to buy Carnegie's interest in Frick Coke, in exchange for Frick's interest in Carnegie Steel. Carnegie refused, saying that the 'company' would take over his interests anyway.

At this, the normally impassive Frick exploded. Jumping to his feet, eyes ablaze, he lunged at the little demon, but Carnegie was too quick for him and scurried off as fast as his short legs would carry him. Frick charged after him, bellowing and shaking his fists. Then the deposed chairman shrugged his shoulders, returned to his office for his coat and hat, and went off to lunch. During the nineteen years of life remaining to them both, Frick and Carnegie never spoke to each other again. The rift was total.

Carnegie made good his threat when he took immediate steps to oust Frick from both the coke and steel companies. Anyone who was well disposed towards Frick, as Schwab had surmised, was removed from the boards of the two companies. The new men in Frick Coke then rubber-stamped the $1.35 contract. By means of the Iron Clad agreement, Carnegie ejected Frick from Carnegie Steel, the company attempting to acquire Frick's stock at the book value of $4,900,000 when, in fact, the annual income from this stock was in excess of that sum. To their everlasting credit, however, three of the partners refused to sign Carnegie's resolution (which could only be activated if three-quarters of the stockholders agreed). Francis Lovejoy, the company secretary, was one of the dissenters. Henry Curry was another. When Carnegie went to see him, Curry was on his deathbed but he still refused to sign, saying, 'Mr Frick is my friend.'

'But am I not also your friend?' asked Carnegie.

'Yes,' was the feeble response, 'but Mr Frick has never humiliated me.'

The last person Carnegie expected to refuse was Henry Phipps, the man who had engineered the Iron Clad agreement in the first place. Carnegie was astounded and enraged at Phipps, the cobbler's son from Slabtown whom he had known – and dominated – all their adult life. But Phipps recognised that if Carnegie were allowed to treat Frick in this despicable manner, none of the partners was safe from the tiny predator. Phipps also had good reason to feel sore at his old friend. The previous year Carnegie had decided to sell his majority interests in the steel and coke companies for $157,950,000 and had granted an option to a syndicate led by Judge W.H. Moore of Chicago. Frick and Phipps had joined in taking the option. The deal fell through, however, and Carnegie had pocketed a forfeit of $1,170,000. Part of the option sum had been put up by Frick and Phipps on Carnegie's assurance that this was a mere formality and that they would not suffer any loss.

In spite of the defection of Phipps, Lovejoy and Curry, Carnegie still had the necessary majority to oust Frick and buy him out at a fraction of the true worth of his stock. Notice to this effect was served on Frick on 15 January 1900. Frick was given exactly fifteen days to sell his interest. He fought back; both he and Phipps immediately sent letters to Carnegie protesting that the value of the Steel Company's properties was considerably in excess of the $250,000,000 which Carnegie had placed on it. It was left to Charlie Schwab to wield the hatchet. On 1 February he wrote formally to Frick informing him that: 'I have today acting as your Attorney in Fact executed and delivered to The Carnegie Steel Company, Limited, a transfer of your interest in the capital of said Company.'

Thus were drawn the battlelines for the most remarkable litigation of its kind ever instituted in America.

In March Frick filed an equity suit. Documents produced at the preliminary proceedings made unedifying reading, as the two captains of industry mocked and derided each other in public like a pair of enraged fishwives. Frick called Carnegie a fraud and a cheat, animated by personal hatred, while Carnegie swore that Frick was 'a man of ungovernable temper'. Too late, Carnegie realised what he had unleashed. As part of the proceedings Frick was required to swear an affidavit estimating the true value of the company. The world gasped when it was revealed that the value of Carnegie Steel, at the close of business on 31 December 1899, was a quarter of a billion dollars – ten times its capitalisation.

The world's press had a jamboree with sensational reports of this giant steel trust, the true extent of which could only have been guessed at. The vast army of workmen at Braddock and Homestead read their newspapers and muttered imprecations against the Little Boss who had forced them to work a twelve-hour shift in hellish conditions in order to pile up these unshared riches. The bosses of rival steel firms, like Bethlehem, chuckled over Carnegie's embarrassment. Even John D. Rockefeller, whose Standard Oil Company had recently been in the spotlight for its attempts to create a monopoly, heaved a sigh of relief and indulged in *Schadenfreude* at the daily revelations. Morale at Carnegie Steel sank to an all-time low and Carnegie, subjected to the jibes and innuendos of the press for the third time in a decade, gnashed his teeth. This time he would not escape to his beloved Skibo so easily.

Frick's trump card was a memorandum in Schwab's fair hand, prepared for a prospectus in 1899 when the Moore–Frick–Phipps

Syndicate was being mooted. In this Smiling Charlie had boasted that Carnegie Steel could sell steel rails abroad at $19, netting a profit of $16 – 'nearly as good as home business has been'. When word got out that Carnegie Steel was making such obscene profits, the whole of American industry howled for Carnegie's blood. Once more he had united every section of the community against him. Realising that the fight was hopeless, Carnegie caved in at once. Hastily he summoned Phipps and begged him to make peace. Frick was a realist and was astute enough to appreciate that prolonged litigation would do no one any good. He proposed a merger of the coke and steel companies and appointed Francis Lovejoy as his representative to decide on a basis of proper valuation.

On St Patrick's Day, 17 March 1900, Phipps, Schwab and Lovejoy met at Carnegie's home. They could not help noticing that the Little Boss was not his usual fiery, pugnacious self. The fight seemed to have gone out of him and he suddenly looked much older than his sixty-four years. 'Boys,' he said wearily, 'work the thing out your own way. I only want what is fair.' Four days later, the partners met in full at Atlantic City, New Jersey. The compromise was, in effect, a total victory for Frick. The two firms were consolidated into a mammoth organisation to be called the Carnegie Company, with an issue of $160,000,000 bonds and $160,000,000 stock, a total capitalisation of $320,000,000. The three principal partners were Andrew Carnegie, with $86,382,000 in stock and $88,147,000 in bonds, Henry Phipps with $17,227,000 in stock and $17,577,000 in bonds, and Henry C. Frick, with $15,484,000 in stock and $15,800,000 in bonds. The rest went to sixty junior partners and the heirs of deceased members of the combined firms. George Lauder got $5,482,000 in stock and $5,593,000 in bonds, while Charlie Schwab got $3,980,000 in stock and $4,061,000 in bonds. The interests of the late Tom Carnegie netted for his widow $2,459,000 in stock and $2,510,000 in bonds.

Schwab celebrated the Atlantic City Compromise with a lavish banquet in Philadelphia. Frick celebrated by sending a terse telegram to a friend:

> Settlement made. I got what is due me. All well. I, of course, have not met this man Carnegie and never expect nor want to. It is not my intention to be officially connected with the reorganized concern.[17]

The Carnegie Steel Company's last month in operations (March 1900) netted a profit of over $5,000,000, an annual rate of $61,000,000. Though keeping well clear of the new company, Frick got his revenge on Charlie Schwab whom he felt had betrayed him at a crucial moment. In July 1900 he sent his last message to Carnegie at Skibo, drawing attention to prodigal mismanagement by President Schwab. He itemised five-year coal contracts 50 per cent above the lowest market price, and 6 per cent higher than even the smallest competitor was paying. He asserted that 'scrap was unloaded on you at fancy prices':

> Look into these and other matters yourself. Do not let them hide things from you. You cannot trust many by whom you are surrounded to give you facts. You need commercial rather than professional ability to cope with concerns managed by brainy and honest men trained to the business. You are being outgeneralled all along the line, and your management of the Company has already become the subject of jest.
>
> Frick

Though he never responded to that message, it doubtless helped Carnegie to make up his mind. The time had now come for him to sell out.

TEN

Spreading the Largesse

1901–10

Ev'n Avarice would deny
His worshipp'd deity,
And feel thro every being love's raptures roll!
Robert Burns, 'Mark Yonder Pomp'

IN 1900 ANDREW CARNEGIE PRODUCED HIS FOURTH BOOK, ENTITLED *The Gospel of Wealth*. It was a compilation of articles which he had published between 1886 and 1899 in the *Youth's Companion*, the *Century Magazine*, the *North American Review*, the *Forum*, the *Contemporary Review*, the *Fortnightly Review*, the *Nineteenth Century* and the *Scottish Leader*. The title itself was taken from an article originally under the simple name of 'Wealth' in the *North American Review* which Gladstone had asked Carnegie to republish in Britain. In due course it appeared in the *Pall Mall Budget* retitled 'The Gospel of Wealth'. After this book appeared Carnegie states that 'it was inevitable that I should live up to its teachings by ceasing to struggle for more wealth. I resolved to stop accumulating and begin the infinitely more serious and difficult task of wise distribution'.[1]

Thus, in his customary simplistic fashion, Carnegie explained away the dramatic change in direction which would govern the last years of his life. It was not the publication of the book (which, in the circumstances, must have raised many a chuckle at the unconscious ironies revealed therein) but the view from the brink of a yawning chasm that made Carnegie shrink back and pause for thought. The long weeks of bitter dispute, so thoroughly ventilated in the world's press, had terrified Carnegie's partners and associates, and the

242

Atlantic City Compromise must have brought immense sighs of relief all round. The settlement was, indeed, a compromise, for both protagonists could regard it as a personal triumph. Frick had not only retained his interest, but added to it beyond his wildest dreams. Carnegie had swallowed the coke company, so there would be no more haggling over prices, and Frick had been permanently exiled from the boardroom. Admittedly Carnegie, who had strenuously resisted large capitalisation, now found himself the largest shareholder in the largest capitalised company the world had ever seen – with three times the capitalisation of its nearest rival, Rockefeller's Standard Oil. But with his usual tenacity the Scot had succeeded in keeping that vast capital entirely within the hands of a small group of associates. Not a single share had slipped through the net, to be traded on the New York Stock Exchange. Still, Carnegie had good reason to congratulate himself as he characteristically took stock of the year just ended. Writing to cousin Dod on New Year's Day 1901, he asked rhetorically, 'Isn't it wonderful we are to have such a good year?'

In one sense, at least, Carnegie was the loser; he had lost the inestimable managerial talents of Henry Clay Frick. Too late, he must have reflected that the squabble over a few cents in the price of coke must have been an enormous price to pay when it meant that he no longer had Frick running the business. Interestingly, Carnegie had looked on the business as his 'family' and in correspondence with George Lauder, when the trouble with Frick erupted, he had stated that he intended to divorce Frick on grounds of 'Incompatibility of Temper'.[2] On this analogy, Carnegie saw himself as the husband and father, the patriarch, the paterfamilias who, in true Victorian tradition, was to be obeyed without question.

But a new century was dawning, and already the Victorian values by which Carnegie had ruled his life and his business were disappearing. On the one hand, the use of fabricated materials in heavy engineering, the erection of skyscrapers, in even larger ships than before, and in a thousand other applications undreamed of a few years earlier, meant that the demand for steel rose astronomically. This had been reflected in the astonishing expansion of Carnegie Steel over the previous decade with profits rising at the rate of $10,000,000 a year. Further expansion of the steel mills and coke plants was urgently required if only to keep pace with the demand, and suddenly Carnegie realised that, without Frick at the helm, the leviathan which he had created would begin to founder.

To make matters worse, Carnegie found others beginning to move in on his territory. His pre-eminence in the steel industry was no longer assured or unassailable when John W. Gates launched the American Steel & Wire Company of New Jersey in 1898. Then, the following year, Judge William H. Moore and his dynamic, thrusting brother James, founders of Diamond Match and National Biscuit, suddenly moved in on the steel industry, gobbling up no fewer than 265 tin-plate mills at a single stroke. J. Pierpoint Morgan, son of Junius the London banker, formed the Federal Steel Company with $200,000,000 capitalisation, with Elbert H. Gary, an energetic young Chicago lawyer, as president. When Carnegie invited Gary to lunch and suggested a rail pool agreement between Carnegie Steel and Federal, Gary said coolly, 'I am willing, Mr Carnegie, if we can do it on an equal basis. I don't think you will have the major part of the rail business long.' Carnegie, who had begun by patronising the much younger man, had no alternative but to agree Gary's terms.

The writing was on the wall, and Carnegie knew that the world was changing rapidly. He was now sixty-five, the age at which most men retire from business. Ever since he had toyed with the idea of selling up and going to Oxford thirty-odd years before, Carnegie had never again considered retirement, but now he weighed up the situation. The battle with Frick had aged him; in the immediate aftermath he no longer had the same zest for the cut and thrust of business. As even bigger sharks than himself swam into his domain he realised the time had come to pull out. But he would not go quietly; he would pull off the stroke of a lifetime, which would show everyone that Carnegie was a force to be reckoned with, right to the end. Carefully he laid his plans.

Far from announcing his impending retirement, he trumpeted a series of new projects that threw the industry into turmoil and confusion. Calmly he announced that he would tackle Gates head-on, by opening a massive rod mill in Pittsburgh. Then he intimated his intentions of constructing a new railroad from Pittsburgh to the East Coast which would rival the mighty Pennsylvania. In midsummer 1901 he revealed that he had purchased land at Conneaut, the terminus of his Bessemer Railroad on Lake Erie, and planned to erect a $12,000,000 tube plant there. This was a shot across the bows of the National Tube Company which had just been launched by J.P. Morgan & Company. Instead of lying back and licking his wounds after the recent Frick dispute, here was Carnegie, more aggressive than ever, launching major assaults on branches of the steel industry which he had hardly bothered with before. What could he be up to? The trade was awash with rumours which Carnegie answered with a bland assertion:

> The policy of the Carnegie Company is to co-operate in every way with its fellow manufacturers in the industrial world, and not to push itself into any new field save in self-defence. We did not leave the National Tube Company. They left us, which they had a perfect right to do, of course. Now we are ready to shake hands and co-operate with them in the most friendly spirit. We are better for them than a dozen small concerns, conducted in a small jealous way. We believe there is room enough for the two concerns.[3]

Hitherto, apart from rails and girders, Carnegie Steel had concentrated on making steel billets, leaving it to other companies to manufacture finished articles from this material, but it had for some time been in Carnegie's mind that he should not be content to let other businesses reap the benefit of the manufactured goods. For the past two or three years he had been arguing strongly in favour of switching to secondary manufacturing, reasoning to Charlie Schwab that 'the company that sells articles finished, will be able to run all weathers and make some money while others are half idle and losing money . . . Our policy should be to make finished articles'.[4] Frick had opposed this policy, but with him out of the way it could now be implemented. Moreover, Schwab was an eager disciple who sincerely believed that diversification into manufacturing projects was the way ahead. Now Carnegie pressed on with plans to start hoop, rod, wire and nail mills. 'Never been time when more prompt action essential, indeed absolutely necessary to maintain property,' he wired Schwab from Skibo.[5] Later he elaborated this in a memorandum which Schwab laid before the board:

245

If I were czar [of the Carnegie Company], I would make no dividends upon common stock, save all surplus, and spend it for a hoop and cotton-tie mill, for wire and nail mills, for tube mills, for lines of boats upon the Lakes for our manufactured articles, and to bring back scrap, etc. You have only to rise to the occasion, but no half measures. If you are not going to cross the stream, do not enter at all and be content to dwindle into second place. Put your trust in the policy of attending to your own business in your own way and running your mills full regardless of prices and very little trust in the efficacy of artificial arrangements with your competitors, which have the serious result of strengthening them if they strengthen you. Such is my advice.[6]

The ambitious plans to build a new railroad arose out of a dispute with the Pennsylvania Railroad, a giant organisation with which Carnegie had had a love–hate relationship all his adult life. The days of Edgar Thomson and Tom Scott were long gone, but in more recent years Carnegie had won highly favourable rates (not to mention secret rebates) from successive railroad presidents, George Roberts and Frank Thomson. But in 1899 Thomson had died and been succeeded by Alexander J. Cassatt, a man of a very different stamp altogether. Cassatt was fiercely opposed to secret rebates and soon let it be known that such preferential treatment would no longer continue. It was this unexpected blow which had caused the price of coke to jump and thus indirectly triggered off the Carnegie–Frick dispute. While Schwab was preoccupied with the construction of new plant at Conneaut and Duquesne, Carnegie himself took over the campaign against Cassatt. When he discovered that Cassatt had contrived a network of interlocking directorships with the New York Central, the Baltimore & Ohio and the Chesapeake & Ohio, he tried to attack him through the courts, on the ground that by owning stock in competing railways he was violating the Constitution of the Commonwealth of Pennsylvania. When this ruse failed, Carnegie planned to rouse public opinion against the railroads, and urge Congress to control freight rates, just as the Board of Trade did in Britain. But the recent revelations in the Frick dispute made Carnegie's anguished outcry against the unfair tactics of the railroad companies ring hollow.

In desperation, therefore, he began drawing up the blueprint for a grand scheme. Taking his Pittsburgh, Bessemer & Lake Erie Railroad as the springboard, he negotiated with the Western Maryland Railroad to carry his freight from the Great Lakes through to Baltimore. At the same time, he opened negotiations with the Buffalo, Rochester & Pittsburgh Railway whose line connected with Carnegie's at Butler, Pennsylvania. This would give him a connection with the Reading Railroad which had access to New York and Philadelphia. Both the Maryland and Buffalo Rochester railroads were available for purchase, though their tracks would have to be relaid on firmer beds to sustain the heavy freight traffic Carnegie envisaged. While these plans were still at a preliminary stage, however, the Western Maryland was acquired by George Gould, son of the notorious Jay Gould. Carnegie, who had dealt with the father to their mutual benefit, had no compunction about hammering out a deal with the son. George Gould dreamed of creating a truly transcontinental railroad from Baltimore to Pittsburgh and thence to St Louis and all points west. It was a prospect that excited Carnegie too, and he entered into the business with all the energy and vigour of a man half his age. It was almost as if he were back at the beginning of his swashbuckling career again. Schwab and the junior partners were caught up in the heady euphoria of the old man's manufacturing and railroad ventures; only cousin Dod and Henry Phipps were appalled at Carnegie's sudden access of creative energy. They were now at an age when they were eager to retire with their stock intact, and looked askance on these reckless gambles.

Carnegie was not the only man to get a new lease of life in his mid-sixties. J. Pierpoint Morgan, the creator of Federal Steel and the National Tube Company, viewed Carnegie's antics with keen interest and mounting disfavour. Once before, in 1885, Morgan had succeeded in blocking Carnegie when the latter had attempted to build a railroad from Pittsburgh to Philadelphia in direct competition with the Pennsylvania. Fifteen years on, however, Carnegie was a much more formidable adversary, with the controlling interest in the largest manufacturing company in America at his back. Now he was posing an even greater threat than before with his plan to ally himself with the infamous Gould syndicate and create totally unnecessary and destructively competitive lines across the country, just to protect his own interests. At this point Gates and the Moore brothers, dismayed at Carnegie's proposed incursion and alarmed at the vulnerability of their own over-capitalised concerns, approached Morgan with a breathtaking offer: nothing less than a buy-out of the Carnegie Steel empire and the reorganisation of the industry into one mighty combine.

Carnegie had already got wind of Morgan's interest. Late in October 1900 Schwab had been approached indirectly. At first he thought that Morgan wished to discuss railroad matters but soon discovered that the great financier was concerned at Carnegie Steel's plans to manufacture tubes in direct competition with one of his own companies. Schwab duly noted Morgan's interest and Carnegie sat back and waited for the next move. Meanwhile Morgan was daily being importuned by frightened railroad backers and steelmen. 'Carnegie must be stopped!' was their slogan. Finally Morgan came to the same conclusion, and the only way to do so was to buy him out. To what extent Morgan was influenced by Carnegie's panicky rivals, and to what extent he was manipulated by the wily Scot himself, will probably never be known. How Morgan arrived at his momentous decision is shrouded in mystery and the stuff of legend. Much has been made of the famous dinner at the University Club in Manhattan on 12 December 1900, at which two New York financiers, J. Edward Simmons and Charles Stewart Smith, entertained Charlie Schwab. If Schwab was the guest of honour, then there, at his right hand, was seated the great J. Pierpoint Morgan himself. Smiling Charlie was on top form that evening. Called upon to speak after dinner, he rose to his feet and over the next thirty minutes expounded his plans for the future of the American steel industry. It should be rationalised and reorganised, a colossus controlling every aspect of mining, refining, manufacture of both raw steel and finished goods, marketing, transportation and distribution. In this streamlined, interlocking, cost-efficient machine, the customer would be offered the world's finest steel at the most competitive prices. In fact, such an organisation should be able to undercut any would-be competitor. Although there were eighty prominent businessmen in the audience (including Carnegie himself, who put in a brief appearance), Charlie was addressing only the man seated at his elbow. Morgan listened impassively, but the fact that his cigar remained unlit spoke volumes.

Shortly afterwards, early in the new year, Schwab was invited to Morgan's house at 219 Madison Avenue. There, in the mahogany-panelled library where priceless works of art hung alongside utter kitsch, the framed souvenirs of foreign travel, Charlie found Morgan's partner Robert Bacon as well as 'Bet a Million' John Gates. The session lasted through the afternoon, all evening and right through the night. A frosty dawn was rising as the meeting finally broke up, but by morning the plans for the creation of that gigantic monolith, the United States Steel Corporation, had been formulated. Only one question remained to be answered: 'Would Carnegie sell?'

Although Carnegie had given his blessing to the dinner in Schwab's honour he was unaware of the subsequent meeting at Morgan's home, for Charlie had simply not consulted him. It is hard to believe, however, that Schwab would have attended that historic all-night session without the Little Boss having some inkling of what was afoot. Morgan hated Carnegie with a manic intensity. He disliked everything about the pushy Scotsman and was infuriated by his bid to 'demoralize railroads just as he had demoralized steel'. It seems probable that Carnegie, realising this antipathy, to some extent engineered the dinner or the seating arrangements, and left the rest to the charm and geniality of Charlie in the hope that Morgan would take the bait.

Word of the secret meeting leaked out in a matter of hours. Midmorning editions of the New York newspapers on 14 January carried reports, with varying degrees of accuracy, concerning rumours of the proposed deal. Carnegie was immediately bombarded by pressmen for confirmation or denial. He remained tight-lipped, refusing to comment on the rumours. Even to someone as close to him as cousin Dod he would write, a few days later, 'There is no substance in the reports anent [concerning] great combination – some talkee, talkee,' and he went on to outline progress on the various ploys then afoot.[7] Simultaneously Schwab was writing to Carnegie mapping out the prospects for Carnegie Steel over the ensuing five years: 'I shall not feel satisfied until we are producing 500,000 tons per month and finishing same . . . If you continue to give me the support you have in the past we'll make a greater industry than we ever dreamed of.'[8] This was an odd letter from a president intent on selling his company; in hindsight, it is not improbable that the letter may even have been written at Carnegie's behest for use as a smoke-screen to conceal his real intentions till the last moment.

Now, however, Morgan was pressing Schwab for an answer. A week later Charlie returned to New York and called at the Carnegie residence. Before seeing the Little Boss, he had a long chat with Louise in private, telling her fully and frankly about his clandestine meeting with Morgan and his associates and of his own concern as to how best to broach the ticklish subject with Carnegie himself. This was an astute move on Charlie's part, for Louise knew better than anyone else the toll which the Frick dispute had exacted. She was anxious for her husband to take things easy, and viewed his new-found energy with dismay. She was eager to channel this burst of creativity into something really worth while. Now was the time for him to devote himself to all those philanthropic schemes of which he had so far only dreamed.

Louise was then preoccupied with the myriad problems connected with the building of the new Carnegie mansion uptown, and it seemed to her that a change of house would go well with a change of direction in business. To Schwab's relief, therefore, Louise proved to be both sympathetic and enthusiastic. She even arranged for Charlie to meet Carnegie the following morning at the St Andrews Golf Club in Westchester County. Carnegie had only recently taken up the game but already he was hopelessly addicted, claiming that a round of golf was 'the best physical therapy in the world'. The following morning found Charlie on the golf course, diplomatically losing to the Little Boss. Afterwards they adjourned for lunch to Carnegie's own little cottage on the edge of the links. Over the meal Schwab blurted out the whole story and waited with bated breath for Carnegie's reaction. The Little Boss merely said that he would have to think it over, and asked Charlie to call on him again the following morning. In the meantime, he asked the company president to consider what might be a fair price in case they decided to sell.

Carnegie appears to have been torn both ways. On the one hand he was on the verge of the most stupendous expansion in his firm's history, with so many exciting projects in train. On the other hand, he realised that the planned expansion would take at least five years, by which time he would have reached his allotted biblical span. Perhaps he would not live that long. Suddenly, the struggle no longer seemed so worth while. Lou was always reminding him that he had a more important destiny to fulfil. There was that idea for a Peace Palace, for example. Then it became clear in his mind. He really had no alternative but to sell out to Morgan – provided, of course, that Morgan would accept his price and his terms.

When Charlie called the next day, Carnegie had prepared a rough estimate; as usual the figures had been jotted down hurriedly with a blunt pencil on a scrap of paper. The $160,000,000 capitalisation bonds would have to be exchanged at par for bonds in the new company. Similarly, the $160,000,000 of stock, in $1000 blocks, would have to be exchanged for stock in the new company. At $1500 a share this put a value on the Carnegie Steel stock of $240,000,000. Adding a modest $80,000,000 for the profit of the past year and estimated profit for the coming year, Carnegie totted up the figures and came to the impressive sum of $480,000,000. There was only one proviso: Carnegie demanded first-mortgage 5 per cent gold bonds in exchange for his personal holdings, as well as those of cousin George and sister-in-law Lucy. He had no desire to end up as the majority shareholder in the new combine. Instead he would require payment in easily negotiable securities as it was his intention to transfer the bulk of this fortune to the great philanthropic works he had in mind.

Schwab took the scrap of paper hotfoot to Morgan and he, without a moment's hesitation, said simply, 'I accept this price.' In this extremely casual manner, the biggest sale in American industrial history was concluded with all the formality of a domestic servant taking dirty linen to the laundry.

A few days later, Morgan decided that he should see Carnegie and shake hands on the deal. He telephoned from his office at 23 Wall Street and asked Carnegie if he would come down to see him. Carnegie, however, insisted that Morgan should come to him. Conceding the point, Morgan jumped into a cab and came up to 5 West Fifty-first Street. The two men met alone for exactly fifteen minutes. On the doorstep, Morgan delivered his parting shot, 'Mr Carnegie, I want to congratulate you on being the richest man in the world!'

On 4 February the managers of Carnegie Steel held a board meeting to ratify the agreement, of which they had been notified in writing by Carnegie. They dutifully minuted:

> Whatever pecuniary benefits we may derive from a new organization such as outlined, our first and most natural feeling is the keen regret to all of us in the severance of our business relations with you, to whom we owe so much. Your sound judgment and profound business sagacity have been the foundation stones on which has been built the fabric of our success . . . With such feeling, knowing you to be sincere in your desire to spend the remainder of your days in those acts of generosity which have endeared you to the world, we reluctantly acquiesce in your decision to retire, and are willing that you should receive bonds of the new Company in payment for your stock in the Carnegie Company, we taking stock of the new company in exchange for our stock in the Carnegie Company.[9]

In due course the United States Steel Corporation was capitalised at $1,403,450,000 divided into bonds, preferred stock and common stock. Carnegie's share was upwards of $250,000,000, all in 5 per cent gold bonds. Together with his vast outside investments, the man who had begun tentatively with a modest stake in Adams Express only thirty-six years earlier now possessed a fortune estimated on Wall Street at up to $400,000,000. When word of the deal was published, reaction was mixed. Ministers preached sermons that railed against Mammon. The press editorialised about a world that was governed by big business, not kings and statesmen. Fortunately for Carnegie, the spotlight was now on his successor, J. Pierpoint Morgan, who was being held up as the new economic emperor.

Meanwhile Carnegie's erstwhile partners reacted in many different ways to their new-found wealth. Henry Phipps was ill in bed with a serious attack of bronchitis when the news of the deal was broken to him by his physician, Dr Jaspar Garmany. Phipps stared at the ceiling, then, tears brimming his eyes, he cried out: 'Ain't Andy wonderful!' After years of pennypinching, ever fearful that the rapacious Carnegie would turn him out as he had done Kloman, Miller,

Coleman and so many others down through the years, Phipps was now a multi-millionaire in fact as well as on paper. Alexander Peacock, the former store clerk, went on a philanthropic spree of his own, seeking out old friends and paying off their debts. Then he hired a 'Peacock Special' and set a new record for the fastest rail crossing of America. Finally he built a great palace on Highland Avenue, Pittsburgh, and filled it with expensive works of art. Thomas Morrison, on the other hand, reinvested his new-found wealth and lived cannily, his only extravagance being his magnificent red sandstone mansion.

Lucy Carnegie netted $6,198,500 with which she purchased an estate at Raquette Lake in the Adirondacks, adding to her extensive properties in Pittsburgh and Florida. Frick put $13,000,000 of his $61,000,000 share into prime Pittsburgh real estate, but indulged his passion for Old Master paintings and other choice works of art, the nucleus of the great New York museum that bears his name to this day. Phipps invested his millions in model tenements in New York City before retiring to his country castle in England. Many of the junior partners went on an orgy of spending that matched the quixotic extravagance of the prospectors who had struck gold in the Klondike a few years earlier. One had portraits of his beautiful wife painted by every American and foreign artist he could find; another presented each of his friends with a brand new motor car, while a third spent lavishly in creating 'the finest mushroom cellar in America'. A fourth designed his own coat-of-arms, and then had it chromolithographed on his cigar-bands. A fifth installed eight bathrooms in his house, one for every bedroom – an unheard-of luxury for that period. A sixth had alternating bouts of extravagance and parsimony, giving Pittsburgh a $100,000 dollar conservatory, then objecting to paying $15,000 for a painting to decorate it, telling a friend that the interest on fifteen grand would be two dollars a day 'and it isn't worth two dollars a day to look at a picture!'.

The big Carnegie Steel bonanza had a crazy effect on prices and values in Pittsburgh for at least a year. Artists, booksellers, antique dealers and importers of Oriental furnishings flocked to the grimy steel city and made a killing as the Carnegie millions percolated down through the system. For a time realtors and interior decorators reaped a golden harvest; but, as the price of milk, bread, fresh fruit and other basic foodstuffs rocketed, people began to question the outcome. 'After-events show that the whole thing was unnatural, harmful and turned out to be very bad for business indeed,' observed the historian Anna Robeson Burr, who concluded that the later good works of the Carnegie foundation hardly compensated for all the debt incurred.

For the fourth time in a decade Carnegie's name was a household word throughout the civilised world. At least on this occasion relatively little opprobrium was now being attached to it. Everyone watched and waited to see whether the little multi-millionaire would honour the gospel of wealth which he had preached in his recent book. In particular, he had pontificated that:

> The day is not far distant when the man who dies leaving behind him millions of available wealth, which was free for him to administer during life, will pass away, 'unwept, unhonored and unsung', no matter to what uses he leaves the dross which he cannot take with him. Of such as these the public verdict will then be: 'The man who dies thus rich dies disgraced.'[10]

The world would have to wait and see, for the Carnegie entourage, which included Lou, four-year-old Baba (as Margaret was known to her doting parents) and Lou's sister Stella, embarked on the *Kaiserin Theresa* for the Mediterranean. On the voyage Carnegie jotted down some disjointed random thoughts, which may have been intended for a speech he never gave. These jottings are quite revealing, and reflect his mixed feelings at selling up:

> Trial bitter – father bereft of his sons – abandoned & alone – no more whirl of affairs, the new developments in – occupation gone. Advise no man quit business – plenty retire upon nothing to return to – misery.[11]

Soon his restless mind was turning to the arduous business of disposing of his riches. In his essay on wealth, which he subsequently used as the core of his book, Carnegie enumerated seven areas in which philanthropy could be practised to good effect. Top of the list was the endowment of universities, something that only the super-rich could hope to do. Next came free libraries which, in Carnegie's eyes, took first place. Then there was the founding or extension of hospitals, followed by the provision of public parks, halls suitable for meetings and concerts, swimming-baths and lastly churches, 'but only the buildings, not the maintenance of the church activities'. Needless to say, the appearance of the book, closely followed by the liquidation of his vast empire, meant that Carnegie was soon inundated by countless good causes and worthy institutions clamouring for a slice of the cake. Ministers and missionaries might grumble that churches had been put at the bottom of the list, though few men of the cloth would go so far as the Revd Hugh Price Hughes, a celebrated Welsh Methodist preacher, who publicly castigated Carnegie as 'an anti-Christian phenomenon, a social monstrosity, and a grave political peril',[12] but there was no shortage of artists, writers, musicians and playwrights who claimed their share of patronage. From 1901 onwards, the number of begging letters that found their way to Carnegie in New York seldom fell below four hundred a day; whenever a particular gift was publicised in the press, the number might rise as high as a thousand. Many thinking men came to the conclusion that charity should not do the work of justice, and pointedly questioned why there should ever be millionaires at all. It was not the disposal of riches that they sought but the fairer distribution of wealth in the first place.

Carnegie had already been practising what he preached, though in a relatively modest way. In addition to the library in Allegheny City and another at Braddock, he had established one in Fairfield, Iowa (in gratitude to Senator James F. Wilson who had been extremely helpful to Carnegie in the construction of railways in that state). In his native land he had furnished a fine library in Dunfermline and provided an endowment fund for the purchase of books and maintenance of the building; but after that he contented himself with paying for library buildings, insisting that the local authorities should match his generosity with the cash to pay for their stock, staff and upkeep out of the local rates or taxes. By the turn of the century further Carnegie libraries, on that basis, had been established in Scotland in Edinburgh, Aberdeen, Ayr, Inverness, Jedburgh, Peterhead, Stirling and Wick. That would be his cardinal rule thereafter, breached on only three occasions, when he paid for the books as well as the buildings in Duquesne, Homestead and the borough of Carnegie, a suburb of Pittsburgh named after him. After 1901 Carnegie free libraries spread like a rash over the United States. A rather quirky stipulation was that each one had to display prominently a bust of Robert Burns, which led to the curious situation, noted in the United States official handbook as late as the 1940s, that there were more statues of Robert Burns in America than anyone else. They have all since disappeared, or been consigned to the basement.

Pittsburgh was put in the embarrassing situation of having to decline the offer of a library as long ago as 1881 because the laws of Pennsylvania did not provide for municipal taxes being used to stock and maintain free libraries. Later, however, Carnegie provided the city with the magnificent Carnegie Institute overlooking Schenley Park (which, incidentally, still boasts a life-sized, full-length bronze statue of the millionaire's favourite bard). Carnegie took an inordinate amount of trouble with this project, fussing over countless petty details of the architecture and fittings, and firing off lengthy memos to the long-suffering William M. Frew of the Carnegie Library Commission on everything from the draping of nude classical statuary to the names engraved on the façade. When the list of names was published, Carnegie subjected Frew to a long tirade:

> I cannot approve the list of names . . . Some of the names have no
> business to be on the list. Imagine Dickens in and Burns out. Among
> painters Perugini out and Rubens in, the latter only a painter of fat,
> vulgar women . . . [13]

Later on, when Carnegie free libraries were scattered hither and yon like religious tracts, the procedure was much brisker and more businesslike. A town council would apply for a Carnegie library and Carnegie's secretary James Bertram would send the local authority the relevant details, specifying the terms and conditions which had to be met before the grant could be disbursed. The council would have to undertake to provide a free site, preferably in the town centre, then pledge an annual appropriation from the rates or taxes, usually 10 per cent of the Carnegie grant, the size of which was invariably based on the civic population at the rate of two dollars a head. This system worked well enough in towns and cities of a reasonable size but left smaller towns with libraries that were woefully underfunded. The sole exception known to the writer, interestingly enough, is the Carnegie library in Dornoch, a Scottish town with a population of about a thousand; but in this case the benefactor had a special interest, for it was the nearest town to his beloved Skibo Castle.

Inevitably this business of bestowing free libraries attracted a great deal of criticism: either that he was doing too much ('better for a community to do for itself') or not enough ('a building without books is not a library'), but of all the brickbats he attracted on account of his philanthropic activities, criticism of his library system bothered him the least. He was secure in the knowledge that, singlehandedly, he transformed the American civic attitude towards free libraries (virtually non-existent before his time). By the 1920s it was estimated that thirty-five million people every day used the Carnegie libraries of America, and Carnegie himself proudly boasted that the sun never set on his libraries. By means of initial funding, therefore, he acquired immortality, and even today these Carnegie free libraries are his most enduring memorial.

Initially no attempt was made to dictate the architectural style of these libraries, but after some bad experiences with substandard structures the Carnegie Corporation of New York devised a standard design which was used thereafter. This explains why, in small towns the length and breadth of the United States, there is to be found to this day a stone building in the style known to architects as Carnegie Classical. Contrary to popular belief, Carnegie did not insist on his name being carved on the façade, though of course he never objected when it was included. He did, however, insist that the ornament over the main doorway should incorporate the sun's rays and the slogan 'Let there be light', although this condition was not always complied with. Whenever possible, he made a point of attending the ceremonies marking the laying of the foundation stone, especially in Britain where the opportunity was invariably taken to confer upon him the freedom of the city, town or borough. In this manner

Carnegie amassed civic freedoms and burgess tickets the way other men collect stamps. He broke all records when he was granted six freedoms in one week. Eventually he held fifty-seven British freedoms, an all-time record. Even Winston Churchill, in the immediate aftermath of the Second World War, never equalled that number. Along the way he also acquired a clutch of honorary degrees. He who had never gone to Oxford University as an undergraduate like he had planned in the 1860s, would eventually collect a doctorate from that august institution. The tiny figure in his scarlet doctoral robes, with his shock of snow-white hair and spade beard, must have reminded many an onlooker of Santa Claus, and indeed the analogy was particularly apt.

Shortly before his departure for Europe in the spring of 1901 Carnegie deposited his vast fortune in a strongbox in a bank vault in Hoboken, New Jersey. Bonds to the value of $5,000,000, however, were detached and sent to the managers of the Carnegie Company, now a subdivision of United States Steel, to be held in trust for the following purposes:

> Income from $1 million to be spent in maintaining Libraries at Braddock, Homestead and Duquesne works.
>
> Income from other $4 million to be applied:
>
> 1st, to provide for employees of Carnegie Company injured in service and for dependents of those killed.
>
> 2nd, to provide small pensions to employees after long service, help in old age. Not to be regarded as a substitute for what the Company is already doing . . . I make this first use of surplus wealth upon retiring from business, as an acknowledgment of the deep debt I owe to the workmen who have contributed so greatly to my success.[14]

Thus the men who had laboured long and hard on his behalf got a little over 1 per cent of his charitable disbursement, which by the time of his death in 1919 had totalled $350,695,653.40. In return, the Homestead workers belatedly presented him with a flowery address which concluded: 'We have personal knowledge of cares lightened and of hope and strength renewed in homes where human prospects seemed dark and discouraging.'[15] The men of the Lucy Furnaces went one better when they presented the Little Boss with a handsome piece of silver plate, tastefully engraved with a similar encomium.

At the same time as he set up the Andrew Carnegie Relief Fund he also left $5,200,000 to New York City to provide for sixty-five branch libraries throughout the five boroughs, and to St Louis $1,000,000 for a similar purpose. In a single day, therefore, he gave away $11,000,000 – equivalent to two-thirds of all his previous benefactions. The interest on his bonds and other investments, however, amounted to more than $15,000,000 a year: clearly he would have to work a lot harder at this business of philanthropy if he were not to die disgraced by his accumulated wealth.

In Pittsburgh, where he had made his fortune, he provided a museum, an art gallery and the Margaret Morrison School for Young Women. Opened in 1895, these buildings and others eventually formed the Carnegie Institute of Pittsburgh to which he had granted about $28,000,000 by the time of his death. In January 1902 he inaugurated an even grander project, the Carnegie Institute of Washington with an initial gift of $10,000,000 in gold bonds, later augmenting this with cash to a total value of $25,000,000. His old friend John Hay, now Secretary of State in the administration of Theodore Roosevelt, was appointed chairman, while Colonel Teddy himself was, *ex officio*, one of the trustees – and a most enthusiastic and hardworking one at that. The Institute was incorporated by Act of Congress on 28 April 1904 'to encourage in the broadest sense and most liberal manner investigations, research and discovery, and the application of knowledge to the improvement of mankind'. Of all Carnegie's benefactions, the Institute received the least criticism in both lay and academic worlds. Indeed, at its inception, it was hailed by the *Independent* as having a more vital role than the Nobel Prize foundation; the latter only rewarded past achievements whereas the Carnegie Institute was having to speculate on the future. One of the Institute's long-term projects was to correct earlier surveys of the world. To this end in 1911 it received from its benefactor a non-ferrous, wood and bronze yacht, named the *Carnegie*, whose mission thereafter was to sail the seven seas and rectify costly (and often tragic) mistakes in maritime charts. Another project was the Carnegie Observatory on the summit of Mount Wilson, California; Carnegie was inordinately proud of the fact that the first celestial photograph taken at this observatory revealed no fewer than sixteen 'new worlds'. The second and third photographs brought the number of hitherto unrecorded stars over the hundred mark.

One day Richard Watson Gilder, editor of the *Century* magazine, sent Carnegie a poem about a mine superintendent named Taylor who had lost his life rescuing men trapped in a coal-pit near Pittsburgh. Carnegie was moved to tears by the poignant couplets entitled 'In the Time of Peace' and there and then he resolved to establish the Carnegie Hero Fund with an endowment of $5,000,000, to reward heroes, or support the families of heroes who perished in the effort to serve or save their fellows. With the prize money, of course, each hero got a large medal which had Carnegie's bearded profile on the obverse. The fund was established in the United States on 15 April 1904, and subsequently extended to the British Isles where it was administered by the Carnegie Dunfermline Trust. Later the scheme spread to the countries of western Europe. In connection with the Hero Fund, Carnegie reproduced in his *Autobiography* fulsome personal letters of praise, including one from Windsor Castle written by King Edward VII in November 1908, sending Carnegie his portrait as a mark of respect. Later King Edward, while travelling in the Highlands, paid a call on the Scots-American philanthropist at Skibo. During the course of this visit the host produced some verses by the Californian poet Joaquin Miller in which Carnegie was extravagantly eulogised at the expense of the crowned heads of Europe. He gleefully pointed out lines referring disparagingly to King Edward and his nephew, Kaiser Wilhelm II of Germany. His Majesty was far too well-bred to comment on this tasteless display. Carnegie, of course, thought that he could get away with anything, thanks to his boyish charm and sparkling wit.

The Carnegie Dunfermline Trust which administered the Hero Fund in the United Kingdom had arisen out of a surprising offer that came, like a bolt from the blue, in 1900, when Colonel Thomas Hunt, the new laird of Pittencrieff, approached John Ross, the Trust's chairman, with an offer to sell the glen to Carnegie if he could meet his price. Ross was astonished at this offer, mindful of the long-running feud between the Hunt and Morrison families which went back more than half a century to the time when the colonel's father, James Hunt, had banned old Tom Morrison and his family (young

Andy included) from the park. Subsequently there had been a lengthy court battle between old man Hunt and the Morrisons, father and son, over the rights of the citizens of Dunfermline to gain access to the glen, as well as Hunt's attempts to encroach on the town's traditional common-grazing land. On one occasion James Hunt had challenged old Tom Morrison to a duel. The latter responded in a voice loud enough for everyone to hear: 'As challenged party I have the right to choose weapons. I'll take my father's shoemaker's knife if you take your grandfather's razor' – a jibe at Hunt's plebeian antecedents, his grandfather having been the town barber.

Colonel Hunt set a high price of £70,000, twice what the land was actually worth. After consulting with Carnegie, Ross had told Hunt that the price was far too high and that Mr Carnegie was not disposed to consider the purchase further. Carnegie, however, was very keen to buy Pittencrieff, but two years passed before he succeeded in his ambition, through the mediation of his friend Lord Shaw. In the end Hunt parted with the glen and its neighbouring park for £45,000. The deal was concluded on 24 December 1902, 'the best Christmas present I ever had,' exclaimed Carnegie ecstatically before rushing a jubilant telegram to cousin Dod: 'Pittencrieff is ours'. To his friend John Morley he wrote at great length, exulting in his new title as Laird of Pittencrieff and only regretting that grandfather Morrison, his uncles and his father had not lived to see that proud moment. In November 1903 he transferred the estate in perpetuity to the royal burgh of Dunfermline, retaining for his lifetime only the mound on which stood the ruins of Malcolm's Tower, so that he might enjoy his lairdship. While the estate was renovated and landscaped for use as a public park, he set up the Carnegie Dunfermline Trust with $2,500,000 worth of United States Steel bonds. Originally it was his intention to select an American town of the same size to be the recipient of a similar benefaction, but this was dropped as impracticable. Unwilling to appear as a sentimentalist where the town of his birth was concerned, Carnegie tried to disguise his gift as a sociological experiment,

> to test the advantages which a community may derive by having placed at its disposal . . . funds dedicated to the purpose of

providing the means of introducing into the daily lives of the masses, such privileges and enjoyments . . . as are calculated to carry into their homes and their conduct sweetness and light.[16]

The Trust was to be ecumenical and representative of all classes in Dunfermline society, but Carnegie's wish that a Roman Catholic priest be included was scotched at the outset by John Ross, the dour Presbyterian chairman. On the score of class, though, Carnegie had his way, and John Weir, secretary of the Fife Miners' Union, rubbed shoulders with the Earl of Elgin and Provost Macbeth.

When it came to the uses to which the Trust put the money, Carnegie often clashed with the trustees. Invariably his wrongheaded stance arose from ignorance of the full facts, as when he opposed an extension to *his* library in the mistaken belief that it was solely for the use of antiquarian scholars. In old age he rediscovered the radicalism of his youth and concocted a grand scheme to provide model housing for the poor, with indoor plumbing as the best medium for bringing 'sweetness and light' into their lives. The trustees pointed out that this scheme, desirable though it might seem, was attended by so many practical difficulties as to be impossible to implement. In one aspect Carnegie got his way, though. When Ross proposed to use Trust funds to establish a textile school as a rival to the Lauder Technical College, Carnegie flatly refused: no other school must be allowed to rival the Lauder Tech. Ross quietly dropped the idea. Considering the constant interference from its benefactor, the Trust worked remarkably well, and in due course was rewarded with an increase in funds to $4,000,000 which yielded an annual income of $200,000 (about £40,000 at the rates of exchange then prevailing). This may not have seemed a lot, but, for a town of only 27,000 people, it represented the largest per capita funding granted to any town anywhere in the world. As a result, Dunfermline could boast a staggering array of amenities that many a much larger town would have envied.

Cornell University elected Carnegie a trustee. Through this appointment he discovered that American academics were very poorly paid, and this led him to create the Carnegie Foundation for the Advancement of Teaching, with total appropriations of $29,250,000. In its first twenty years this foundation disbursed more than $20,000,000 to retired professors and many millions more to lecturers and their widows. As in all the other trusts and foundations, payments came from the income, the capital sum remaining intact.

One of the more bizarre beneficiaries of Carnegie largesse was the Brander Matthews project for simplified spelling. An examination of Carnegie's handwritten correspondence reveals a cavalier approach to spelling – 'riten' for 'written' is a recurring example of his abhorrence of unnecessary or silent letters. He not only pumped $280,000 into the Matthews project but persuaded Theodore Roosevelt to give it his presidential blessing, thus ensuring the maximum publicity. When the scheme was lampooned in the humorous periodicals, Carnegie's enthusiasm waned. Typical of the satirical verse that greeted his latest good cause was written by Wallace Irwin:

> Grate scot! I kannot spel the wurdz
> That sizzle 'neath my brow
> Sins A. Karnaygy spoyld the rulz
> We ust to have in gramar skulz.[17]

Of infinitely more lasting benefit was the Scottish Universities Trust, which was primed with $10,000,000. Half of the annual income of $500,000 from the appropriated Steel bonds was used to pay the tuition fees of poor students, while the rest went to improve the facilities of the four Scottish universities. Not only did they confer honorary doctorates on their little benefactor but the students of the oldest university, St Andrews, elected Carnegie their Lord Rector in 1902:

> Few incidents in my life have so deeply impressed me as the first meeting of the faculty, when I took my seat in the old chair occupied successively by so many distinguished Lord Rectors during the nearly five hundred years which have elapsed since St Andrews was founded.[18]

Poring over previous rectorial addresses to get some ideas for his speech, he was touched to find that the great Dean Stanley no less had advised the students to 'go to Burns for your theology'. Later Carnegie would entertain the principals of the four universities in grand style at Skibo.

The success of the Scottish Universities Fund encouraged Carnegie to establish a similar fund, known as the United Kingdom Trust, for the universities in England and Ireland. Both foundations continue to do excellent work to this day. Like other Carnegie benefactions, however, there are strings attached; for, not unreasonably, beneficiaries are expected to repay their loans once they are established in their chosen careers.

The statistics of Carnegie's benefactions are numbing. During his lifetime, total disbursements on libraries amounted to $50,364,808. Of the 2811 free libraries, 1946 were located in the United States, 660 in the United Kingdom, 156 in Canada, twenty-three in New Zealand, thirteen in South Africa, six in the British West Indies, four in Australia and one apiece in the Seychelles, Mauritius and Fiji. Carnegie presented 7689 organs to churches at a total outlay of $6,248,000. Even in this act of generosity Carnegie was fiercely criticised – this time in Scotland by the Free Presbyterians, a rather dour sect who savaged him from their pulpits for forcing the Devil's kist o' whistles on God-fearing congregations, instead of relying solely on the human voice as God Almighty intended.

As the richest man on earth, as the press liked to style him, Carnegie was an object of considerable curiosity. As the man who had devoted so much time in piling up all those millions began to spend all his time in giving them away, he became the target of even more intense scrutiny. He revelled in this interest and never shied away from press publicity, even when it was condescending if not downright hostile. Over the years, he had developed his own method of dealing with the more patronising newspapermen; one ploy was to play the idiot or simpleton. The journalists who fell for this would then marvel all the more at how such a dolt could have made such an enormous fortune. Typical of the pressmen who were fooled by Carnegie's japes (of which grandfather Carnegie would have heartily approved) was W. Orton Tewson, one of America's most prominent literary critics and, at one stage in his career, the London correspondent of the *New York Times* and the *American*:

> I never could make him out. His general ignorance seemed colossal, and yet he was so successful. At heart, I don't believe any man has

been more surprised at his own success than was Carnegie. I used to see the old boy twice a year regularly in London . . . where he always stayed at the Coburg Hotel on his way to Skibo and when returning to New York. I never got anything very intelligent out of him – maybe it was my incompetence, but I don't believe so. I remember one occasion when I found him chuckling over a clipping from one of the London morning papers which quoted him in its 'Shafts of Wisdom' column for some saying ascribed to him. He placed the clipping in front of the clock on the mantelpiece, and kept on marching up and down the room, returning each time to look at the clipping, rub his hands with glee and chuckle to himself, saying: 'Shafts of Wisdom, Shafts of Wisdom.' Then the telephone bell rang, and instead of picking up the instruments, he got down on his knees – the 'phone was on a small table – and put his ear to the mouthpiece and talked into the receiver. Of course, nothing happened, except that after a bit he said to me: 'I never could manage one of these, can you?' I think perhaps he was play-acting, but he was always the same with me, at all events so simple-minded and ignorant of what seemed the barest necessities for getting anywhere in this world, that I have always marvelled at his success. But I never tried to sell him anything!'[19]

The boy-telegraphist who became one of the first to read Morse signals by sound could not have been the near cretin whom Tewson observed. Of course, Carnegie was playing games, no doubt the most effective way of dealing with such a pompous correspondent.

Inevitably Carnegie attracted a great deal of criticism as a vain self-publicist, and it was frequently argued that if he were a true philanthropist he would do good by stealth and not reveal his identity when making donations to worthy causes. Carnegie, on the other hand, argued that publicity was sought not for himself but for the good that his money could do, and to help spread his gospel of wealth. To an anonymous friend he once wrote, 'Of course it's disagreeable work & puts me forward as a vain trumpeter but one who isn't willing to play this part *for the good* to be done, isn't much of a man.'[20] But Carnegie enjoyed his 'trumpeting' far too much to be convincing on this score. He took inordinate delight in the testimonials and civic freedoms, the honorary doctorates, the medals and decorations, and the honorary memberships of over two hundred academic institutions – but then he would not have been human had he not revelled in the limelight which his bounty produced. Poultney Bigelow, son of John Bigelow who had worked closely with Carnegie in setting up the New York branch libraries, left an extremely jaundiced view of Carnegie's philanthropy:

> Never before in the history of plutocratic America had any one man purchased by mere money so much social advertising and flattery. No wonder that he felt himself infallible, when Lords temporal and spiritual courted him and hung upon his words. They wanted his money, and flattery alone could wring it from him. Ask him for aid in a small deserving case or to assist a struggling scientific explorer – that would be wasted time. He had no ears for any charity unless labelled with his name . . . He would have given millions to Greece had she labelled the Parthenon Carnegopolis.[21]

This was as inaccurate as it was unjust. Although Carnegie usually ignored such unfair and uninformed criticism as this, occasionally he felt impelled to defend himself. When he offered to match the $600,000 endowment of the Franklin Institute in Boston he was upset when Charles Eliot, president of Harvard and one of the trustees, enquired if he expected the name to be changed to the Franklin Carnegie Institute. With some asperity Carnegie replied that the idea of tampering with Franklin's name had never entered his mind, any more than it had done when he duplicated Peter Cooper's gift of $600,000 to the Cooper Union. When told of the Boston fund he had been glad to do something for Boston 'for which it isn't easy to do much, blessed as she is with a very rich and gift-getting University and Public Library'.[22]

He went on to point out that when he gave the magnificent concert hall in New York which today bears his name, he had wanted merely to call it the Music Hall; but that the board of management had changed the name while he was absent in Europe, without consulting him, because foreign artistes refused to appear in a mere music hall. He rounded off his reply to Eliot in a rather aggrieved tone. The way of the philanthropist was hard, but he did nothing for popularity, just to please himself:

I never reply to attacks. Although I confess I was surprised that you
should have for a moment imagined there was a man living who could
dream of coupling his name with Franklin or with any founder.

Peter Cooper (1791–1883) built America's first steam engine, *Tom
Thumb*, in 1829 and introduced the Bessemer steel process to the
United States in 1856. Eventually he had iron foundries, steel mills
and railroads in New Jersey and Pennsylvania and, as president of the
North American Telegraph Company, controlled more than half the
telegraph lines of the United States at one time. He was one of
America's first great philanthropists, campaigning for free school
education and founding the Cooper Union for the advancement of
science and art (1859). His name was linked with that of his son-in-
law Abraham Hewitt in the creation of the Cooper-Hewitt Museum.
Carnegie increased the financial resources of the Cooper Union by
generous gifts from 1900 onwards. When the Museum was forced to
seek a new home, it was the Carnegie Corporation of New York that
came to the rescue. Since 1976 the Cooper-Hewitt Museum has been
housed in Carnegie's former mansion.

Many of Carnegie's benefactions honoured men whom he greatly
admired, and in these cases he expressly forbade the use of his own
name. Thus he established the Conway Hall at Dickinson College in
memory of Moncure D. Conway whose autobiography had impressed
him. The Stanton Chair of Economics at Kenyon College, Ohio, was
named after Edwin M. Stanton who had greeted little Andy so kindly
when he delivered his telegrams. There were also the Hanna Chair at
Western Reserve University, Cleveland, the John Hay Library at
Brown University, the Elihu Root Fund at Hamilton College, the Mrs
Grover Cleveland Library for Wellesley, and many others. In fact,
there were numerous instances in which Carnegie expressly forbade
publicity of any kind. More than $250,000 a year, for example, was
set aside for emergency distribution to 'deserving cases' while a
similar sum was disbursed in private pensions, ranging from old
school chums in Dunfermline, fellow-telegraphists in Pittsburgh and
colleagues from the early days of the Pennsylvania Railroad, to
deserving celebrities such as Rudyard Kipling and several former
Presidents of the United States or their wives and dependants. It has
been claimed that Booker T. Washington was the recipient of

Carnegie largesse. In fact the great Negro educationist actually declined a personal gift, claiming that the sum which Carnegie wished to set aside for the future support of Mr and Mrs Washington was 'far beyond our needs and will seem to my race a fortune. Some might feel that I was no longer a poor man giving my services without thought of saving money.'[23] But he was quite happy to accept $600,000 from Carnegie for Tuskegee Institute, dedicated to 'the education and advancement of the colored race'.

Applications for Carnegie funding were not always granted. There was a grain of truth in Poultney Bigelow's jibe about the 'struggling scientific explorer' being turned down, for such was the response given to an appeal from Dr Wilfred Grenfell, the medical missionary who laboured among the fisher folk of Labrador. Grenfell was brought to Carnegie's attention by Joseph B. Gilder (brother of the magazine editor mentioned earlier). As a result, Carnegie sent $1000 and hinted that this might become an annual payment. Sure enough, a cheque for the same amount was forthcoming the following year. Gilder subsequently arranged for Grenfell to meet his benefactor and the two men had an hour-long meeting in Carnegie's study in New York. Carnegie later escorted the missionary to the front door, urging him to call again whenever he was in town. Imagine the astonishment and chagrin of Gilder and Grenfell when, a year later, the cheque was reduced to $250. Gilder's impassioned appeal to Carnegie to restore the full amount went unheeded.

Later on, when Grenfell was making a heroic effort to reorganise the Seamen's Union at St John's, Newfoundland, and build a new home for it, adequate to the needs of tens of thousands of fishermen who put in at that far northern port every summer, Gilder tried to interest Carnegie in the provision of a heated swimming-pool in the basement, with the laudable intention of teaching the fishermen to swim. Owing to the coldness of the rivers, lakes and sea in and around Newfoundland, people never had the opportunity to acquire this skill. Consequently, when a man fell overboard, he invariably drowned. To Gilder's great disappointment, Carnegie was unresponsive, objecting to the cost of heating the water. Gilder explained that waste steam from the heating plant would be utilised, but Carnegie was unmoved. About a year later Gilder raised the matter again, and regretted that Carnegie had not seen his way to aid Grenfell.

Carnegie sought an explanation and got it. 'I never understood the situation before,' he confessed; but in the meantime Grenfell had succeeded, after herculean efforts, in raising the necessary funds without Carnegie's aid. It is probable that Gilder's request had fallen on deaf ears because Carnegie had anticipated being importuned regularly for the maintenance of this heated pool. In general, his benefactions were one-offs that required no long-term commitment on his part. Even eminent friends such as Herbert Spencer and William Ewart Gladstone were sometimes turned down when they applied to Carnegie on behalf of deserving cases.

In 1904 Carnegie's splendid mansion, occupying a full block on Fifth Avenue between Ninetieth and Ninety-first Streets, was ready for occupation. When he and Lou originally inspected the site he was astonished to find cattle and goats browsing amid mounds of rubbish, and a community of ramshackle shanties in a sea of mud that reminded him forcibly of Slabtown. In the space of eighteen months this eyesore had been cleared and tastefully landscaped and a great mansion, the worthy residence of the world's richest man, soon rose from the rubble. Carnegie's study was a cosy sunlit room overlooking the garden, and here he busied himself with a thousand and one projects. He usually worked in the mornings and after lunch took a couple of turns round the reservoir in Central Park near by, returning for formal conferences in his stately library overlooking Fifth Avenue. Over the vast fireplace was carved his favourite motto, 'The hearth our altar: its flame our sacred fire'. When the builder told him that this was too long for the fireplace, Carnegie retorted, 'You mean the fireplace is too short for the motto. Make it longer; and if the room is too small for the fireplace, make the room bigger; and if the house is too small for the room, pull it down and build a bigger one. But at your peril, don't cut a letter out of that motto.'

As in Skibo Castle, a singular feature of the new mansion was the knobs and handles, set low on the doors for the convenience of the little man, if for no one else in the house. The new mansion was formally inaugurated with a dinner of the Carnegie Veterans' Association, an annual gathering of Carnegie's 'young geniuses' who invariably presented the Little Boss with a loving cup, suitably inscribed to mark the occasion. Frick, who lived only a few blocks away, was never invited; and, of course, any of the junior partners who had sided with him were likewise excluded.

After a decade of *ad hoc* disbursement of his bounty, Carnegie put the philanthropic business on a proper footing by establishing the Carnegie Corporation of New York with an endowment of $125,000,000 to support and develop existing and future institutions and act as a clearing house for the whole range of Carnegie charities. This giant charitable corporation derived its income from the interest on its Steel bonds; by 1931 it had expended the equivalent of the sum originally invested, and still had the capital intact. The bulk of the money had gone to the lesser foundations in support of educational surveys, economic research, medical education and public health, legal education and law reform and a wide variety of scientific research projects. In 1951 the original Steel bonds matured and the resulting cash was promptly reinvested. Twenty years later the Corporation estimated that its grants over its first half-century were almost as much as Carnegie's total fortune at its height. The latest quarterly report available at the time of writing, indicates that the Corporation currently has assets of almost a billion dollars – all from an endowment of $125,000,000.[24]

In 1913 Carnegie set up a similar body, the Carnegie United Kingdom Trust, with a much more modest endowment of $10,000,000. Originally he thought that he could simply transfer funds from the Carnegie Corporation for this purpose, but it was pointed out to him that he was debarred by the terms of his own endowment to the Corporation. Consequently, he was obliged to dip into what still remained of his personal fortune. Like its much larger American brother, this Trust continues to forge ahead, funding many libraries, educational projects, scientific and economic research and myriad lesser causes with cash that has now far exceeded the original endowment.[25]

In his 1931 biography of Carnegie, John K. Winkler had written sourly: 'Did he wish to benefit humanity? To make his name immortal? To wipe out the stains of the past with the pure brush of sincere philanthropy? Who can tell?'[26] Who indeed? But surely the immense good that has come of the Carnegie millions must outweigh any reservations about the manner in which they were amassed.

ELEVEN

Saint Andrew, Apostle of Peace

1901–14

I murder hate by field or flood,

Tho Glory's name may screen us;

In wars at hame I'll spend my blood –

Life-giving wars of Venus.

      Robert Burns, 'Lines at the Globe Tavern, Dumfries, 1793'

PACIFICISM WAS INSTILLED IN ANDREW CARNEGIE FROM A VERY early age. Although there would be times, at the beginning of the Civil War and during the Spanish-American War, when he let his pacifist ideals be muted by the justice of the cause, he never wavered in his sincere belief that world peace was essential to human progress. In 1869, when Britain launched HMS *Monarch*, then the largest and most powerful battleship afloat, Carnegie impetuously sent an anonymous telegram by the recently established transatlantic cable to John Bright, a Radical of the old school who was now in Gladstone's Liberal Cabinet. The one-liner read: 'First and best service possible for *Monarch*, bringing home body Peabody.' This was a laconic reference to the American merchant and philanthropist George Peabody who had recently died in London. Without ascertaining the identity of his correspondent, Bright arranged for Peabody's coffin to be taken to America aboard the pride of the Royal Navy. Many years later, at a small dinner party in Birmingham, Carnegie met his hero and informed him that it was he who had sent the telegram. On one of his early visits to England, Carnegie had become interested in the Peace Society of Great Britain and attended many of its meetings, and later on he was especially drawn to the

Parliamentary Union founded by William Randall Cremer. In 1887 Cremer and his Arbitration Committee visited Washington, and Carnegie had the pleasure of introducing them to President Cleveland.

Over the ensuing decade Carnegie devoted more and more of his free time to the furtherance of peace, and when Tsar Nicholas proposed the great Peace Conference at The Hague, Carnegie was voluble in his support. The Hague Conference had the relatively limited objective of getting the leading powers to agree to scale down their armament programmes, and although it failed signally in that respect, it nevertheless created the notion of having some kind of supra-national body to settle disputes between countries. Hitherto great international gatherings of statesmen and diplomats had only been called into being whenever a major crisis loomed, as, for example, the Berlin Congress of 1878 which addressed the Balkan question and the imminent collapse of the Ottoman Empire.

'We have already Peace Societies and Arbitration Societies,' wrote Carnegie in October 1900 to W.T. Stead, editor of *The Review of Reviews* who had urged him to use some of his great wealth in founding a new international society for world peace, and he added, 'There is nothing that robs a righteous cause of its strength more than a millionaire's money – especially during his life. It makes a serious, holy cause simply a fad. Its life is tainted thereby.' In a remarkably short time, however, he would change his mind. Just as he had started in business with eggs in many baskets, but eventually concentrated the bulk of his wealth and energy in steel, so too the random, sometimes irrational or even quixotic, disbursement of money to good causes eventually took second place to a goal so stupendous in its magnitude that it took the breath away merely to contemplate it. The goal which Carnegie would set himself was nothing less than the eradication of war, the curse of mankind since the dawn of time.

Prior to this earth-shaking decision he had strenuously campaigned for an arbitration treaty between Britain and the United States, but the Venezuela boundary dispute of 1895 showed how fragile such an agreement might have been. Sometimes his dreams of peace were oddly at variance with his public pronouncements. One would have thought that the four thousand miles of undefended, open frontier between the United States and Canada were a practical demonstration of the pacificist's ideals; but Carnegie passionately felt that Canada should become part of the United States, and these intemperate outbursts, widely publicised of course, did nothing to endear him to the Canadians or to diminish their demands for greater imperial funding for their defence against their powerful neighbour. The same may be said of Mexico, which Carnegie also saw as a potential extension of the United States with the ultimate aim of bringing the entire continent under American rule. Carnegie could be remarkably wrongheaded at times, but in pursuit of the Canadian bee in his bonnet he definitely overstepped the mark, especially when, in 1903, he prophesied that 'Canada will someday annex the Republic, just as the northern part of Great Britain, called Scotland, actually annexed the southern part, called England, and has blessed it ever since.' By these intemperate remarks he succeeded in upsetting Scotsmen, Englishmen, Canadians and American jingoists alike – quite a remarkable feat, even by Carnegie's standards.

It is not surprising, therefore, that the mainstream pacifist movements tended to be wary of the little man, keeping him at arm's length. Only when the size of his immense fortune was realised, and especially after he began giving most of it away, did the pacificists make really serious overtures to him. As a consequence, between 1903 and 1914 Carnegie endowed four trusts and built three impressive 'temples of peace' as he called them, at a personal cost of $25,250,000. This was not the largest sum expended on a single cause by any means, but it was undoubtedly the project dearest to the old man's heart. Two of these endowments, discussed in the preceding chapter, were the Simplified Spelling Board and the Hero Fund which do not at first glance appear to have furthered the cause of world peace; but Brander Matthews had converted Carnegie to his concept of simplified spelling as a necessary prelude to English becoming the lingua franca of the entire world. When people could communicate freely with each other, all the disagreements that arose from simple misunderstanding would vanish and wars would no longer arise. (Almost a century on, however, English is closer to becoming a global language than ever, yet the world is no nearer to peace as a result.) In the end, all it achieved was the modified spelling of words like honor and favor – a reform which had been advocated more than a century earlier and which had been enthusiastically adopted by Robert Burns in his own prose and poetry.

Not until 1910, when Carnegie created his Endowment for International Peace, did he allay the suspicions of serious pacificists that he was nothing more than a muddle-headed eccentric with far more money than sense. Carnegie chose his seventy-fifth birthday, 25 November 1910, as the occasion to announce this endowment with a trust fund of $10,000,000. The annual income from this money was to be used 'in any way appropriate to hasten the abolition of war'. Such was Carnegie's optimism concerning the attainment of that aim within the foreseeable future that he included a proviso that 'when the establishment of universal peace is attained, the donor provides that the revenue shall be devoted to the banishment of the next most degrading evil or evils, the suppression of which would most advance the progress, elevation and happiness of man'.[1] Carnegie assembled an impressive board of trustees, headed by President Taft. Within two years this body had organised several divisions dealing with such specific aspects as international law, economics, education and 'intercourse' which dealt with publicity and propaganda for the peace movement. Ironically, one of the Endowment's most concrete achievements was the exhaustive survey of conditions prevailing in the Balkans in the aftermath of the Second Balkan War, 1913–14. At the end of 1913, the Endowment's first full year of operation, its chairman, Nicholas Murray Butler, could claim with a measure of satisfaction that the infrastructure was in place for the long-term realisation of its goals, though he was faintly critical of his own government and the other leading powers for not taking positive steps to reduce international tension. In particular, he singled out the naval rivalry between Britain and Germany, the traditional enmity of Germany and France, the actions of the American government in the Pacific which would lead to friction with Japan, and a series of misunderstandings between the United States and Mexico.

The fourth and last of the Carnegie endowments with a pacificist element was the Church Peace Union, founded in February 1914. Unlike the previous endowments, this was funded by the Carnegie Corporation rather than the man himself, and was given the comparatively modest sum of $2,000,000. Given Carnegie's antipathy towards organised religion, this endowment seems rather surprising.

In fact it was Louise Carnegie who was the driving force, having been converted to the idea by two ministers, her own pastor Dr William P. Merrill of the Brick Presbyterian Church in New York, and Frederick Lynch, a Congregational clergyman in Pittsburgh. Once her husband was sold on the idea of the different religious denominations uniting to oppose war, he entered into the spirit of the thing with characteristic enthusiasm. In his own way, therefore, he felt he was doing something positive to break down the artificial barriers of religions and create a truly ecumenical spirit in the cause of world peace. He was particularly pleased when his latest endowment recruited an impressive board which included Cardinal Gibbons, the Episcopal Bishop Greer and a couple of prominent rabbis as well as leaders from the Universalists, Baptists and other sects. At the inaugural meeting it was decided to hold an international conference in Europe that summer. In due course this was fixed, and Carnegie hoped to join the American delegation bound for Konstanz, Germany, on 1 August 1914. As it turned out, 'the best laid schemes o' mice and men', as Carnegie's favourite bard so pithily put it, were sent agley by factors beyond their control.

These four foundations may have received a vast amount of cash, but they did not get the same degree of thought and energy as Carnegie expended on his 'temples of peace'. Of the three, the Palace of Peace at The Hague was the first to be undertaken and the last to be completed, and was by far the largest and most important. The impetus for this building – to house a permanent tribunal to settle international disputes – arose from the disarmament conference of 1899. Frederic de Martens, a Russian diplomat of Dutch origins, Frederick Holls, secretary of the American delegation, and Andrew White, American ambassador to Germany, were the prime movers in this project. Carnegie was decidedly lukewarm when the idea was first broached by Holls, but White adopted a more subtle, psychological approach and gradually the notion became clearer in Carnegie's mind. Even so, he was too preoccupied with his first great acts of philanthropy, not to mention moving house, to give the idea much serious attention. 'Please let the idea rest for the moment,' he wrote to Holls in the spring of 1902; but within months Holls and White had persuaded him to make at least a tentative move in that direction, with a grant of $250,000 for a library on international law for use by the Permanent Court of Arbitration at The Hague. This was an exceedingly generous sum of money for a library, but even so it fell far short of what Holls and White had in mind.

They continued to press Carnegie, and in the end he conceded that if he were approached by the Dutch government he might consider building a 'temple of peace' rather than just a library. Holls wrote to the American ambassador to Russia, admitting that Carnegie was rather slow to make up his mind, 'beside being given to changing it with lightning quickness'. Through diplomatic circles, however, the desired result was achieved; Baron de Gevers, Dutch minister to the United States, let it be known that his government would be pleased to accept the gift of a court house for the Hague Tribunal, and would provide a suitable site for the building. At Skibo Castle on 7 October 1903 the formal deed for the creation of a trust under Dutch law was signed by Carnegie and Baron de Gevers. Interestingly, the pump was to be primed with $1,500,000 drawn by Carnegie out of his personal bank account on a bank draft of the Netherlands government. Holls communicated with Baron de Bildt, the Swedish minister to the Court of St James, concerning this matter and warned the diplomat that Carnegie was 'a very peculiar man but you will know exactly how to get along with him'. If invited to Skibo, Holls advised him strongly to go up there 'for it is one of the most charming places in Scotland'. Meanwhile Andrew White pressed home the advantage by congratulating Carnegie in fulsome terms: 'The gift which fairly takes my breath away is your provision for the Temple of Peace. That will result undoubtedly in saving hundreds of thousands of lives. It is an immense thing, to have made such a provision.'[2]

Sadly, Holls was accidentally killed shortly afterwards and did not live to see the laying of the foundation stone of the great Peace Palace. He was, however, spared the heartaches and tribulations which dogged and daunted his colleagues. These arose primarily over a protracted wrangle between the Dutch government and the planning commission over the choice of a site. This contentious issue was not resolved until May 1905 when it was finally agreed to erect the building on the outskirts of the Zorgvliet Park near The Hague, and the Dutch parliament voted the 700,000 guilders (about $290,000 or £75,000) required to purchase the land. There then ensued a long and acrimonious argument over virtually every detail of the construction, from the prize-winning architectural drawings to the actual materials used. In every aspect of this long-drawn-out and, at times, exceedingly bitter, saga, Carnegie played a central and highly opinionated role. The unfortunate man at the centre of this epic storm was David Jayne Hill, the American minister to the Netherlands, who was the target of incessant critical and querulous letters, memoranda and telegrams from Carnegie. Blithely ignoring his earlier intentions, Carnegie fiercely criticised the original plan because it included a library which, he alleged, had not been in the original scheme at all. Reading between the lines in this lengthy and increasingly acrimonious exchange, one gets the impression that Carnegie was blowing hot and cold on the project. Money was at the heart of the matter, Carnegie clamouring for a small, simple structure and arguing that a large, showy building would be incongruous. In particular, he urged that the court chamber should be so small that the members would be forced to huddle close together, 'in touch with each other mentally and almost physically, proximity being always conducive to friendly conference and harmony. It dampens excited oratorical discussion'.[3] When the jury selected a design by W.M. Cordonnier of Lille, Carnegie objected that no American architect had been chosen. Again he took umbrage at the jury referring to the proposed building as the Library and Court of Arbitration. In a long letter of complaint he conceded: 'I have neither the right or desire to counsel the Jury,' although counsel was the one commodity of which there seemed an endless stream coming from Skibo. Within a fortnight, he was on the warpath again, demanding that Cordonnier's plan be scrapped completely and insisting on a fresh start. In particular he criticised Cordonnier's façade: 'To me the building proposed is no temple of peace, but shows all over of pomp, pride and vain circumstance of inglorious war.'[4]

Ambassador Hill was inclined to agree with Carnegie on that score, preferring something smaller, in the neo-classical mode, rather than the proposed fussy structure resembling a medieval Flemish guild hall. Samuel Harden Church of the Carnegie Institute in Pittsburgh was drafted across to confer with Jonkheer Van Karnebeek, the director of the Peace Palace, and explain to him the preferred Carnegie Classical style. Van Karnebeek appeared to give way regarding the design, but in one area he remained obdurate; the structure must be built in Flemish red brick, arguing that stone or marble were unsuited to the damp Dutch climate. In the end, Van Karnebeek made the pilgrimage to Skibo to put his arguments to Carnegie in person. Considering the circumstances, the meeting was remarkably cordial. In the end Carnegie gave way, after some modification of the towers, and finally conceded that a library was an indispensable appendage to the proposed court. On the question of building materials, however, he would not budge. The Peace Palace must be built of honest Scottish stone. At first he insisted that the stone used to build Skibo should be employed, but when it was discovered that the castle had exhausted the local quarries, he recommended granite from Aberdeen. In the end he was silenced by the estimated cost of quarrying and shipping the required amount of granite, and so Van Karnebeek finally had his way.

The foundation stone was not laid until the summer of 1907, in nice time for the opening of the Second Hague International Conference. Actual construction of the palace took a further six years, delayed and exacerbated by constant bickering over details, specifications and materials. For an entire decade the Peace Palace was bedevilled by controversy, but finally, on 28 August 1913, the opening ceremony was performed. The correspondent from *The Times* cynically noted that: 'There was glorious sunshine and, more importantly, the present lull between the last war and the next has been a propitious opportunity for offering to the world the noble gift of Mr Andrew Carnegie.' Into the Great Court crowded Queen Wilhelmina and the Carnegies, as well as statesmen and diplomats, over four hundred people in all. The man from *The Times* also commented cryptically that the building itself 'is certainly unlike anything else in the world'.[5]

The following day Carnegie took centre stage, unveiling busts of King Edward the Peacemaker and Sir William Randall Cremer. In his address, Carnegie praised the Palace as 'a perfect gem'. He then boarded his favourite bandwagon and extolled the virtues of the Teutonic nations (Germany, Britain and the United States) joining forces to secure world peace. In particular he urged Kaiser Wilhelm to summon the leading nations of the world to a peace conference:

> The greatest advances have appeared to burst upon us suddenly although the ground has been well prepared. So it will probably be with the change from barbarous war to civilized peace ... One small spark often creates the flame. The German Emperor holds in his hand the torch.[6]

Within a twelvemonth Carnegie would be regretting this unfortunate turn of phrase.

By contrast, the other temples of peace caused relatively little trouble in their planning and construction. Carnegie was flattered when Elihu Root, Secretary of State, asked him to consider providing a new and more commodious building for the Bureau of American Republics that would be worthy of its role in bringing the countries of the Western Hemisphere closer together. This was a deeply cherished aim of Carnegie, and he responded to the invitation with alacrity and enthusiasm. Within three weeks he had replied to Root, offering $150,000 for the purpose. This time there was no nonsense with foreign architects, and in due course the building was erected in the neo-classical style favoured for public edifices in the District of Columbia. The foundation stone of the Pan American Union Building was laid on 11 May 1908 and almost exactly two years later it was formally inaugurated.

Root was also the instigator of the third, and smallest, of the peace temples. In 1907 the five republics of Central America signed an agreement at Washington to establish a Central American Court of Justice where their differences and boundary disputes could be settled. On 27 May 1907 Root communicated this decision to Carnegie, who agreed to put up the $100,000 for the temple which was to be built at Cartago in Costa Rica. This building progressed with the minimum of fuss and was formally inaugurated in May 1910.

These endowments and institutions which Carnegie funded are still in existence, and over the years they have done much good work and helped to settle all manner of disputes great and small; but in the larger context it is now realised that they could never achieve anything of lasting importance, and Carnegie was singularly naïve in supposing that he could use his money to play God. In fairness, however, far greater organisations than he could ever have envisaged have tried and failed. The League of Nations, with its splendid Palais des Nations on Lake Geneva, was the great white hope of the world after the First World War, but it was powerless to stop the relentless march of fascism in the 1930s, and the Second World War brought it to an ignominious end. Rising from its ashes at the end of that war, the United Nations Organisation has achieved even more, especially through its specialised agencies like UNICEF and the Food and Agricultural Organisation; but, like its predecessor, it has so far been unable to check or prevent major conflagrations in many parts of the world, from Bosnia to Zaire. Three-quarters of a century after Carnegie embarked on this particular brand of philanthropy, world peace seems to be as elusive as ever.

As President of the Peace Society of New York, an office which he accepted with great reluctance and soul-searching in 1907, Carnegie hosted a peace banquet in April 1908 at which, to his pleasant surprise, he was invested with the insignia of Chevalier of the Légion d'Honneur by Baron d'Estournelles de Constant. 'Such honors humble, they do not exalt;' he wrote, 'so let them come.'[7] Subsequently he received the Grand Cross of the Order of Oranje-Nassau from the Netherlands and the Grand Cross of the Danish Order of Danebrog. Strangely enough, no British decoration ever came his way nor, for that matter, the Nobel Peace Prize, though no man ever did more (in the pecuniary line at any rate) to promote world peace.

Carnegie was not content to provide money for endowments and temples of peace; he yearned also to play a personal part in achieving world peace. The first inkling that he was a force to be reckoned with came on 17 October 1905, when he made a stirring, impassioned denunciation of war 'as the foulest fiend ever vomited forth from the mouth of Hell' in his rectorial address at St Andrews, inaugurating his second term as Lord Rector of the university. The climax of this address reviewed the progress of the Permanent Court of Arbitration which had been set up at The Hague. Though it had not yet obtained a home of its own, this institution had already been the means of averting war between the United States and Mexico, and bringing the Venezuelan crisis of 1902 to a peaceful conclusion. It had mediated successfully between Britain and Russia over the recent

Dogger Bank incident and was engaged in a series of talks involving the United States, Russia and Japan over their clash of interests in the Far East. 'There sits the divinest conclave that ever graced the earth,' he concluded, though he also drew attention to the fact that the Hague Court had not been able to prevent three major wars – the Russo-Japanese conflict, the Boer War and the American campaign against the Filipinos who, having seen the Spaniards depart, were now clamouring for freedom from the Americans. Carnegie wound up by proposing a League of Peace, in which the world's five great powers – the United States, Great Britain, Germany, Russia and France – would agree never again to go to war with each other. Where the great powers set an example, lesser powers would surely follow.

This speech was reported all over the world and made a tremendous impact; it was enthusiastically acclaimed by pacificist groups everywhere because it not only highlighted the evils of war but offered a constructive solution to the problem. Within twelve months several hundred thousand copies of the speech, translated into thirteen languages, had been disseminated at Carnegie's expense by Baron d'Estournelles de Constant and his Society for International Conciliation. In France alone, a hundred thousand copies were distributed to school teachers; by 1909 the speech had gone through five editions and over three million copies. This established Carnegie as one of the world's most prominent and ardent peace propagandists, and over the ensuing years he wrote numerous articles and pamphlets with such titles as 'The Anglo-French-American Understanding', 'The Cry of Wolf', 'The Next Step for Peace', 'Peace versus War', 'The Crime of War is Inherent', 'Armaments and Their Results', 'The Path to Peace Upon the Seas', 'War as the Mother of Valor and Civilization', 'The Baseless Fear of War' and 'The Decadence of Militarism'. These polemical writings were widely circulated and reprinted in newspapers and magazines all over the world, and placed Carnegie in the forefront of peace activism. His arguments were always closely reasoned and his words had greater impact than those of many other peace propagandists because he adopted a down-to-earth, commonsense approach.

The same spirit of pragmatism and realism pervaded his dealings with politicians and presidents, particularly in his one-man campaign to get the major powers to reduce the size of their Dreadnought battleship fleets. At that time, Britain maintained a policy of having a battle fleet which must be larger than the world's second and third navies combined; but by 1906 the Royal Navy had a tonnage of 2,100,000 whereas the next four European powers combined had only 600,000 tons of capital shipping. The Second Hague Conference, in 1907, proved a great disappointment to Carnegie because the issue of disarmament foundered on Britain's naval policy and the objection raised by Germany which had recently embarked on a costly programme of battleships in order to reduce the threat from Britain. Britain, of course, perceived this move by Germany as a threat and reacted by stepping up its building programme. Carnegie viewed the posturing and bellicose antics of the major powers with mounting despair. His only consolation was that the Peace Court, as a last resort, would prevent war. In this respect he opposed the smaller countries having an equal say: 'I incline to the plan of five or six Powers agreeing to the Court, and let the smaller Powers alone. They can't go far, a joint word – what we Scotch call an intimation will serve to keep them from disturbing the world's peace.'[8] Thereafter he switched tactics and concentrated on a consortium of major powers who would police the world and began promoting the idea of a Legion of Peace. In an article in *Outlook* late in 1907 he wrote: 'I believe the next step to universal peace to be the formation of a League of Nations similar to that formed in China recently for a specific object.' This seems to have been a reference to the Treaty of Portsmouth which Theodore Roosevelt engineered between Russia and Japan in 1905. This, incidentally, added considerably to Roosevelt's prestige at home and abroad and secured for him the Nobel Peace Prize the following year. Carnegie promoted his idea of a League of Nations with Roosevelt, and when the latter went to Christiania (now Oslo) to collect his prize in 1910 he spoke eloquently and forcefully about a future League of Nations for the prevention of war. For this reason he is often regarded as the progenitor of the great world body brought to fruition by Woodrow Wilson in 1919; but credit for the idea in the first place belongs to Andrew Carnegie.

Early in 1907 a new International Peace Society was formed and Carnegie was elected its first president. At the first National Arbitration and Peace Congress held in April he waxed eloquent on the theme of an international police force. But, he argued, force should only be the ultimate deterrent. Before matters came to that, an international policy of non-intercourse with the offending country should be pursued: 'No exchange of products, no loans, no military or naval supplies, no mail – these restrictions would serve as a solemn warning and probably prove effective. Force should always be the last resort.'⁹

Subsequently he refined his ideas of the League of Nations consisting of the five leading powers, with the authority to enforce economic sanctions, with an international police force to coerce the aggressor nation if required. This League would operate in conjunction with the Peace Court to which all nations would submit international disputes for arbitration. As a start, he advocated closer co-operation between the British Royal Navy and the United States Navy in the policing of the high seas. This notion received a very sympathetic hearing from Carnegie's old corporation lawyer, Philander Knox, who was now Secretary of State, and it was also well received by his friend John Morley, who succeeded in interesting the British Foreign Secretary, the Marquess of Lansdowne. President Roosevelt, initially receptive, surprised and disappointed his friend when, in November 1907, he changed his mind and initiated a policy of building up the US Navy. The reason for Roosevelt's sudden change of heart was the 'Yellow Peril', the fear of Japanese expansion across the Pacific, and this would become a major obsession in ensuing years. The following month the two men had a meeting to discuss the matter. When Roosevelt revealed the reason for demanding a futher three battleships, Carnegie brushed it aside, saying that Japan was really a negligible quantity. Roosevelt said nothing at the time, but sent Carnegie a curt note in January 1908 saying that it 'would be the very highest unwisdom' to treat the Japanese threat so lightly. Despite this sharp difference in opinion, however, Carnegie remained one of Roosevelt's most ardent admirers, though he was often sorely pressed to defend Colonel Teddy against the criticism of his pacificist colleagues.

From 1907 also dates Carnegie's obsession that the key to world peace lay in the palm of Kaiser Wilhelm II. Throughout his life, Carnegie had had his idols: grandfather Morrison, uncle George Lauder, his sainted mother, Tom Scott. As his horizons widened the objects of his worship became more eminent: James Blaine, Grover Cleveland, William Jennings Bryan and Elihu Root in America, and John Bright, William Ewart Gladstone and John Morley in Britain. But all of them paled into insignificance before Theodore Roosevelt (whom he had begun by distrusting but later admired unreservedly) and Kaiser Bill (whom he began by admiring, but by whom he would later be bitterly disillusioned). Although Roosevelt dazzled Carnegie with his larger-than-life personality, the President privately had no time for the other man and once wrote to his friend Whitelaw Reid (1905): 'I have tried hard to like Carnegie, but it is pretty difficult.' Fortunately Carnegie never discovered what Roosevelt really thought of him.

One of Carnegie's fantasies was to effect a meeting between these two superheroes, the Kaiser and Roosevelt – with himself, of course, centre stage. He would sketch his plan for world peace and these two men, perceived as the most powerful rulers of the time, would agree his proposals: war would be banished, the lion would lie down with the lamb, swords would be beaten into ploughshares, and all would be right with the world.

Roosevelt, however, had one disadvantage: his second term of office was due to end in March 1909. Though easily the most popular American president in recent times, he had promised in 1904 that he would not seek a third term, and in the presidential campaign of November 1908 he had backed his friend William Howard Taft, who was duly elected. A subsequent bitter quarrel with Taft induced him to throw his hat into the ring when the next presidential contest arose in November 1912, but all that he and Taft succeeded in doing was to split the Republican vote, demoralise their party, and concede a landslide victory to the Democrats led by Woodrow Wilson. Nevertheless, the years after he demitted office, especially 1910–12, witnessed the emergence of Roosevelt as the world's outstanding figure. During an extensive tour of Europe he was fêted everywhere. In London he attended the funeral of King Edward VII as Taft's special envoy and in Paris he addressed the Sorbonne, but in Berlin he stood alongside the Kaiser as they reviewed the imperial guards. Roosevelt was the only civilian ever accorded this exalted privilege, and Carnegie's only regret was that he could not have been there on the podium, alongside his two heroes. He did the next best thing, by sending Roosevelt detailed instructions on how to behave and what exactly to say to the Kaiser; amazingly, Roosevelt took Carnegie's advice very much to heart. It should perhaps be noted that Roosevelt's great world tour, which included many months in Africa slaughtering wild animals in the name of science, was actually funded by Carnegie, J.P. Morgan and a few other wealthy backers.

Despite his global popularity and great charisma, however, Roosevelt was now a man without real power. That lay with German's All-Highest. Still a relatively young man, Wilhelm celebrated the twentieth anniversary of his autocratic rule in 1908. He was in the prime of life, with a firmer control over Germany than ever before, and seemed destined to reign over his Empire for many years to come. The Kaiser was increasingly regarded by Carnegie as his chosen instrument in conferring the greatest of all benefits on mankind, not just for the present, but for posterity. Thus it was that, in his speech at the New York Peace Conference on 17 April 1907, Carnegie spoke movingly:

> It lies today in the power of one man to found this league of peace. Perhaps our President may yet have that part to play. He seems born for great roles in the world drama . . . At this moment, however, it is not in his hands, but in those of the German Emperor, alone of all men, that the power to abolish war seems to rest . . . Much has been written and said of the Emperor as a menace to the peace of Europe, but I think unjustly. So far, let me remind you, he has been nearly twenty years on the throne and is guiltless of shedding blood. No war can be charged to him. His sin hereafter may be one of omission, that having been entrusted with the power to abolish war, he failed to rise to this transcendent duty.

Carnegie's perception of the Kaiser was no gut feeling. He had studied his hero thoroughly, and had been schooled by such men as Nicholas Murray Butler, Andrew White and David Jayne Hill, as well as White's successor as American ambassador in Germany, the aptly named Charlemagne Tower. Without exception, these men were ardent admirers of the Emperor, though Carnegie outdid them all. In his article 'The Cry of the Wolf' he lashed out against the fear and distrust of Germany which had developed in recent years in Britain and, to a lesser extent, in America. In emphasising the peace-loving nature of the Kaiser, however, Carnegie differed sharply from his British friends, particularly Morley and Bryce, but his comments did not pass unnoticed at Potsdam. The Kaiser was not getting too good a press generally at that time, so Carnegie's fulsome praise stood out. Soon after the publication of this article the Kaiser informed Ambassador Tower that he would be pleased to welcome Mr Carnegie at the annual fleet review at Kiel. There was an exchange of correspondence between Tower and Carnegie late in April 1907 and a few weeks later he prepared to leave America for Europe. On the eve of his departure in early June he wrote to Morley expressing his view of the Kaiser: 'No other man has the power to draw a League of Nations competent to keep the peace for an agreed upon period just as an experiment. Even if nations didn't accept he holds the Stage as world's apostle of Peace.' He was extremely impressed with the Kaiser's devout piety; Wilhelm had sent Carnegie a copy of the address to his son on his consecration as crown prince 'and it wouldn't discredit a Holy Father of the Catholic Church'. Then he concluded, 'Well, never was a Holy Father more convinced of his Mission than I am of mine. I *know* I offer H.I.M. the plan that makes him the greatest agent known so far in human history. The Peace Maker.'[10]

On 19 June the Carnegies arrived at Kiel and the little peace zealot went straightway with Tower to register aboard the imperial yacht *Hohenzollern*. Unexpectedly, they bumped into the Kaiser himself, neatly clad in nautical rig. Unabashed, Carnegie greeted the object of his hero-worship warmly and cried: 'This has happened just as I could have wished, with no ceremony, and the Man of Destiny dropped from the clouds!'

'Ah, but I understand you do not like kings,' observed the Kaiser with a smile.

'No, Your Majesty, I do not like kings,' riposted Carnegie. 'But I do like a man behind a king when I find him.'

That evening they toasted each other and got on famously. Wilhelm even let his guest get in a word or two occasionally. The meeting was an unqualified success, so far as Carnegie was concerned. In his journal he observed:

> The Emperor is fine company, and I believe an earnest man anxious
> for the peace and progress of the world. The peace of the world has
> little to fear from Germany. Her interests are all favorable to peace,
> industrial development being her aim.

Subsequently he expanded this brief, first impression in a long letter to Sir James Donaldson, Principal of St Andrews University:

> I had three interviews with the German Emperor and dined with
> him twice – a wonderful man, so bright, humorous and *with a sweet
> smile*. I think he can be trusted and declares himself for peace.[11]

Thereafter Carnegie never flinched from his belief in the Kaiser; nothing and no one could ever shake this unbounded faith. As late as 8 June 1913 he was writing an effusive article the *New York Times* Sunday magazine entitled 'Kaiser Wilhelm II, Peace Maker'. But long before that date the terrible chain of events that would lead to global catastrophe had been set in motion.

The emergence of the great power blocs, with Britain, France and Russia in the Triple Entente, and Germany, Austria and Italy in the Triple Alliance, polarised the situation. Nevertheless the first major clash of these power blocs – over Austria's annexation of Bosnia in 1908 – eventually passed off without war. In fairness to the Kaiser, he had been shocked and outraged at Austria's action, taken without consulting or even notifying her ally. He had accused Vienna of duplicity and felt himself deeply wounded in his sentiments of an ally; but his chancellor, Von Bülow, feared that Germany would lose her last reliable ally, and backed Austria at all costs. Similarly, it was not the Kaiser but one of his ministers, Kiderlen-Wächter, who was primarily responsible for the collision with France which arose in 1911 when the French began to bring Morocco under their rule. Wilhelm was dead against letting a fresh quarrel develop between Germany and France over Morocco. Against his own better judgement, however, the Kaiser was persuaded to send the gunboat *Panzer* to the Moroccan coast. Even after the so-called Agadir Incident, which only drove Britain and France closer together and alienated public opinion in much of Europe as well as in America against Germany, Carnegie continued stoutly to uphold the Kaiser as the one man on whom world peace depended. Rather lamely, he concluded that had the Morocco crisis of 1911 occurred a decade earlier, it would immediately have plunged Britain, France and Germany into war. That it did not lead to war, he claimed, was due to the efforts of the German Emperor.

Now the Kaiser was held up by Carnegie more than ever as the 'Hero of Peace'. When Nicholas Murray Butler proposed that Wilhelm be given an illuminated testimonial, signed by the leading officials of seventy American societies and institutions, on the occasion of his Silver Jubilee in June 1913, it was Carnegie who journeyed to Berlin to present the memorial to the Kaiser in person. As he handed the precious document to the Emperor, Carnegie emotionally hailed him as 'our strongest ally in the cause of peace'.

In 1906 Theodore Roosevelt had been awarded the Nobel Peace Prize, largely on account of his role in ending the Russo-Japanese War. Three years later Baron d'Estournelles de Constant was the recipient of the prize and in 1912 it was the turn of Carnegie's friend Elihu Root, in respect of his position as president of the Carnegie Endowment for International Peace. Carnegie himself was actually nominated for the prize, and, though bitterly disappointed when he did not get it, he tried to console himself that it had gone to his favourite candidate. It seems incredible that the Norwegian Storting, which provided the jury for the Peace Prize, ignored the claims of Andrew Carnegie. To be sure, the prize was then worth no more than £8000 in cash, together with a gold medal, but the honour and prestige, not to mention recognition for his efforts to secure world peace, would probably have meant more to Carnegie than all his other honours and decorations put together. Even the first Pan-American Gold Medal, presented to him in 1911, must have seemed a poor substitute, despite the elaborate ceremony attended by President Taft, Secretary Knox and the ambassadors of the twenty-one American republics. It was the crowning honour of his long and busy life.

Nevertheless, Carnegie could console himself with ample evidence of the high regard in which he was held by the world's greatest and most influential figures. No less a personage than the Pope himself addressed a public letter to Carnegie hailing him as the Peacemaker, surely the first step in the long process of canonisation. Baroness

Berthe von Suttner, Nobel's secretary and the first woman to hold the Peace Prize, wrote to him in May 1909, saying: 'America is in advance of Europe in many things over Europe – but in the peace-movement the advance is a stupendous one. And most of it is due to *you*.'[12]

As time passed, Carnegie lulled himself into a false optimism about world peace, despite a series of wars and revolutions in Mexico, right on America's own doorstep, since 1911, as well as the Italo-Turkish War of the same year and the Balkan Wars of 1912–13. Carnegie would argue that these were limited conflicts, which had been contained within specific areas, and the fact that these wars had not spread to neighbouring countries was surely proof that the world, at large, had matured. At the end of 1913 the Carnegies sent out New Year greetings cards inscribed:

> . . . strong in the faith that International Peace is soon to prevail, thru several of the great powers agreeing to settle their disputes by arbitration under International Law, the pen thus proving mitier [*sic*] than the sword . . . Be of good cheer, kind friend.
>
> It's coming yet for a' that!
> When man to man the world o'er
> Shall brothers be and a' that.

On 23 May 1914 the Carnegies set off on what was Andrew's sixty-fourth crossing of the Atlantic. They disembarked at Plymouth a week later and began a hectic social round which included a brace of freedoms (at Coventry and Lincoln) to add to the bag, before heading north for rest and recreation at Skibo. Carnegie, who had never paid any heed to Britain's internal politics, was appalled to find much talk of trouble in Ireland, where the smooth transition to Home Rule was bedevilled by the arming of Protestant paramilitaries in Ulster and a much-publicised 'mutiny' of senior army officers at the Curragh camp near Dublin. Carnegie had nothing but contempt for 'organised religion' and the bigotry it so often spawned, and he pressed a great deal of well-meaning advice on John Morley and Prime Minister Asquith. On the very day, 28 June, that he wrote a long letter to *The Times* about 'the perils in which the Mother Country is becoming involved', a tubercular student named Gavrilo Prizip assassinated the heir to the Habsburg dominions, the Archduke Franz Ferdinand, and his wife as they rode in an open carriage through the streets of the Bosnian capital, Sarajevo.

The Carnegies passed an idyllic, tranquil fortnight at Skibo before retiring to their shooting-lodge on the moors at Aultnagar, where Andrew put the finishing touches to the *Autobiography* he had been writing over the three preceding years. He was engaged in this congenial task, ironically concluding a chapter entitled 'Meeting the German Emperor', when word reached him on 4 August that war had broken out in Europe. He had just described his last meeting with the Kaiser, at Berlin in June 1913, when he had presented the American testimonial, and hailed the Kaiser as 'our chief ally' in the quest for world peace. Now he appended a sorry paragraph:

> He had hitherto sat silent and motionless, taking the successive addresses from one officer and handing them to another to be placed upon the table. The chief subject under discussion had been World Peace, which he could have, and in my opinion, would have secured, had he not been surrounded by the military caste which inevitably gathers about one born to the throne – a caste which usually becomes as permanent as the potentate himself, and which has so far in Germany proved its power of control whenever the war issue has been presented. Until militarism is subordinated, there can be no World Peace.[13]

Carnegie was stunned by the news of war. Suddenly his magnificent obsession was shattered and all hopes of creating a world of peace seemed to vanish for ever. One may imagine the anguish he felt as he penned the following lines: 'The world convulsed as never before! Men slaying each other like wild beasts!' But then he perked up. There was something of that old, indomitable resilience in the words:

> I dare not relinquish all hope. In recent days I see another ruler coming forward upon the world stage, who may prove himself the immortal one. The man who vindicated his country's honor in the Panama Canal toil dispute is now President. He has the indomitable will of genius, and true hope which we are told.

'Kings it makes god, and meaner creatures kings.' Nothing is impossible to genius! Watch President Wilson! He has Scotch blood in his veins.

To which John C. Van Dyke, who edited Carnegie's memoirs for publication in 1920, added: 'Here the manuscript ends abruptly.'

TWELVE

Last Years

1914–19

John Anderson my jo, John,
We clamb the hill thegither,
And monie a cantie day, John,
We've had wi ane anither;
Now we maun totter down, John,
And hand in hand we'll go
And sleep thegither at the foot,
John Anderson my jo!

      Robert Burns, 'John Anderson, My Jo'

IN THE PREFACE TO HIS *AUTOBIOGRAPHY* CARNEGIE'S WIFE LOUISE explained how he was engaged in writing his memoirs when news of the outbreak of the First World War reached him at Aultnagar. He immediately packed up his writing materials and returned to Skibo to be more in touch with the situation:

> These memoirs ended at that time. Henceforth he was never able to interest himself in private affairs. Many times he made the attempt to continue writing, but found it useless. Until then he had lived the life of a man in middle life – and a young one at that – golfing, fishing, swimming each day, sometimes doing all three in one day. Optimist as he always was and tried to be, even in the face of the failure of his hopes, the world disaster was too much. His heart was broken.[1]

Carnegie's immediate concern was the Church Peace Union whose first World Conference opened at Konstanz, Germany, on 1 August.

292

From Aultnagar the following day Carnegie sent a telegram to J. Allen Baker, leader of the British delegation, saying: 'We shall be with you today in spirit, and full in the faith that our cause is righteous,' and ending: 'We know that man is created with an instinct for development, and that from the first he developed to higher and higher standards and that there is no limit to his future ascent.'[2] Events were moving at such a rapid pace that the pious hopes expressed in this telegram were shattered almost before they were wired. With the German declaration of war on Russia on 1 August, France (under the terms of the Triple Entente) was automatically at war with Germany and Germany, in execution of the Schlieffen plan for the invasion of France, demanded from Belgium the right of transit for its troops through that country. On 3 August King Albert of the Belgians gave his formal refusal, whereupon the Germans invaded Belgium the following day. In defence of the treaty of 1839 which had guaranteed Belgian neutrality, Britain was now sucked into the conflict, and declared war on Germany at midnight. At a Cabinet meeting earlier that day John Morley, true to his pacificist principles, resigned from the Liberal government. On that same evening, Morley wrote to Carnegie describing the poignancy of his last Cabinet meeting as Britain teetered on the edge of the abyss: 'But what a black panorama! To nobody will it seem blacker than to you. Hell in full blast. This is a sorrowful night for me – probably the last of my public life.'[3]

Meanwhile the British and American delegations to the peace conference had managed to escape from Germany aboard the last train to leave the country before the frontiers were sealed. On Sunday, 2 August, delegates had met three times for prayers and impassioned speeches. While the armies of France, Germany and Britain were being mobilised, the delegations from these countries met for the last time in 'perfect brotherhood and affection', as Frederick Lynch, leader of the American group, described the unforgettable scene. From London on 6 August he wrote to Carnegie at great length, vividly describing the horrors he had witnessed on the appalling journey across Europe. Nothing daunted, the travel-stained delegates reconvened on 7 August in the Westminster Palace Hotel, London, feeling that their peace deliberations were more urgently needed than ever before, and an address to the American

Federal Council of Churches was drafted. The American delegation would head for home, more convinced than ever of the horrors of militarism and determined to keep the United States out of the conflict at all costs.

As soon as he heard that the forty-strong American delegation had reached London, but was stranded there without sufficient funds to proceed, Carnegie immediately wired the Royal Bank of Scotland in London to provide them with whatever cash they needed, and he would reimburse the bank. In his letter Lynch concluded:

> I hope you have not lost courage. You must have felt heart-sick and dejected as have we all. But I believe this catastrophe will witness the beginning of the end of trust in might and brute force. That trust has failed at last.

Suddenly and brutally, Carnegie was confronted with the stark fact that all the millions he had expended on the promotion of world peace had been blown away in the twinkling of an eye. His vast fortune suddenly seemed a widow's mite when compared with the billions being spent each day in the prosecution of this dreadful war. Lynch's letter, with its grim accounts of drunken youths howling for the blood of their enemies, shattered Carnegie's illusion that the ordinary, decent people wanted peace and that it was only their leaders who were hellbent on waging war. Even as they were being confronted with such unpalatable truths, however, Lynch and Carnegie were taking refuge behind barricades of platitudes. While the latter proclaimed the 'onward and upward' progress of mankind, the former was calling on the United States 'to be Moses to lead Europe out of this awful wilderness she has become'. The metaphor was singularly unfortunate, for Moses wandered forty years in the wilderness and died without reaching the promised land.

The shock of war was forcibly brought home to the Carnegies as their horses and traps were requisitioned and the young men from the farms on the Skibo estate, either reservists or territorials, were mobilised in the first few days of the war. Those left behind had to struggle to get in the harvest with fewer hands than usual – and the harvest that glorious autumn was more abundant than usual. The womenfolk were kept busy sewing and knitting troop comforts. John

Morley came north and spent two weeks at Skibo, and from him the Carnegies got a first-hand account of the rapid descent into the 'Trough of Despair', as Morley termed it. If Carnegie had any lingering illusion about the war being short and the prospect of a stronger peace movement arising from the ashes, it was soon dispelled by Morley, who subsequently wrote from London that 'For the moment, there is nothing for people like you and me, but *an iron silence*. We can keep a vigilant eye upon events – Words are vain or worse than vain.'[4]

For several weeks Carnegie fumed and fretted, as his plans to make a quick return to America were constantly frustrated and aborted. Eventually, in mid-September, he and his family managed to secure berths on the *Mauretania*. They took a poignant farewell of the staff at Skibo on the morning of 14 September. As he drove to the railway station at Bonar Bridge, Carnegie took comfort from the magnificent autumn colours; little did he realise that he would never see his beloved Skibo again. Morley joined them for dinner at their hotel in Liverpool that evening before they boarded the ship. The two men furnished a stark contrast, Morley in the depths of despair and Carnegie resilient and optimistic as ever. Already his hyperactive mind was planning the world peace council which he hoped to propose to Woodrow Wilson as soon as he returned to America. But even his buoyant spirits were dashed on the homeward voyage. Because of the ever-present fear of attack by German submarines, the ship steamed at half speed, her lights extinguished. Louise, not a good sailor at the best of times, made herself even more sick with worry about travelling on a British ship in time of war. Carnegie whiled away the time by formulating his peace proposal and despatched this to President Wilson as soon as the liner docked. Wilson acknowledged receipt on 29 September: 'I am warmly obliged to you for lodging in my mind a suggestion which may later bear fruit.' Thus the seeds of the League of Nations were sown.

The immediate problem was to open peace negotiations among the leaders of the belligerent powers, and to this end Wilson despatched his close friend, Colonel Edward M. House, to Europe. Meanwhile Morley poured cold water on Carnegie's plans, pointing out that war fever had now reached such a pitch in Britain that any talk of peace would instantly be howled down. Ignoring this advice, Carnegie sent off an article to the *Independent* in October entitled 'A League of Peace – Not Preparation for War'. In this article it was evident that Carnegie's grasp of the current situation was weak. Comparing war to fighting a duel on a grand scale, he praised the Kaiser for having reduced the amount of duelling among Prussian officers. But he doggedly continued to advocate his League of Peace, even though he himself must have become very disheartened at times. His antidote to the war was to ignore it, to carry on as if nothing was happening. As the months passed, his ideas of turning back the clock became less and less realistic. There was no shortage of people in America who, perhaps out of ignorance, had no more realistic assessment of the European situation than he himself had. One of these was William Jennings Bryan, the Secretary of State and an old friend of Carnegie. Between them, Bryan and Carnegie concocted a preposterous scheme whereby the latter would liaise between the State Department and Kaiser Wilhelm in person to secure a cooling-off treaty. To this end, Carnegie sent a letter to the German Emperor in October 1914. Telling the Kaiser that he was convinced 'of your earnest desire for World Peace. This you probably know, since I have not failed repeatedly to proclaim it here', Carnegie reminded His Imperial Majesty of their meeting at Kiel. Then he outlined his plan for a cooling-off period between the belligerents. Reminding Wilhelm of 'your devotion to International Peace', Carnegie informed him that the main political parties in America were remarkably unanimous 'in the belief that this unparalleled war is at last to result in a stern resolve among the best of nations that men shall no longer be permitted to slay each other as they are now doing'.[5]

Wilhelm, alert to the potential benefits to be gained from securing American neutrality, let alone goodwill, readily assented to Carnegie's scheme. A conciliation treaty was consequently drafted, but it foundered when the American Senate refused to ratify it after the *Lusitania* was torpedoed in 1915 with the loss of 1200 lives. Having failed to negotiate this treaty, Carnegie now found himself fighting a rearguard action against the faction which regarded American involvement in the war as inevitable, sooner or later, and that the United States would have to prepare for action. The leader of this faction was Theodore Roosevelt who stumped the country whipping up war fever and savagely denouncing 'the pacifist crowd . . . above all Carnegie' for having 'occupied a peculiarly ignoble position . . . and who seemingly are willing to see the triumph of wrong if only all physical danger to their own worthless bodies can thereby be averted'.[6]

The scales had fallen from Carnegie's eyes at last, and he, in turn, had nothing but contempt for 'that mad militarist' Roosevelt. Now he pinned his faith on the Democrats, Woodrow Wilson and William Jennings Bryan. Asked by the *Pittsburgh Dispatch* for a New Year message, he gave a closely reasoned argument in favour of American neutrality, brushing aside the view that America needed to increase the size of her army and navy. With 16,000,000 men capable of bearing arms in a national militia for the country's defence, there was no need for a large standing army. 'Our beloved Republic has no enemies in the world: neither personal nor national . . . She is the foremost of nations in longing for international peace . . . ' And he reiterated his upbeat slogan in his closing sentences: 'Our Republic has nothing to fear, her march is onward and upward. She leads the procession, other nations must follow.' This bullish statement was the last he ever delivered to the American people at large.

Those closest to Carnegie, who appreciated the extent and magnitude of his obsession with peace, feared for his sanity, and life itself, when the cataclysmic blow struck in August 1914. For a time, to be sure, he was assailed by despair and the lowest of spirits, but it was not in the nature of the man to be downcast for long. On the ship home, he had had a chance to take stock of the situation, and by the time he landed at New York he had begun to plan what might have been the great masterstroke of his entire career, nothing less than the formation of the League of Nations, with himself, of course, as its acknowledged leader. Over the ensuing months he commuted between New York and Washington, and found in Wilson and Bryan kindred spirits, but just as he felt that he might be getting somewhere with his plans for a conciliation treaty as a prelude to his grand design for permanent world peace, something came out of the blue to interfere with the most important work of his life.

On 5 February 1915 he was subpoenaed to appear before the United States Commission on Industrial Relations. This commission started quite innocently as an enquiry into the relationship between management and labour right across the industrial spectrum, but one of the aspects which the commission targeted was the philanthropic foundations created by very wealthy men. There was a suspicion that such foundations might become a menace to human liberty and the democratic government of the country. Both Carnegie and Rockefeller were summoned on the same day, Rockefeller in the morning and Carnegie after lunch. A hearty meal, however, had not mellowed the audience gathered in the chamber, which seems to have been made up of 'socialists, single-taxers and members of the I.W.W.' (Industrial Workers of the World, known derisively as the Wobbly-wobblies) according to the *New York Herald*. Carnegie, impeccably dressed as befitted the occasion in a black frock coat, black bowtie and starched white shirt, sensed this hostile atmosphere, and summoned up every last ounce of charm to win over his audience.

The resulting performance was one of Carnegie's best. He read from a carefully worded statement, pausing only to make impromptu wisecracks. With the Little Boss ad libbing wildly and getting an appreciative chuckle, then a guffaw, from the assembled throng, he knew that they were melting towards him. With increasing confidence he raced through his dazzling performance, certain in the knowledge that he now had them eating out of his hand. At the outset, when asked what his occupation was, he quipped, 'To do as much good in the world as I can.' At the end he sat down with the affable comment that 'I haven't spent a more agreeable afternoon in I don't know when.' The hundreds crammed into the assembly hall of the Metropolitan Life Building in New York shook with laughter at the little man's sallies. Frank P. Walsh, chairman of the commission, soon gave up all attempts to conduct the meeting in a proper and decorous manner and laughed as loudly as the others. Carnegie interspersed his witticisms with homespun aphorisms. Asked for his views on the relations between capital, labour and management, he said that they were a three-legged stool, 'each necessary for the other, neither first, second or third in rank, all equal'. Eventually Walsh interjected while Andrew was in full flow: 'Now, I just want to ask you a question or two, Mr Carnegie, and then we will excuse you.'

'Oh, I am not in any hurry. I am enjoying this immensely.' And he turned his dazzling smile on the audience, which included a large number of women. The little charmer had never been on better form, and no one present could imagine that he was only months away from his eightieth birthday. The *Herald* reporter neatly summed it up when he said the interrogation of Andrew Carnegie had become almost a love feast. 'He had met them and they were his.' It was Carnegie's last public appearance and he left the stage on a high note, like the consummate actor he was.

All afternoon the adrenaline had been pumping, but as he returned home, he felt suddenly drained of energy. In the crowded, overheated room, he had caught a viral infection. Extreme tiredness overcame him and he scurried off to bed where he remained for several days nursing a bad cold, which developed into bronchitis and then pneumonia. By mid-March he was gravely ill, though his physician, Dr Jaspar Garmany, reassured his wife that he had a stout heart and good stamina. Garmany's confidence was rewarded when, with the advent of spring, the patient slowly recovered. Physically his health was restored, but Louise noted with mounting concern that mentally her husband was at a low ebb. He would sit listlessly in his sunlit garden in New York, a pathetic little bundle cocooned in blankets, staring vacantly into space for hours on end, manifesting no interest in anything or anyone around him. For months he had busied himself in the forlorn quest for world peace, but his prolonged illness had confronted him with the futility of it all. Now it seemed to him that he had nothing left to live for. This gloomy viewpoint was reinforced by the letters from friends in Britain which made increasingly grim reading. Too late, they realised the negative effect these letters were having upon him and tried to make light of the darkening situation.

Carnegie's depression deepened still further when May gave way to June, a time when he would normally have been making preparations to leave America for Scotland. As a compromise, the Carnegies spent the summer at Pointe d'Acadie, Bar Harbor, Maine, where they took a short lease of George Vanderbilt's summer home. They had gone there at the behest of Dr Garmany, but the choice was disastrous as Bar Harbor proved to be cold, clammy and foggy. Here, nevertheless, something of the old Carnegie briefly resurfaced, and he even felt well enough to go for short cruises in his yacht. But the true test came when he picked up a pen and paper to write a letter to Morley or some other old friend, and then, after a few words, would drop the paper and lapse into vacant silence once more.

His eightieth birthday fell on Thanksgiving Day, 1915. Newspapermen, calling for the usual annual message and affable session in

Carnegie's study, were surprised and disappointed when he merely
sent out his greetings and a brief message:

> Say to the reporters who usually call on my birthday that all goes
> well with me. Dr Garmany marvels at the splendid return to health
> which a summer on the Maine coast has wrought.
>
> The world grows better and we are soon to see blessed peace
> restored and a world court established when, in the words of Burns:
>> Man to man the world o'er
>> Shall brothers be for a' that.

But as hopes of an early return to world peace faded, Carnegie's
spirits sank even further. The messiah of world peace increasingly
gave way to long bouts of melancholy.

The winter of 1915–16 was spent in Florida, much of it aboard the
yacht. The mild sea air was invigorating, and Carnegie was gradually
regaining his old equilibrium when news came that Lucy Coleman
Carnegie had died. 'Mr Carnegie bore the news better than I
expected,' wrote Louise to Robert Franks, his financial secretary. 'I
tried to break it very gently, and his quiet acceptance of it was very
pathetic. He does not say much, but he is not brooding over it.'[7]

In April they returned to New York. The following month their
daughter Margaret graduated from Miss Spence's school and the
family moved to new quarters for the summer, the Brick House in
Noroton, Connecticut, overlooking Long Island Sound. This too
proved to be an unfortunate substitute for the cool, bracing climate
of Skibo, for Noroton was hot and humid, which exacerbated
Carnegie's misery and wretched longing for his Scottish home.
Louise was getting desperate, realising that he would never survive
the hardships of another Atlantic crossing. It was vital that she find
somewhere in the States that replicated the Skibo climate, and she
enlisted her friends in this desperate quest. As 1916 drew to a close,
she found the solution, near Lenox, Massachusetts. This was a fifty-
four-roomed greystone mansion called Shadowbrook, built some two
decades earlier for Anson Phelps Dodge. At the time, it was the
second-largest private residence in America, being surpassed only by
Mrs George W. Vanderbilt's Biltmore at Asheville, North Carolina.
Perched on the summit of a craggy hill overlooking Lake Mahkeenac,

with the beautifully wooded Berkshire Hills beyond, Shadowbrook offered a tolerable substitute for Skibo. Louise first visited it in the autumn and was captivated by the riot of colour. The estate was purchased in October and this gave Carnegie incentive to make plans for the following summer. At the same time, the deterioration in relations between Germany and the United States gave him renewed interest in the world at large. He began reading the newspapers once more and resumed dictating letters to President Wilson, a sure sign that he was getting back to normal at last. Now, the old pacificist was more and more convinced that peace could only be assured if America came into the war against Germany. There was something of the old fire in the letter sent to Wilson on 14 February 1917:

> Some time ago I wrote you 'Germany is beyond reason'. She has ever since become more and more so until today she shows herself completely insane . . . Were I in your place there would soon be an end to this. There is only one straight way of settlement. You should proclaim war against her, however reluctantly, and then settlement would soon come. Britain and France co-operating with us, would ensure peace promptly beyond question, and at the next meeting at the Hague, we would abolish war forever . . . Let me predict you will have the greatest of all careers before you; hope it will be soon clearly defined. Be of good cheer.[8]

Carnegie was not the only prominent pacificist who now saw American involvement as the only way to bring this war of attrition to a speedy conclusion. Both J. Allen Baker and Lord Bryce in Britain urged the United States to end its neutrality. The Carnegie Endowment for World Peace passed a resolution giving its backing to Wilson's increasingly tough stance against Germany. When Congress declared war on Germany on 6 April 1917 Carnegie sent a wire to the President: 'You have triumphed at last. God bless you. You will give the world peace and rank the greatest hero of all.' And putting his money where his mouth was, he immediately subscribed for $200,000 worth of Liberty Bonds. Louise's brother Harry was commissioned lieutenant in the army, and Carnegie himself made a valiant personal sacrifice when he let his valet Robert Morrison enlist in the Marines.

Through that summer the Carnegies spent an idyllic time at Shadowbrook. They went for long drives in their new motor car most afternoons, and after he acquired the *Sheila*, an electric launch, Carnegie resumed his passion for fly-fishing on the lake. By October that year he was writing pugnaciously to Lord Bryce, forecasting an imminent end to the war, with Germany's defeat before the year was out; but as 1917 closed and the defeat of the Central Powers seemed as remote as ever, Carnegie sank once more into depression. One of the few highlights of this period was the arrival of a copy of Viscount Morley's memoirs, which Carnegie avidly devoured. It rekindled old memories of happier times, and the old man was especially touched by those passages which mentioned him: 'Your references to me are all too flattering, but I am not altogether displeased, though you know my modest nature.'[9]

Carnegie longed for the end of the war when he would at long last be able to return to his beloved Skibo. As 1918 dragged on, however, and American involvement in the war seemed to bring its end no nearer, he gave way to violent mood swings, now exuberantly optimistic, now depressed and fretful at the President's canny attitude. Still, he continued to look forward to the resumption of peace. He and Louise had intended to return to New York at the end of October, but Massachusetts was enjoying an Indian summer so they remained in the Berkshires till the first week of November. Their return to New York coincided with the collapse of the Habsburg empire and the abdication of Kaiser Wilhelm, who fled from Germany and sought asylum in Holland. On 10 November, only hours before the Armistice, Carnegie wrote jubilantly to Woodrow Wilson:

> Now that the world war seems practically at an end I cannot refrain from sending you my heartfelt congratulations upon the great share you have had in bringing about its successful conclusion. The Palace of Peace at The Hague would, I think, be the fitting place for dispassionate discussion regarding the destiny of the conquered nations, and I hope your influence may be exerted in that direction.[10]

It is interesting to speculate that, had Carnegie's recommendation been followed, the peace conference might have had a very different outcome, without the long-term repercussions which the world was to suffer barely two decades later. The atmosphere at The Hague, in a country which had managed to remain neutral throughout the conflict, would also have been very different from that which prevailed at Versailles, with its echoes of French glory in the reign of Louis XIV, and bitter memories of the peace imposed on France by the Prussians in 1871. As Woodrow Wilson publicly announced his Fourteen Points and made plans for the League of Nations, Carnegie ecstatically celebrated his eighty-third birthday, his happiest in several years. The war was over and all his hopes for world peace seemed suddenly within reach. His happiness was crowned with the announcement that his only daughter Margaret had fallen in love with a dashing young naval ensign, Roswell Miller, whose sister Dorothy had been a close friend of Margaret's at Miss Spence's school. Miller came from sound commercial and industrial stock, his father having been the president of the Chicago, Milwaukee & St Paul Railroad for many years. Their engagement was formally announced at Carnegie's birthday party. The old man was in fine fettle all that winter, with plans for the return to Skibo the following spring as well as the preparations for Margaret's wedding.

On 22 April 1919, the thirty-second anniversary of her parents' wedding, Margaret Carnegie married Roswell Miller at the Carnegie mansion in New York. Her father was frail and feeble, but his spirit was gay as he insisted on escorting the bride down the staircase to the altar erected in the dining-room. After the brief ceremony, Carnegie kissed his daughter, shook Roswell's hand warmly and retired upstairs to rest. In the evening he arose and played backgammon with Louise.

Mentally Carnegie was as alert as ever, but to Louise's dismay she realised that he was now in far too poor shape to make the Atlantic crossing. By the beginning of May it was painfully obvious that there would be no return to Skibo this summer. Louise quietly broached the subject with him. They would return to Shadowbrook this summer. Next year, perhaps . . . She brightly explained the predicament: difficulties in transportation and wartime food shortages still prevailing in Britain made the trip impracticable. At that point Carnegie looked up sharply and said evenly, 'There won't be a next year for me.' Neither of them ever mentioned the return to Skibo again.[11]

Towards the end of May the Carnegies returned to Shadowbrook. Margaret and Roswell came up from Connecticut for a few days. On 4 June they set off on the journey home, and Louise noted regretfully in her diary: 'I am left alone with Andrew, so frail and feeble and so very weak.' It was some consolation when Robert Morrison, recently demobilised from the Marine Corps, returned to Shadowbrook to take care of the old fellow. The lazy, hazy days of summer passed in total idlenesss. Carnegie was now too weak to go fishing, and spent his time swathed in blankets, seated on the veranda, waiting, waiting. On Thursday, 7 August, his strength rallied and he spent some time that day under a group of pines near the lakeshore trying unsuccessfully to land a black bass. Next day he complained of a cold which went down into his chest. On Saturday he spoke of difficulty in breathing but spent the afternoon with Louise among his flowers. The following morning his cold was no worse than usual. He had breakfast and decided to remain in bed that day.

On Sunday night he was struck down by bronchial pneumonia. This time there were no reserves of strength to fall back on, and Carnegie himself had no wish to go on. About six o'clock on the morning of Monday, 11 August, Louise was hastily called to his bedside. 'I remained with my darling husband, giving him oxygen until he gradually fell asleep at 7:14,' she wrote in her diary. 'I am left alone . . . Margaret and Roswell such comforts, relieving me of details. Telegrams pouring in. I think he knew me but he did not speak.'

The private funeral service took place on 14 August. Only members of the family and intimate friends attended the simple twenty-minute ceremony, and at least half of the sixty people clustered around the flower-decked coffin were members of the Carnegie household. Although Andrew belonged to no church, the service was conducted by Louise's pastor, the Revd Dr William P. Merrill of the Brick Presbyterian Church in New York, and a local minister, the Revd Dr Benson N. Wyman of Lenox Congregational Church. A prayer, a bible-reading and hymns from the Brick Church choir completed the service. There was no eulogy.

At his own request Carnegie was buried in the Sleepy Hollow Cemetery in North Tarrytown, New York. His grave was marked by a Celtic cross, carved from stone quarried near Skibo. On the cross was cut a simple inscription:

Andrew Carnegie

Born in Dunfermline, Scotland, 25 November 1835

Died in Lenox, Massachusetts, 11 August 1919

In 1924 Samuel Gompers, head of the American Federation of Labor, was buried in a nearby plot. The villagers claim that the great capitalist and the great trade union leader lie at peace, and there are no new tales of ghosts to add to the Legend of Sleepy Hollow.

When the terms of Carnegie's will were revealed the world waited with bated breath. Had the old man succeeded in divesting himself of his vast wealth, or had he died in disgrace, according to his gospel of wealth? There was wild speculation in the press that his fortune might have amounted to $600,000,000 and that the residue might be in excess of $250,000,000. In point of fact he left less than a tenth of that sum, his estate being appraised at $22,881,575 net. Two-thirds of that sum was left to the Carnegie Corporation, but under New York state law not more than half an estate of a person having a husband, wife, child or parent could pass in public bequests. This left Louise as automatic co-legatee with the Corporation, giving her a personal fortune, from her husband's New York property, of $11,338,538.

The will, executed on 13 February 1920, gave to his widow 'all my real estate forever, together with all books, pictures, works of art, furniture, horses, carriages, motor cars, stables, garages, dwellings, etc' and added:

> Having years ago made provision for my wife beyond her desires and ample to provide for our beloved daughter Margaret, and being unable to judge at present what provision for our daughter will best promote her happiness, I leave to her mother the duty of providing for her as her mother deems best. A mother's love will be the best guide.[12]

Louise also had a life interest in a trust fund, established in 1912, of $4,643,750, which on her death in 1946 passed to her daughter. Carnegie left $4,250,000 to be disbursed as pensions, gifts and annuities among some four hundred beneficiaries. They included $5000 annuities to the widows of Grover Cleveland and Theodore Roosevelt, in the hope that this act would shame the federal government into making adequate provision for the wives of late presidents. Annuities of $10,000 were left to ex-President Taft, Viscount Morley and David Lloyd George. Robert Franks, Carnegie's long-term financial secretary, received an annuity of $20,000 and was placed in charge of the Home Trust Company of New Jersey, a corporation established to administer Carnegie's estate. Among the $17,480,839 of stocks and bonds administered by this trust there was only one worthless security, a tranche of 1520 shares in the Keokuk & Hamilton Bridge Company (a forerunner of the Keystone Company) which Carnegie had retained out of sentiment. Under Franks's careful administration, this trust fund actually increased in value over the ensuing years, and as the beneficiaries of the annuities died, the annuity fund grew correspondingly, with half of the net sum reverting to Louise Carnegie.

She was sixty-two when her husband died, and faced the prospect of widowhood with equanimity. She was comfortably off, and she resolutely stuck to the old Carnegie routine. In the summer of 1920 she made the long-promised return to Skibo, and thereafter spent the summer months there each year right up until the outbreak of the Second World War. On the day that the German forces invaded Poland she packed her luggage, took a tearful farewell of her staff, and left Skibo, never to return. It was a reprise of the sad parting a quarter of a century earlier. In New York she gave Christmas parties for British evacuees and visiting servicemen, raised funds for the Red Cross and bought war bonds. When the war ended, she herself was too frail and feeble to contemplate an Atlantic crossing. She made plans to return to Skibo in the summer of 1946, but on 24 June that year she died peacefully at her mansion in New York.

Margaret Carnegie Miller would carry on the family tradition a few years longer, spending her summers at Skibo and her winters in New York. In 1982 she sold the estate to Derek Holt who subsequently disposed of it to Peter de Savary. Skibo, restored to its fomer glory, is now a luxury hotel and country club. Margaret died at her home in Fairfield, Conneticut, on 11 April 1990, shortly after her ninety-third birthday.

Andrew Carnegie was the most extraordinary character thrown up by the volcanic eruption of American industry. He set a new standard of wealth and, in real terms, his vast fortune has seldom been equalled, far less surpassed. Even from the grave he reached out to claw back one of every dozen dollars earned by the United States Steel Corporation. He was the last of the great tsars of industry. At the time of his death the encomiums were mixed. Charlie Schwab put it charitably when he observed that: 'He possessed the faculty of inspiring others to unusual efforts in a greater measure than any man I ever knew.' And Elihu Root dutifully recorded: 'He belonged to that great race of nation builders who have made the development of America the wonder of the world.' The platitudes came thick and fast . 'He made vital, in our country at least, the conception that the owner of great wealth is a trustee for the public, obligated to divide his wealth for the public use,' wrote Henry Pritchett. Only Herbert N. Casson struck a faintly sour note: 'Carnegie's career, whether we regard it with complacency or as a social menace, was possible only in this country and in the last generation.'

Carnegie had successfully divested himself of the bulk of his wealth. Through the corporations, trusts and endowments, the things on which he set the greatest store have continued to flourish. His death spared him the crushing disappointment of seeing the United States Senate refusing to ratify the great work which he had begun and which Woodrow Wilson completed. There was a cruel irony in the fact that the League of Nations should be established as Carnegie would have wished – but it was a League marred by the studied refusal of the United States to participate. While Carnegie's adopted country withdrew into blinkered isolationism, the League was left to founder. Louise worked tirelessly in the interwar period on behalf of the League, but it must have broken her heart to see it powerless to halt the rise of militarism in Japan, Italy and Germany, with fatal consequences.

In November 1935 the centenary of Carnegie's birth was widely celebrated throughout the English-speaking world, wherever there was a Carnegie library, in fact. On the centenary date Louise made one of her increasingly rare public appearances and echoed her late husband's optimism and idealism:

I believe the day will yet come when his hopes shall be realised and the world shall become a family of nations. For many years the subject of internationalism has interested me more deeply than any other, and if the years have taught me anything it is that no man or nation can do any effective work in the world alone. It is only by working together for a common cause that civilization can be carried forward.[13]

Sadly, that optimism would all too soon prove to have been as misplaced as Carnegie's was when he presented his peace testimonial to the Kaiser at Kiel in the summer of 1913.

Today, as we approach the second millennium, the quest for world peace may be as much a chimera as it was in 1913 or 1935, but in many other ways Carnegie's legacy has been more tangible, and conferred more lasting benefits on mankind. The libraries that he endowed flourish as strongly as ever and are, perhaps, what he will best be remembered for; although the great Peace Court at The Hague is still performing the functions envisaged for it by its originator almost a century ago, while the principles of international arbitration which he enunciated, and for which he fought so ardently, are now well established and perhaps offer the best hope for the future stability of this planet. The Carnegie Institutes, the Carnegie Corporation and the Carnegie trusts roll on for ever, thanks to the miracle of capitalism.

It is said that a man may gain immortality in three ways: by fathering a son, writing a book or planting a tree. Carnegie never managed to pass on his surname to a son, but he wrote books that would repay reading even today, and he not only planted trees that flourish at Skibo to this day but had the rare distinction of a plant named after him. In 1848 the botanist Engelmann had given the Saguaro, largest of all the cacti, the scientific name of *Cereus giganteus*; sixty years later the botanists Britton and Rose, financed by the Carnegie Institute of Washington, repaid their patron and sponsor by renaming it *Carnegiea giganteа* in his honour. Somehow it seems appropriate that this giant among succulents, standing up to seventy feet in height and thriving in the harsh environment of the Arizona desert, prickly on the outside and soft on the inside, should be named after Andrew Carnegie.

It is not recorded what Carnegie himself thought of this honour, but doubtless the Little Boss saw the humour of it, and heartily approved.

Notes

Abbreviations

ACLC: Andrew Carnegie Papers, Library of
Congress, Washington, DC

ACUSC: Andrew Carnegie Papers, United
States Steel Corporation, New York

1.Dunfermline, 1835–48

1. J.B. Mackie, *Andrew Carnegie, his Dunferm-
line Ties and Benefactions* (1916), pp.5–6.
See also Eric Simpson, *The Auld Grey
Toun: Dunfermline in the Time of Andrew
Carnegie, 1835–1919* (Dunfermline, 1987),
for useful general background.

2. *Autobiography of Andrew Carnegie* (1920),
hereafter referred to as *Autobiography*, p.2

3. Burton J. Hendrick, *The Life of Andrew
Carnegie* (New York, 1932), hereafter
referred to as Hendrick, vol. 1, p.1

4. Dunfermline parish registers, West
Register House, Edinburgh

5. Ibid.

6. Dunfermline parish registers, op. cit.,
show the children of Andrew Carnegie
and Elizabeth Thom as Elizabeth (1793),
Charlotte (1795), Ann (1796), Margaret
(1799), James (1801), William (1804),
Henrietta (1806) and Andrew (1808).
Family legend states that there were ten
children, not eight; and that Ann was the
eighth child, but these myths are dis-
proved by the parish records.

7. Mackie, op. cit., p.7

8. *Autobiography*, p.2

9. Ibid., p.3

10. The heart of Bruce had been placed in a
silver casket interred in the wall of
Melrose Abbey. This was plundered by
the English in 1385 and rediscovered in
1996.

11. John Pattison, *Genealogy of the Morrison
Family* MS, dated Pittsburgh 1935, in

Carnegie papers, Carnegie Museum,
Dunfermline, but inaccurate and with
many gaps.

12. Dunfermline parish registers, op. cit.,
give the births, but not the marriages, of
families which did not adhere to the
established Church of Scotland. The
marriage registers of the period are, in
fact, remarkably scanty, indicating that a
high proportion of the weavers, fishermen and seamen and their families
belonged to various seceding sects.

13. Mackie, op. cit., p.9

14. Dunfermline parish registers of
marriages, West Register House, Edinburgh, make no mention of this wedding,
which would have been performed in a
dissenting chapel and therefore not
registered.

15. Dunfermline parish registers of births,
West Register House, Edinburgh

16. *Autobiography*, p.8

17. Ibid., p.6

18. John K. Winkler, *Incredible Carnegie* (New
York, 1931), hereafter referred to as
Winkler, p.33

19. *Autobiography*, p.23

20. Ibid., p.2

21. Ibid., p.16

22. AC MSS, 28 December 1889, in ACLC
vol. 10

23. *Autobiography*, p.21

24. Hendrick, vol. 1, p.26

25. *United States Handbook* (1946) recorded
4,350 of them. They all seem to have
vanished in more recent years.

26. Hendrick, vol. 1, p.27. The lines Morley
had in mind were from Burns's 'A Man's a
Man for a' that', Carnegie's favourite poem

27. *Dunfermline Journal*, 26 February 1841

28. *Autobiography*, p.13

29. Annie and Andrew Aitken to William and Margaret Carnegie, 10 October 1840
30. Hendrick, vol. 1, pp.42–3
31. Expanded in *Autobiography*, p.26, and considerably embellished in *An American Four-in-Hand in Great Britain* in which the farewell to Dunfermline occupies some 600 words.

2. Allegheny City, 1848–53

1. *Autobiography*, p.28
2. Ibid., p.30
3. Ibid., p.30
4. Ibid., p.31
5. AC, 'How I Served my Apprenticeship as a Businessman', in *The Youth's Companion*, 25 April 1896, p.217
6. *Autobiography*, p.13, previously quoted
7. AC, 'The Road to Business Success, a Talk to Young Men', reprinted in *The Empire of Business* (New York, 1902)
8. *Autobiography*, p.32
9. Ibid., p.33
10. Ibid., p.34
11. Ibid., p.35
12. Ibid., p.36
13. Thomas N. Miller to AC, 1903, quoted by Hendrick, vol. 1, p.53
14. Speech of Henry Phipps, Jr. at Dunfermline, 27 July 1881
15. Joseph Frazier Wall, *Andrew Carnegie* (New York, 1970), hereafter cited as Wall, p.89
16. Hendrick, vol. 1, p.35
17. *Autobiography*, p.36
18. In his *Autobiography*, p.37, AC gives the location of the O'Reilly Telegraph Office at the corner of Fourth Avenue and Wood Street. Some historians think that it was in the old Odeon Building nearby, but David N. Bates stated authoritatively that it was on Third and Wood. See his very informative article 'The Turning Point of Mr Carnegie's Career' in *Century Magazine*, vol. 76 (July 1908), p.335.
19. *Autobiography*, p.37
20. Ibid., p.39
21. Ibid., p.43
22. David McCargo to AC, 20 May 1903, ACLC vol. 96
23. *Autobiography*, p.44
24. Ibid., p.56
25. Ibid., p.57

26. Ibid., pp.62–3
27. Ibid., p.60
28. Winkler, p.55
29. Carl Engel to Robert M. Lester, 24 April 1935, in archives of the Carnegie Corporation, New York
30. *Autobiography*, p.61
31. Ibid., pp.45–6
32. Ibid., p.48
33. Quoted by Hendrick, vol. 1, p.66

3. My Boy Andy, 1853–59

1. *Autobiography*, p.63
2. T.B.A. David to AC, 20 May 1903, ACLC vol. 96; J.P. Glass to AC, 15 March 1858, ACLC vol. 1
3. AC to George Lauder, Sr., 14 March 1853
4. *Autobiography*, p.65
5. Ibid., pp.65–6
6. Ibid., p.66
7. Ibid., p.67
8. Ibid., p.68
9. Ibid., pp.73–4
10. Ibid., p.72
11. Ibid., p.82
12. Ibid., p.82
13. Ibid., p.73
14. Winkler, p.60
15. *Autobiography*, p.77
16. Ibid., p.79
17. Winkler, p.66
18. *Autobiography*, p.79
19. ACLC vol. 1
20. Ibid.
21. Ibid., which also includes a letter from I. Bennett to AC regarding Margaret Carnegie's sojourn in East Liverpool, 11 March 1858
22. *Autobiography*, p.80
23. Ibid.
24. Ibid., p.84
25. Ibid., p.85. Wall (p.136) says that the informer told AC who the ringleader was and promised a list of the signatories, but this is an embellishment of the bare details given by AC himself. The likelihood is that mention of a list was pure bluff on Scott's part.
26. Ibid. p.86
27. Ibid., p.89
28. Ibid., p.90
29. Thomas Miller to AC, 10 April 1903, in ACLC vol. 95

30. *Triumphant Democracy* (1886), pp.297–9
31. Theodore T. Woodruff to AC, 12 June 1886
32. AC to Woodruff, 15 June 1886, in ACLC vol. 9
33. *Autobiography*, p.87
34. Hendrick, vol. 1, pp.94–5; Winkler, pp.66–8. Only Wall (pp.134–41) ascertained the truth.
35. H.W. Schotter, *The Growth and Development of the Pennsylvania Railroad Company*, Philadelphia, 1927, p.87
36. Hendrick, vol. 1, p.96
37. *Autobiography*, pp.87–8

4. The Spoils of War, 1859–65

1. *Autobiography*, pp.91–2
2. Copy in ACLC, vol. 1
3. *Autobiography*, pp.93–4
4. Ibid., p.96
5. Ibid., p.97
6. Ibid., p.98
7. Ibid., p.93
8. G. Alexander to T. Miller, 2 May 1903, ACLC vol. 96
9. Ibid.
10. *Autobiography*, pp.82–3
11. AC, 'Stanton the Patriot', address at Kenyon College, Ohio, 1906, reprinted in *Miscellaneous Writings of Andrew Carnegie* (New York, 1933), vol. 1, p.217
12. *Autobiography*, p.83
13. *Pittsburgh Gazette*, 13 April 1861
14. 'Stanton the Patriot', op. cit., p.233
15. J.A. Mackay, *The Eye Who Never Slept: A Life of Allan Pinkerton* (Edinburgh, 1996), pp.99–101
16. *Autobiography*, p.100
17. Bates, David Homer *Lincoln in the Telegraph Office* (New York, 1907), p.22
18. Transcript from AC to John C. Cowan (editor of the *Pittsburgh Chronicle Telegraph*), 29 April 1911, in ACLC vol. 192
19. AC to W.H. Holmes, 26 July 1861, in ACLC vol. 1
20. *Autobiography*, p.101
21. AC to Enoch Lewis, 4, 5, 9 and 10 October 1861, in ACLC vol. 1
22. AC to Lewis, 5 October 1861, op. cit.
23. *Autobiography*, p.137
24. Hendrick, vol. 1, p.120
25. *Autobiography*, p.110

26. Ibid., p.111
27. Ibid., p.113
28. Ibid., p.114
29. Butler's receipt of 19 June 1864 and the certificate itself, dated 19 July, are preserved in the Miscellaneous Papers File, ACUSC
30. ACLC vol. 1

5. Many Fingers, Many Pies, 1865–73

1. Quoted by Winkler, p.81
2. Ibid., p.82
3. Ibid., p.83
4. Hendrick, vol. 1, pp.138–9
5. Ibid., p.141, based on an interview (1928) with John Walker who was an eyewitness
6. AC to Thomas Miller, 3 June 1867, in Letterbook 1866–9, ACUSC
7. Miller to AC, 2 April 1903, in ACLC vol. 95
8. *Pittsburgh Leader*, 25 September 1903
9. J. Edgar Thomson to AC, 12 March 1867, ACUSC
10. AC to W.B. Ogden, 12 March 1867, ACUSC
11. *Autobiography*, p.143
12. Photocopy in AC Papers, New York Public Library
13. *Autobiography*, p.160
14. Contract in AC's handwriting, Letterbook 1866–69, ACUSC
15. AC to Pullman, 4 March 1868, ACUSC
16. For a full account of this episode see James D. Reid, *The Telegraph in America* (New York, 1886)
17. *Autobiography*, p.174
18. AC to Miller, 10 April 1903, ACLC vol. 95
19. *Autobiography*, p.152
20. Thomson to AC, 3 October 1873, AC Papers, New York Public Library
21. Hendrick, vol. 1, pp.196–7

6. Man of Steel, 1873–81

1. AC to William Shinn, 21 May 1873, Letterbook 1872–77, ACUSC
2. Winkler, p.137
3. *Autobiography* p.203
4. Ibid., p.192
5. Ibid., p.202
6. Ibid., p.196
7. Winkler, p.129
8. AC to Shinn, 10 April 1876, ACLC vol. 4

9. AC to Shinn, 1 May 1877, ACLC vol. 4
10. AC to Shinn, October 1877, ACLC vol. 4
11. AC to Shinn, 4 April 1879, ACLC vol. 4
12. AC to John Scott, 7 April 1879, ACLC vol. 4; see also the William Shinn Suit File, ACUSC
13. AC to Shinn, 14 September 1879, in the Shinn Suit File, op. cit.
14. *Round the World* (New York, 1884), p.306
15. W.R. Jones to AC, 5 November 1880, ACUSC
16. AC to Jones, 8 November 1880, ACUSC
17. Jones to AC, 19 December 1880, ACUSC
18. Quoted by Winkler, p.154

7. The Rise of Henry Clay Frick, 1881–92
1. Hendrick, vol. 1, pp.294–5
2. For biographical details see George Harvey, *Henry Clay Frick, the Man* (New York, 1936)
3. Winkler, p.162
4. Hendrick, vol. 1, pp.296–8
5. Winkler, p.167
6. *Autobiography*, p.213
7. William Roscoe Thayer, *The Life and Letters of John Hay*, vol. 2, p.74
8. *Autobiography*, p.321
9. Harvey, op. cit., p.90; Winkler, p.175; Wall, p.495
10. Harvey, p.90

8. Homestead, 1892
1. Winkler, pp.192–3
2. Ibid., p.194
3. *Autobiography*, p.228
4. Ibid., pp.240–54
5. Winkler, p.196
6. Ibid., pp.197–8
7. Quoted in Harvey, op. cit., p.134
8. Quoted by Winkler, p.208
9. AC to George Lauder, 17 July 1892, ACLC vol. 17. Hendrick, vol. 1, p.404 omitted the phrase beginning 'such a fiasco' without inserting ellipsis to indicate a passage omitted. This completely altered the sense of the letter. Wall, p.561, quotes the letter in full.
10. Quoted by Winkler, p.208
11. *New York Times*, 16 July 1892
12. Burton Hendrick quaintly put this as 'his intellect and sense of justice, however, at once supervened'. Hendrick, vol. 1, p.408

13. Quoted by Hendrick, vol. 1, p.408; Wall. p.566
14. Quoted in Bridge, op. cit., pp.233–4; Wall, p.573
15. AC to William Ewart Gladstone, 24 September 1892, in Gladstone Papers, vol. 437, Additional MS 44.522, folio 302, British Library, London
16. *Autobiography*, p.228
17. Ibid., p.232
18. Winkler, p.219
19. AC to John Morley, 16 April 1893, ACLC vol. 20

9. The Greatest Business in the World, 1893–1900
1. *Autobiography*, p.254
2. Winkler, p.226
3. Quoted by Winkler, pp.227–8
4. AC to Grover Cleveland, 20 December 1893, ACLC vol. 23
5. Quoted by Winkler, p.233; Grover Cleveland to H.A. Herbert, 10 January 1894
6. *New York Tribune*, 31 August 1894
7. AC to Grover Cleveland, 27 December 1893, ACLC 24
8. AC, 'Some Important Results of the Jubilee', *North American Review*, vol. 165, October 1897, p.506
9. *Autobiography*, p.217
10. AC to Frick, 29 August 1892, quoted by Bridge, *The Inside History of the Carnegie Steel Company*, New York 1903, p.259
11. AC to Henry W. Oliver, 25 September 1897, ACUSC
12. Nelson A. Miles, *Serving the Republic* (New York, 1911), p.274
13. Andrew D. White to AC, 18 June 1900, ACLC vol. 75
14. Quoted by Winkler, pp.243–4
15. Minutes of board meeting, Carnegie Steel, 20 November 1899, ACLC vol. 70
16. Quoted by Winkler, pp.249–50
17. Quoted in Harvey, op. cit., p.172

10. Spreading the Largesse, 1901–10
1. *Autobiography*, p.235
2. AC to George Lauder, 25 November 1899, ACUSC
3. Quoted by Winkler, p.263
4. AC to Charles Schwab, 22 December 1898, ACLC vol. 58

5. AC to Schwab, 7 July 1900, ACLC vol. 76
6. AC to Schwab, 11 July 1900, minuted at the board meeting of 31 July 1900, ACLC vol. 76
7. AC to George Lauder, 24 January 1901, ACLC vol. 81
8. Schwab to AC, 24 January 1901, ACLC vol. 81
9. Letter of the Board of the Carnegie Company, 4 February 1901, ACLC vol. 81
10. *The Gospel of Wealth*; see also AC 'Wealth' in *North American Review*, June 1889
11. Undated memo in ACLC vol. 81
12. Revd Hugh Price Hughes, *Irresponsible Wealth*, Part III, p.891
13. AC to William M. Frew, 24 October 1894, ACLC vol. 28
14. AC to President and Managers of the Carnegie Company, 12 March 1901, ACLC vol. 82
15. Employees of Homestead Steel Works to AC, 23 February 1903, reprinted in *Autobiography*, p.257
16. Records of Carnegie Dunfermline Trust, Abbey House, Dunfermline
17. Quoted by Winkler, p.282
18. *Autobiography*, p.271
19. Quoted by Winkler, pp.285–6
20. AC to an anonymous 'Dear Friend indeed', 11 July 1912, ACLC vol. 207
21. Poultney Bigelow, *Seventy Summers* (London, 1925), vol. 2, p.194
22. AC to Charles Eliot, 32 December 1904, ACLC vol. 110
23. Quoted by AC in *Autobiography*, p.276
24. Carnegie Corporation quarterly accounts, July 1996
25. For a detailed survey of the Carnegie millions and how they have been used, see Simon Goodenough, *The Greatest Good Fortune: Andrew Carnegie's Gift for Today* (London, 1985)
26. Winkler, p.276

11. Saint Andrew, Apostle of Peace, 1901–14
1. *The Times*, 15 December 1910
2. Andrew White to AC, 30 April 1903, ACLC vol. 96
3. AC to David Hill, 18 June 1906, ACLC vol. 130

4. AC to David Hill, 10 July 1906, ACLC vol. 131
5. *The Times*, 29 August 1913
6. *The Times*, 30 August 1913
7. *Autobiography*, p.286
8. AC to James Bryce, 18 November 1907, ACLC vol. 145
9. AC's speech to the National Arbitration and Peace Congress, New York, 17 April 1907
10. AC to John Morley, undated, but about 5 June 1907, ACLC vol. 142. Morley replied by return, on 14 June.
11. AC to Sir James Donaldson, 3 July 1909, ACLC vol. 166
12. Berthe von Suttner to AC, 22 May 1909, ACLC vol. 166
13. *Autobiography*, p.371

12. Last Years, 1914–19
1. Preface to the *Autobiography*
2. AC to J. Allen Baker, 2 August 1914, ACLV vol. 225
3. John Morley to AC, 4 August 1914, ACLC vol. 225
4. John Morley to AC, 28 August 1914, ACLC vol. 225
5. AC to Kaiser Wilhelm II, 19 October 1914, ACLC vol. 226
6. Theodore Roosevelt to James Bryce, 31 March 1915, reproduced in Elting E. Morrison, *Letters of Theodore Roosevelt* (Cambridge, 1952), vol. 8, pp.913–16
7. Louise Carnegie to Robert Franks, 20 January 1916, Franks Papers, Home Trust Company, Hoboken
8. AC to Woodrow Wilson, 14 February 1917, ACLC vol. 234
9. AC to John Morley, 21 January 1918, ACLC vol. 237
10. AC to Woodrow Wilson, 10 November 1918, ACLC vol. 237
11. Louise Carnegie to Margaret Carnegie Miller, 2 May 1919, quoted by Wall, p.1039
12. *New York Times*, 29 August 1919, for the full text of AC's will
13. Quoted by Burton J. Hendrick and Daniel Henderson, *Louise Whitfield Carnegie* (New York, 1950), p.265

Select Bibliography

Carnegie, Andrew, *Our Coaching Trip, Brighton to Inverness* (private circulation) (New York, 1882)

    An American Four-in-Hand in Great Britain (New York, 1884)

    Round the World (New York, 1884)

    Triumphant Democracy (New York and London, 1886)

    The Gospel of Wealth and Other Timely Essays (New York, 1900)

    The Empire of Business (New York, 1902, reprinted 1935)

    Problems of Today: Wealth – Labor – Socialism (New York, 1908)

    Autobiography (New York and London, 1920)

Alderson, Bernard, *Andrew Carnegie: From Telegraph Boy to Millionaire* (London, 1902)

Bridge, James H., *The Inside History of the Carnegie Steel Company* (New York, 1903)

Casson, Herbert N., *The Romance of Steel* (New York, 1907)

Giddens, Paul H., *The American Petroleum Industry – Its Beginnings in Pennsylvania* (Princeton, 1959)

Goodenough, Simon, *The Greatest Good Fortune: Andrew Carnegie's Gift for Today* (London, 1985)

Grodinsky, Julius, *Jay Gould, 1867–1892* (Philadelphia, 1957)

Harvey, George, *Henry Clay Frick, the Man* (New York, 1936)

Hendrick, Burton J., *The Life of Andrew Carnegie*, 2 vols. (Garden City, NY, 1932)

Hendrick, Burton J., and Henderson, Daniel, *Louise Whitfield Carnegie* (New York, 1950)

Husband, Joseph, *The Story of the Pullman Car* (Chicago, 1917)

Mackay, James, *The Eye Who Never Slept: A Life of Allan Pinkerton* (Edinburgh, 1996)

Mackie, James B., *Andrew Carnegie, His Dunfermline Ties and Benefactions* (Dunfermline, 1916)

Miles, Nelson A., *Serving the Republic* (New York, 1911)

Morrison, Elting E., *Letters of Theodore Roosevelt* (Cambridge, 1952)

Plum, W.R., *The Military Telegraph During the Civil War* (Chicago, 1882)

Pritchett, Henry S., *The First Twenty Years of the Carnegie Corporation* (New York, 1931)

Reid, James D., *The Telegraph in America* (New York, 1886)

Root, Elihu, *Andrew Carnegie 1835–1919* (New York, 1920)

Schotter, H.W., *The Growth and Development of the Pennsylvania Railroad* (Philadelphia, 1927)

Schwab, Charles M., *Andrew Carnegie, His Methods with his Men* (Pittsburgh, 1919)

Simpson, Eric, *The Auld Grey Toun: Dunfermline in the Time of Andrew Carnegie, 1835–1919* (Dunfermline, 1987)

Thayer, William R., *The Life and Letters of John Hay* (New York, 1911)

Wall, Joseph Frazier, *Andrew Carnegie* (New York, 1970)
    Skibo (Oxford, 1984)

Winkler, John K., *Incredible Carnegie* (Garden City, NY, 1931)

Index

INDEX

319